Christians in the American Empire

Faith and Citizenship in the
New World Order

VINCENT D. ROUGEAU

2008

OXFORD
UNIVERSITY PRESS

Oxford University Press, Inc., publishes works that further
Oxford University's objective of excellence
in research, scholarship, and education.

Oxford   New York
Auckland   Cape Town   Dar es Salaam   Hong Kong   Karachi
Kuala Lumpur   Madrid   Melbourne   Mexico City   Nairobi
New Delhi   Shanghai   Taipei   Toronto

With offices in
Argentina   Austria   Brazil   Chile   Czech Republic   France   Greece
Guatemala   Hungary   Italy   Japan   Poland   Portugal   Singapore
South Korea   Switzerland   Thailand   Turkey   Ukraine   Vietnam

Copyright © 2008 by Oxford University Press, Inc.

Published by Oxford University Press, Inc.
198 Madison Avenue, New York, New York 10016

www.oup.com

Oxford is a registered trademark of Oxford University Press.

Library of Congress Cataloging-in-Publication Data
Rougeau, Vincent D., 1963–
Christians in the American empire : faith and citizenship in the new world
order / Vincent D. Rougeau.
    p. cm.
Includes index.
ISBN 978-0-19-518809-7
1. Christianity—United States—21st century.   2. United States—Moral conditions.
3. Christian sociology.   I. Title.
BR526.R67 2008
261.80973—dc22   2008003861

9 8 7 6 5 4 3 2 1

Printed in the United States of America
on acid-free paper

To Robin
with all my love

Preface

I have spent the better part of the last two decades teaching law at two Catholic universities in the United States. Although I myself am Catholic, before I began my career in academia I had never attended a Catholic school, nor had I ever been officially associated with Catholic education in any formal capacity. I am pleased to say that, after a lifetime in secular settings, I found teaching in Catholic institutions intellectually stimulating and personally invigorating in ways entirely new to me. For the first time, I was able to integrate my faith commitments with my intellectual life in a way that was not purely private. Moreover, with students and faculty from a wide range of faith traditions, I was free to discuss the contributions of religious thought to our understandings of legal concepts to a degree that had not been possible in other academic environments.

After the tragedies of September 11, however, I sensed a fundamental change in the climate on many Catholic university campuses. It became increasingly apparent to me that religious believers—Catholics in particular—were being asked to declare their allegiance to religious "truth" in a way that seemed to align rather conveniently with the political program of the Republican Party. Of course, the American "culture wars" had long been simmering and subsequent to these battles, and evangelical Protestantism and the Protestant mainstream had further divided themselves into conservative and liberal camps that in fact closely tracked the agendas of the Republican and Democratic parties. Yet, up to this point, the situation

within Roman Catholicism in the United States had been a bit more complicated. Although American Catholics had long been heavily Democratic, the
cultural conflict over abortion, rising post–World War II affluence, and widespread assimilation had moved many of them to the political Right. Indeed, the
election of Ronald Reagan marked an important milestone in the emergence of
Catholics as an important part of the Republican political coalition. On the
other hand, the strong association of the Catholic Church with the interests of
labor, immigrants, and the poor, as well as its heavy involvement in peace and
justice movements in response to various military conflicts around the world,
made it difficult to argue that Catholic belief would necessarily incline someone to declare allegiance to one or the other side of the American political
divide. During the 1990s, however, powerful new voices arose that actually
began to make some headway with the argument that only one political party
in the United States was consistent with a serious Catholic faith commitment.

As the Republican revolution gathered strength and eventually triumphed
in the party's 1996 accession to power in Congress, many Christians began to
see their position on abortion as the sine qua non of their political views. To
some extent the emergence of this litmus test was the Democrats' doing, for the
Democratic leadership had made it extremely difficult for anyone who opposed
the Supreme Court's decision in Roe v. Wade to have any meaningful voice in
the party. When Governor Bob Casey of Pennsylvania was not given a speaking
slot to deliver a pro-life speech at the 1992 Democratic convention, many people believed that this signaled the beginning of the end of any coherence to the
descriptor "pro-life Democrat." This placed many Catholics in an extremely
awkward political position. Catholic teaching on the immoral nature of abortion was well established, and the church had made clear its opposition to the
ruling in Roe v. Wade when the decision came down in the early 1970s.

Where, then, did this leave Catholics who did not share the Democratic
position on abortion but supported many other core party positions? By the
1990s an emerging group of Catholic thinkers was gaining increased attention
for the argument that, because abortion went to the basic question of respect for
human life, opposition to abortion was the only issue that really mattered when
it came to selecting a political party to support, particularly in presidential
elections. How could voters who were serious about their Catholic belief support a party that endorsed a legal decision that allowed for the taking of innocent life? Put another way, since the Republican Party opposed Roe v. Wade and
the Democrats supported it, how could a Catholic vote for the Democrats?

An extensive literature takes up this debate in more detail, and it would not
be helpful to reproduce it here. Nevertheless, it is useful at this point to make a
few general observations about the controversy and to examine some of the

assumptions underlying the pro-Republican position. For a democracy to function in a pluralist society, citizens must make prudent choices about their political representation, recognizing full well that not every value that they hold dear will find meaningful expression through the law or politics. Compared to many other models of democratic governance, the two-party system in the United States exerts an extremely limiting influence on the content of political expression. To argue that one party's position on one issue must decide a citizen's vote is somewhat simplistic given these limiting realities. *Roe v. Wade* is a legal opinion that offers women in the United States the right to obtain an abortion through a significant portion of the term of a pregnancy. Nevertheless, the choice to exercise this right is one that individual women make, and the existence of the legal right to an abortion does not by itself cause abortions. Indeed, in other countries where similar abortion laws exist, many fewer women choose to have abortions than is the case in the United States. This fact suggests that there are additional influences on American women that encourage them to seek abortions, some of which may be the result of economic, social, and cultural conditions unique to the United States. Certainly it is arguable that these other conditions have at least as much effect on a woman's decision to terminate a pregnancy as does the existence of a legal right to do so.

Might Catholic citizens, fully informed of the Catholic Church's position on abortion and in an appropriate exercise of their prudential judgment, decide that economic, social, and cultural changes would be a more effective way to decrease and ultimately prevent abortions than the use of raw political power to outlaw them against the will of the majority of the American people? What should Catholics and other Christians do if they believe that the Republican Party represents a collection of interests that are working to reinforce the economic, social, and cultural conditions that make the United States the leader in the developed world in the number of abortions performed every year? What should Christians do if they see the economic agenda of the Republican Party as rooted in libertarian and free-market ideas that are inconsistent with core values elucidated in Christian social teaching, ethics, and theology?

In addition, what if a Christian sees the Republican Party's agenda as supporting a role for the United States in international affairs that has unleashed an immoral and unnecessary war in Iraq and made future wars more likely, actions that have already resulted in death and untold suffering for millions of people? Are babies in the womb any more deserving of protection than children living under the constant threat of death in Baghdad, a danger directly attributable to the decisions of Republican political elites in the United States? During the period immediately preceding both this war and the 2004 presidential elections, tremendous pressure to support a military attack was exerted on Catholics and other Christians who questioned its legitimacy, pressure that was often applied not on the basis of political arguments but on challenges to the seriousness of the faith commitment of those who disagreed.

One goal of this book is to offer Christians and other religious believers a richly layered argument that provides both theoretical and practical reasons for rejecting core intellectual commitments of right-wing politics in the United States. In particular, I hope to respond to attempts by the Religious Right, notably Catholic neoconservatives, to claim that the two political parties in the United States serve as meaningful proxies for distinguishing religious belief from unbelief or serious faith commitments from nominal ones. In order to do this properly I must also consider the political Right as a whole, beyond its powerful constituency of religious conservatives. It is here that one finds the influence of secular ideas such as libertarianism, social contract theory, and free-market economics, ideas to which no thoughtful Christian owes any particular allegiance and which in some cases might even be seen as antithetical to orthodox Christian intellectual traditions. Upon closer examination, the pervasive influence of these theories on the Republican agenda undermines any claim that the American Right is particularly sympathetic to the core values of Catholicism in particular and Christianity more generally.

My analysis of these issues is rooted in my training as a legal academic, one who in particular sees serious jurisprudence as driven by a need to understand the philosophical and theoretical commitments of key actors in a society—most notably its social, economic, and political elites. I believe this is the best way to understand why certain legal regimes are put into place, why particular policies are developed to support them, and why certain assumptions and arguments are employed to justify them. This type of analysis requires the engagement of ideas from disciplines outside the law, at least law narrowly construed as the examination of legal rules. Yet, in general, it is impossible to understand the law in any meaningful way without some sort of engagement with the intellectual traditions and the history of the society that the legal system regulates, and it is hard to imagine a serious academic and intellectual inquiry about "the law" divorced from this broader perspective.

Thus, in this work, I draw heavily from the disciplines of theology, philosophy, and history in an effort to explain the key commitments and beliefs of those who wield economic and political power in this country. In doing this, I reveal rather starkly how certain American elites, many of whom have little use for religious belief, manipulate religious values and use the language of religious commitment as a means of justifying current economic, social, and political arrangements and of staving off attempts to reconsider or reorder them. For example, the tragic events of September 11 have been employed by political elites in the United States not as opportunity to demonstrate the strength of America's democratic institutions or to forward the vision of human dignity promised by our Constitution but as an opportunity to sow fear and suspicion among the citizenry, to wage war, and ultimately to consolidate power in the presidency. Since September 11, Americans have been encouraged to direct more hostility at immigrants, economic migrants, and the poor. They have also been implored to tolerate stunning invasions of their privacy by the government, to support aggressive efforts to undermine the independence of the judiciary, and to acquiesce in broad assertions of executive power.

Although the United States has emerged as the world's wealthiest and most powerful nation, it is riven internally by an increasingly profound ideological divide, popularly represented in the image of the "culture war" or the "red state/blue state" dichotomy of presidential election results. Of course, "red state/blue state" differences are vastly oversimplified. For the most part, few American states have cohesive cultural identities that bear any real relationship to the worldviews of their citizens, and the divide of which I am speaking has little to do with the geopolitical boundaries of the fifty states. The real source of this division is rooted in responses to modernity and the challenges of global economic and social change. For some Americans, the response to these changes is rooted in the past, and they seek solace primarily in concepts that flourished in the nineteenth and early twentieth centuries—triumphant, authoritarian religion; laissez-faire, free-market economics; and aggressive national sovereignty. For others, hope lies in the future—freedom of conscience and respect for religious pluralism, global commitments to human dignity and human rights, and increasing balance in the global economic order between the haves and the have-nots.

I have become concerned about the growing tendency of those whose vision for the future draws heavily upon the past—let us call them conservatives—to attach the moniker "Christian" to themselves and their views in ways that suggest religious concordance with their political positions and, therefore, a certain unchallengeable "truth." Since the mid-twentieth century, orthodox Christian thinking has moved in directions that are much more consistent with the potential promise of the emerging transnational global order than with the positivist constructs of power rooted in the parochial sovereignty of nation-states and the whims of their leaders. Furthermore, the Christian intellectual tradition is far too rich and complex to allow it to be captured by the peculiar cultural experiences and responses of certain religious groups in the United States. Christianity can never be allowed to serve as an apologia for American power and the American way of life. Authentic Christianity must challenge the

United States to reckon more honestly with its failures and push the nation to use its awesome wealth and power in ways that promote global peace and human dignity. I hope that this book will empower Christians and others of good will who share this vision for the United States to confront those political and religious conservatives who claim to speak in their name—those who assert that they are defending "freedom," promoting "family values," preserving "law and order," and protecting us from "terrorists"—and to challenge their claims to religious authority for their aggressive, antidemocratic assertions of power over the rest of us.

This book would not have been possible without the help of many people. Although it would be impossible to recognize all of them (and I apologize to those I am unable to acknowledge here), there are nevertheless a few individuals whose help was essential in bringing this book to press. I am particularly indebted to my colleague Cathleen Kaveny, who first proposed to me the idea of writing a book and whose review of drafts, encouragement, and friendship have been absolutely invaluable during this process. I would also like to thank my colleagues Jay Tidmarsh, for his comments on drafts of several chapters, and Teresa Phelps, whose book, *Shattered Voices: Language, Violence, and the Work of Truth Commissions,* and good counsel on writing helped spur me forward on this project. I also extend my heartfelt appreciation to James Boyd White, Michael Perry, and Thomas Kohler, all of whom were instrumental in getting my book idea approved by Oxford University Press.

Much of my writing was done during my year in residence at Notre Dame's London Law Centre in the United Kingdom, and I would like to thank my dean, Patricia O'Hara, and my colleague Geoffrey Bennett, director of the London Law Centre, for everything they did to make my experience in London possible, comfortable, and enjoyable. I would also like to recognize my secretary at Notre Dame, Gloria Krull, and my research assistants who were most heavily involved in work on the book: Nicholas Danella, Joseph Rompala, and Eric Thomason. Finally, I would like to thank my reader, whose careful review of the manuscript provided a number of important insights and suggestions, many of which I incorporated into the book's final drafts.

Contents

Christians in the
American Empire

Introduction

Americans have long accepted the notion of the United States as
an exceptional nation. For a country born out of a revolutionary experiment in eighteenth-century democratic liberalism, the idea of
uniqueness comes naturally and is not without some basis in fact.
Typically, Americans view exceptionalism as a positive trait, and
it is often the source of an overriding sense that the United States
is a "better" nation than any other—the most democratic, the freest,
the most faith filled, the strongest—the list goes on. But the word
"exceptional" is Janus-like, and its negative face rarely receives the
attention of the positive. Not only does American exceptionalism often degenerate quickly into an unthinking, bellicose nationalism,
but, more darkly for the nation's future, it often blinds Americans
to the reality that the United States is no better protected from
the vicissitudes of the human condition than is any other place on
earth. Indeed, the 2005 hurricane season demonstrated that the
United States may be particularly *ill* prepared for predictable, everyday challenges like the weather, with Hurricane Katrina in particular exposing deep dysfunction in the nation's social and physical
infrastructure.

American culture has a particular propensity for celebrating notions of freedom that are rooted in extreme versions of individual
autonomy. Increasingly, this has driven American law and politics
away from understandings of the human person that are situated
in communal values like solidarity and sharing. Hurricane Katrina

and the near destruction of New Orleans exposed an American governing elite that was shockingly cavalier in its disregard for meaningful emergency preparedness and virtually incapable of demonstrating the kind of community-bonding leadership and compassion one would expect in a crisis of such magnitude. American politics has continued to descend to shocking new lows, with corruption scandals enveloping prominent members of Congress from both parties, as well as some of President Bush's closest advisors. Nevertheless, American power elites continue to nurture a culture of self-promotion and greed in order to maintain their social and economic dominance, to justify current structural inequalities in American society, and to promote the creation of economic and political structures around the world sympathetic to their interests.

The political and legal developments that have grown out of this culture present unique challenges to orthodox Christians who are more inclined toward social democracy than free markets and individualism and who find that visions of freedom and human dignity rooted in community provide a more compelling link to the conception of the human person developed in the Gospels and through Christian tradition. I use the term *social democracy* to describe a political theory that recognizes the essential nature of groups and structures–for good and for ill—in people's lives. It also acknowledges that justice cannot flourish in human communities without a recognition of certain limitations we face in our ability to shape our own existence.

I also use the expression *social democratic* to identify an understanding of liberalism that does not proceed from an assumption of individuals as fully formed rights bearers who must diminish themselves in order to enter into necessary but ultimately unfortunate community with others. Rather, this concept of liberalism celebrates community as an essential and beneficial aspect of the human condition. Thus, social democrats recognize that there are limits to what individuals can do to affect the direction of their lives because structures exist that enhance or inhibit our ability to make choices. By way of example, one can imagine that, when presented with the same "freedom" to choose, the poor are not able to make the same choices as the rich and that women and men have different, although perhaps overlapping, sets of choices.

In speaking of Christianity, I use the term *orthodox* to identify those Christian traditions that root their theology not only in scripture but also in a respect for an authoritative tradition that reaches back to the Hebrew, Greek, and Roman influences on the Church fathers. Another way to identify this group would be through its adherence to the Apostle's Creed. Thus, one might also call orthodox Christians "creedal Christians." Orthodox or creedal Christianity teaches that human dignity is both God given and a reflection of the creation of human beings in God's image and likeness.[1] Only in community with others can it be fully realized.

This is not, however, to ignore the centrality of individual autonomy to any meaningful understanding of human dignity, and much of Christianity's awakening to the full implications of true respect for the individual is a result of its encounters with democracy and liberalism.[2] Nonetheless, for orthodox Christians, individual freedom is meaningful only in the context of a web of communal relationships that nurture both rights and duties, and this relational understanding of freedom is linked with the concept of a triune God of Father, Son, and Spirit acknowledged in the creed. Men and women, created in the image and likeness of a God in three persons, are communal beings from inception. Although the full implications of the meaning of the Trinity may be a mystery, the idea that the complete dignity of the human person cannot be conveyed by an emphasis on individuality seems to jibe intimately with the way most cultures have understood human interdependence.

Because of its emphasis on the relational aspects of human community, orthodox Christian theology, particularly Catholic thought, parts sharply with the contract-based theories of rights that find strong support in the Anglo-American world, most notably in the United States. These philosophies tend to nurture notions of individual autonomy that are skeptical of, if not hostile to, claims of community.[3] More specifically, Catholic social thought, which represents Catholicism's most comprehensive exploration of the church's relationship to the modern world, sees the individual, the state, politics, and the economy proceeding from understandings of freedom rooted in theological and philosophical traditions that stress human interdependence. It also rejects as a theoretical starting point for understanding democracy and human liberty any notion of a completely autonomous individual. Furthermore, since the Second Vatican Council, Catholicism has engaged other Christian traditions in a far-reaching ecumenical dialogue on these issues, and Catholic perspectives have both influenced and been shaped by encounters with serious thinkers from the Eastern Orthodox and mainline Protestant denominations that share a similar intellectual tradition.[4]

Despite denominational differences, orthodox Christian thinking on these questions is relatively consistent. Nevertheless, key groups within American Christianity, particularly certain Protestant evangelical and fundamentalist congregations that are increasingly influential in American politics, do not share the intellectual tradition of Christian orthodoxy, and their emphasis on a personal relationship with Christ and individual interpretations of scripture has achieved a comfortable complementarity with American individualism and free-market liberalism.

In this book I argue that the social, economic, and political life of the United States has reached a crisis point that will require many Christians to make some difficult choices about the nature of their participation in American democracy and society. I base this assertion on a thorough reading of the rich tradition of social thought that has developed in Roman Catholicism since the late nineteenth century and on my conclusion that much of Catholic social thought is in deep tension with the current direction of American economic, political, and cultural life, particularly as it has developed during the last quarter century. Many other Christians, religious believers of other traditions, and even those of no faith tradition at all have found the reasoning of Catholic social teaching compelling or, at the very least, view it as a touchstone for important dialogue about religious engagement with the modern world. For Catholics, the social doctrine is a fundamental teaching of the faith that rejects the radical secularism and moral relativism of the American political Left, as well as fundamentalist God-talk and the money-centered individualism of the Right.

Nevertheless, the current locus of power in American politics is in right-wing or "conservative" ideologies, so the intellectual inconsistency of Catholic social teaching with the current political program of the Right deserves particularly close attention. As free-market liberalism, libertarianism, and religious traditionalism have become driving intellectual forces in the Republican Party, certain American Catholics have attempted to link Catholic teaching to a right-wing political agenda in hopes of moving more Catholic voters into the Republican Party and aligning American Catholicism more comfortably with American power. Some of the most prominent proponents of these views are Rev. Richard John Neuhaus, editor of the influential journal *First Things;* George Weigel, a senior fellow with the Ethics and Public Policy Center; and Michael Novak, a scholar supported by the American Enterprise Institute. All three are often included in a group loosely identified as "neoconservatives," a contested moniker but one that typically identifies a primarily right-wing political stance that is staunchly free trade and sees a unique, morally grounded role for the United States as the standard-bearer of democracy and free-market liberalism around the world.

In general, neoconservatives are supportive of unilateral action by the United States in international affairs, due in part to a belief in the moral superiority of the nation's mission, values, and institutions. In this regard, neoconservatives draw on a long tradition of messianic exceptionalism in U.S. culture that has suggested a special destiny for the nation since the Puritan settlement of Massachusetts. Neuhaus, Weigel, and Novak have been extremely vocal in their support of the Republican Party as the most appropriate political "home" for American Catholics, on the basis of their strong belief that the "moral truth" of the founding ideals of the United States is rooted in a vision of natural law that links these values to the Christian truths of Roman Catholicism.

It should not be particularly surprising that American neoconservatism is highly controversial both at home and abroad. I argue in particular that it is somewhat disingenuous for Christians who align themselves with the Republican Party to claim that their political choice is demanded by a meaningful understanding of the intellectual traditions of Christianity. The Republican political program is driven not only by neoconservatives but also by ideologues who embrace libertarianism, nativism, free-market capitalism, militarism, and moral absolutism in ways that are completely at odds with modern understandings of orthodox Christian theology. Indeed, close scrutiny of the use of Catholic social teaching by some Catholic neoconservatives reveals a selective emphasis on isolated themes rather than an analysis of contemporary problems in light of the scope and ongoing development of the tradition. How else, for example, could Neuhaus and Weigel claim with so much conviction that the war in Iraq was "just" in the face of intense opposition to the unleashing of the conflict from the Vatican, the American bishops, and most of the world's prominent Christian theologians? What explains the deafening silence of these same voices in the face of growing evidence that the case for the war was based on weak or false information that was fed to the American public by duplicity within the Bush administration?[5] Worst of all, who has come forward to take responsibility for the ever-more horrific lot of the Iraqi people, whose current condition is directly attributable to the United States' decision to start a war?[6] The protection and promotion of peace are always the preferred Christian alternatives to military conflict, and "just war" theory must always be read in this light.[7] Despite its being cast as a "crusade" by President Bush and neoconservative intellectuals, the Iraq War has little to do with Christianity, properly understood. It is simply one step in a broader process of bolstering America's world power and creating a civil religion sympathetic to the social, political, and economic objectives of key elites in the United States.[8]

Thoughtful American Christians must recognize that, regardless of who occupies the White House, the United States has not been selected to be a special recipient of divine favor, nor has God chosen the United States to play a unique role among the world's nations. Attempts to justify U.S. economic and military hegemony by likening the nation's foreign policy to a divinely inspired moral role in world affairs should be dismissed out of hand as irresponsible political pandering by people anxious to preserve their grip on power. Why is the United States more deserving of God's favor than any other nation on earth? Are our wealth and military power proof of our favored position?

Orthodox Christian theology rejects any attempt to link wealth and temporal power to God's favor. Indeed, if any group can lay claim to a special relationship with God, it is the poor. In the final analysis, no U.S. political party or presidential administration has any right to claim a Christian mandate for a quest to maintain world dominance.

By exposing some of the powerful imperatives that drive legal and political choices in the United States, I hope to explain why key priorities of America's governing and social elites part with the ethos that should underlie Christian citizenship in a democratic society. I also argue that religious influences on political choices in pluralist democracies have certain pragmatic limits and that it is absurd and dangerous for Christians to see American politics as a means for creating a coherent Christian culture in the United States. Diverse societies filled with people of varying beliefs represent the current reality for most liberal democracies worldwide. It is a political and cultural environment that Christians committed to human dignity and respect for individual conscience should embrace, and it is one in which a Christian can both survive and thrive. Working from a vision of active and respectful Christian participation in pluralist, secular democracies, I propose an approach to political engagement and civic life for Christians that nurtures human dignity through the enhancement of community life and social solidarity and rejects the heavy-handed power of military violence, the social emptiness of radical personal autonomy, and the winner-take-all mentality of loosely regulated free-market capitalism.

A Christian's public life must be rooted in charity and love. In a democracy, Christian citizens should look closely at the assumptions and values that shape law and public policy and then determine whether, on balance, the apparatus of state strives to promote the dignity and participation of citizens in the nation's common life. Specific policies or actions will doubtless fail this test, but traditional Christian theology rejects the notion that the civil order is ever a perfect reflection of the celestial one. The Christian's role is to assess the overall direction of the society and ask hard questions about what type of community the nation's political and legal actors are attempting to create. How do our leaders understand what supports a decent and dignified human existence, and how does this vision affect our nation's relationships to other human communities around the world?

The United States is not the "new Israel," and the promotion of this idea in American public life by certain Christians shows not only hubris but also an inexcusable disregard for the all-encompassing salvation message of the New Testament. The United States is a secular, pluralist democracy grounded in shared understandings among the majority of its citizens about privileged roles for personal freedom, democratic governance, and free-market liberalism. As

Jeffrey Stout has argued, "democracy is a culture, a tradition, in its own right. It has an ethical life of its own, which philosophers would do well to articulate."[9] Christians can and should participate in this process of articulation, and indeed they have much to contribute. As an initial matter, however, Christians must recognize that there will always be important areas in which U.S. civil society does not comport with their faith traditions.

Nevertheless, those Christians who share strong communal and humanist values can turn their attentions to engagement with the world in ways that bring a richer understanding of human dignity and social justice to public discourse. The call to a lived Christian faith, particularly as it is embodied in Catholic social teaching, announces understandings of justice and human dignity that require an embrace of a universal humanistic vision. Through a meaningful engagement with the tradition of Christian humanism, Christians in the United States could exhort their fellow citizens to be less materialistic, nationalistic, and self-centered and challenge them to become more charitable, more cosmopolitan, and more open to the transformative power of engagement with others, both at home and abroad. Indeed, the Christian should be what Anthony Appiah calls a "rooted cosmopolitan," respectful of local differences, historical circumstances, and traditions but unwilling to become a servant of a project dependent on the exceptionalism or celestially favored status of one particular nation.[10] Unfortunately, it appears that the United States has taken up an imperial project on the basis of just such a premise.

The American Empire

Applying the term *empire* to the United States tends to raise eyebrows, if not righteous anger, among Americans, no doubt because of the largely antidemocratic tendencies of many of history's imperial projects and a strong ideological association of the nation's founding with an anti-imperialist quest for "freedom." Nevertheless, there has probably never been a similar time in U.S. history in which the description of the United States as an empire has been more widely accepted around the world. What does it mean to call the United States an empire? To answer this question, it seems particularly useful to begin with a prominent Canadian's impression of the United States. Any nation's assessment of itself has to be balanced against the impressions of those looking at the country from a critical distance.

Because of Canada's geographic proximity and cultural similarity to the United States, it is hard to imagine another nation whose citizens are in a better position to assess America with a balance of respect, fear, envy, and disdain.[11]

In 1963 George Grant wrote *Lament for a Nation: The Defeat of Canadian Nationalism,* in which he described the inevitable absorption of Canada into an American individualist and capitalist "empire." At that time he defended this description of the United States: "The use of the concept 'American Empire' is often objected to, particularly by those who like to believe that the age of empires is over. They associate an empire with earlier patterns—the British, the Spanish, and the French—when Europeans maintained rule in distant parts of the globe by superior control of the sea. But an empire does not have to wield direct political control over colonial countries. Poland and Czechoslovakia are as much part of the Russian Empire as India was [of] the British, or Canada and Brazil of the American. An empire is the control of one state by another. In this sense, the United States of America has an empire."[12]

Lest one be tempted to think that this more than 40-year-old view of U.S. power might be grounded in political conceits that are now dated, a book written in 2002 by an American author makes Grant seem remarkably prescient. In *American Empire: The Realities and Consequences of U.S. Diplomacy,* Andrew Bacevich comes to the same conclusion as Grant on the imperial status of the United States. He argues that America's frayed social fabric and weak civic identity have made constant economic growth the balm for the country's social and political dysfunction. This constant push toward "more and better" in the material lives of American citizens is supported by an aggressive international diplomatic strategy of "openness":

> In the age of globalization, economic considerations have become inseparable from those of national security. . . . Both peace and prosperity require order. Both demand adherence to particular norms: respect for private property, financial transparency, and some semblance of checks on corruption.
>
> Although the strategy of openness implies expansion, it does not qualify as "imperialistic," at least in the conventional sense of the term. It is, for example, strongly averse to acquiring territory or colonies. But the strategy does seek to consolidate and even enlarge a particular conception of global order. More specifically, it seeks to make permanent the favored position that the United States enjoys as victor in two world wars and the Cold War, the furtive hegemony to which most Americans purport to be oblivious, but that others recognize as the dominant reality of contemporary international politics.[13]

In Bacevich's terms, "openness" means "the removal of barriers to the movement of goods, capital, people, and ideas, thereby fostering an integrated international order conducive to American interests, governed by American norms, regulated by American power, and above all, satisfying the expectations of the American people to ever-greater abundance."[14] If Grant's description of the American empire contained a weakness, it was that he did not define what constituted "control" of one state by another when there has been no direct political or geographic conquest. Bacevich, however, provides an important rationale for viewing economic and social control as an alternative route to empire.

Michael Hardt and Antonio Negri have taken a more traditionally "leftist" view of U.S. power and have differentiated *empire* from *imperialism*. In their view, "the sovereignty of the nation-state was the cornerstone of the imperialisms that European powers constructed throughout the modern era. . . . Imperialism was really an extension of the sovereignty of the European nation-states beyond their own boundaries."[15] Hardt and Negri see empire as a new form of global sovereignty that has arisen with the decline of the dominion of territorial nation-states. Whereas nation-state supremacy was the linchpin of the imperialism that European nations constructed throughout the modern era, today's empire "establishes no territorial centers of power and does not rely on fixed boundaries or barriers. It is a *decentered* and deterritorializing apparatus of rule that progressively incorporates the entire global realm within its open, expanding frontiers."[16] Drawing on the classic works of Thucydides, Livy, and Tacitus and anticipating key underpinnings of U.S. justifications for the Iraq war for four years before it was launched, they maintain that "empire is formed not on the basis of force itself, but on the basis of the capacity to present force as being in the service of right and peace. All interventions of the imperial armies are solicited by one or more of the parties involved in an already existing conflict. Empire is not born of its own will but rather it is called into being and constituted on the basis of its capacity to resolve conflicts."[17]

The instability of the civil and social order has long led governments into various foreign adventures in an effort to direct popular attention elsewhere. In his 2003 Clarendon lectures at Oxford University, David Harvey observed that the decade preceding September 11, 2001, saw U.S. civil society declining into an "aimless, senseless chaos of private interests."[18] He went on to observe that

> during the 1990s there was no clear enemy and the booming economy within the United States should have guaranteed an unparalleled level of contentment and satisfaction throughout all but the most underprivileged and marginalized elements of civil society. Yet . . . the 1990s turned out to be one of the most unpleasant decades in US history. Competition was vicious, the avatars of the "new

economy" became millionaires overnight and flaunted their wealth, scams and fraudulent schemes proliferated, scandals (both real and imagined) were everywhere embraced with gusto, vicious rumors circulated about scandals plotted in the White House, an attempt was made to impeach the president, talk-show hosts Howard Stern and Rush Limbaugh typified a media totally out of control, Los Angeles erupted in riots, Waco and Oklahoma symbolized a penchant for internal opposition that had long remained latent, teenagers shot and killed their classmates in Columbine, irrational exuberance prevailed over common sense, and corporate corruption of the political process was blatant.[19]

If an expanding economy and the constant enlargement of the scope of the material benefits of American capitalism could not keep the population satisfied, what was to be done? Harvey argues that the "war on terror" provided "the political opening not only to assert a national purpose and to proclaim national solidarity, but also to impose order and stability on civil society at home. It was the war on terror, swiftly followed by the prospect of war with Iraq, which allowed the state to accumulate more power."[20]

In his most recent book, *The New American Militarism: How Americans Are Seduced by War*,[21] Bacevich provides a broad-ranging analysis that lends a great deal of support to Harvey's view. Bacevich argues that since World War II, the U.S. political elite, along with much of the American public, has developed a siege mentality that initially was the result of a need to stand resolute before the threat of communism. Over time, however, this has produced a willingness to "use all of the instruments of executive and military power, instantly and without hesitation, to keep our enemies at bay."[22] This has led to the creation of what Bacevich calls "the national security state," which is sustained by an "imperial presidency": "The Soviet threat was real and an American response was necessary, but one unanticipated consequence was that crisis became a seemingly permanent condition. With anxious citizens looking to the commander-in-chief to keep them safe, presidents accrued—and exercised—an ever-expanding array of prerogatives.... Although the Cold War eventually ended, the symbiotic relationship between the national security state and the imperial presidency did not."[23]

The events of September 11 have emboldened the Bush administration to assert breathtaking privileges for the executive branch. In testimony before the Senate Judiciary Committee in February 2006, Attorney General Alberto Gonzales claimed that the "plain language" of a congressional resolution giving President Bush the authority to use "all necessary and appropriate force" against al-Qaeda granted the executive branch broad, unchecked authorization to spy on the private communications of American citizens despite the existence of extremely detailed, specific legislation that requires the executive branch to seek a warrant for such monitoring.[24] If this were not enough to suggest an imperial presidency run amok, during the very same week, the Bush administration announced a recharacterization of the war on terror into "the long war." Congress was told in the Pentagon's quadrennial defense review that Americans should prepare for a "large-scale, potentially long duration, irregular warfare campaign" that would require a budget of $550 billion. This was coupled with statements to the press by then Defense Secretary Donald Rumsfeld that suggested that the United States and its allies were locked in new crisis comparable to the Cold War, in which the enemy was seeking to establish an Islamic empire around the globe.[25]

On the basis of any number of definitions, the United States is a modern imperial nation. To some extent, its governing elites are attempting to control domestic instability by expanding U.S. global power through the assertion of a great, new crisis for the twenty-first century: Islamic fundamentalist fascism. They combine this with a claim to a unique ability to keep the international peace because of the country's unassailable military superiority. The peaceful goal of the exercise of imperial power—the *mission civilatrice* of American imperium—will be the aggressive encouragement of the American versions of democracy and free-market capitalism, which will secure international peace over the long term. The foot soldiers for the military campaigns necessary to prosecute a "long war" have been drawn primarily from the segments of the population least likely to benefit from free-market liberalism and social individualism at home—the rural and urban poor, recent immigrants, and low-skilled, blue-collar workers. There has never been a hint of a suggestion that America's middle and upper classes would ever be asked to bear the costs of empire—certainly not with their children's lives.

This lack of any real sense of responsibility or duty among America's privileged for the power the nation wields and for the benefits that power confers upon them is a troubling sign for the future. What sacrifices are Americans as a group willing to endure in order to maintain the world's most materially indulgent lifestyle? What are America's responsibilities when it comes to protection of the global ecosystem? What are the nation's obligations to the poor at home and abroad? The lack of a strong domestic cultural or moral consensus on important questions like these has led to an increasingly shaky civil society that relies heavily on the promise of expanding economic opportunity. This would suppress the social discord and economic instability that would likely follow any restraints on American consumerist consumption or any requirement that the burdens of empire be shared across the social spectrum. On the basis of the current preeminence of U.S. military and economic power, the Bush administration in particular has drawn the United States into an unsustainable unilateralist posture with much of the world, leaving the nation's overextended military in the difficult position of being ill prepared to respond to direct attacks on the nation's domestic security, a use of the military that would be licit with regard to international law and tend to receive widespread political support.[26]

Given the historical record, it is arguably naïve to think that the United States would work so hard to maintain its dominance in the world because of some spiritually grounded zeal to "free" the world's people from dominance and oppression. "Freedom," however, is an important justification for the current aggressive use of U.S. power around the world because it sends a strong message about the nation's exceptionalism that resonates with the American people. In American public discourse, "freedom" is rooted in highly stylized national foundation myths of great rhetorical power, and the concept has long been able to withstand real scrutiny in order to announce a vision of peace and prosperity for world's oppressed with which it is hard to disagree. George Bush's second inaugural address is an excellent example of the use of this freedom rhetoric to announce imperialistic objectives in moralistic terms:

> The survival of liberty in our land increasingly depends on the success of liberty in other lands. The best hope for peace in our world is the expansion of freedom in all the world. America's vital interests and our deepest beliefs are now one. From the day of our founding, we have proclaimed that every man and woman on this earth has rights and dignity and matchless value because they bear the image of the maker of heaven and earth. Across the generations, we have proclaimed the imperative of self-government, because no one is fit to be a master, and no one deserves to be a slave. Advancing these ideals is the mission that created our nation. . . . Now it is the urgent requirement of our nation's security, and the calling of our time. So it is the policy of our nation to support the growth of democratic movements and institutions in every nation and culture, with the ultimate goal of ending tyranny in the world.[27]

Despite this high-minded vision of the United States' role in the world, many who have taken the time to ask what Americans have meant throughout history when they have praised freedom and excoriated tyranny have found the answers wanting. For example, in unpacking some of the freedom myths surrounding the creation of the American republic, British historian Robert Harvey noted in his book *A Few Bloody Noses:*

> It is asserted that a fundamental motive for the [American Revolution] was an ideological love of liberty reacting against British military oppression. The motives were in fact much more complex—ranging from a love of liberty, certainly, to economic self-interest, and above all to the extraordinarily rapid transformation undergone by American society, both in numbers and in material wealth.... It is widely believed that Americans overwhelmingly rallied to the patriotic cause of resistance to the British. There is no evidence to support this.... Independence was a minority cause, support for which was whipped up by a group of committed political ideologues supported by sympathetic commercial interests.[28]

Freedom, of course, has meant different things to different people. America was a slave society in which economic and social freedom for some was inextricably linked to bondage for others through the maintenance of a socioeconomic system in which human beings were chattel. "Freedom" for some also depended on the ruthless suppression, removal, and eradication of the native Indian tribes. Respect for and responsibility to others have long been expendable in the quest for personal gain, and in this sense, the "revolutionary" story of the founding of the United States has a lineage that can be traced to Cain and Abel. After the Revolution, at least eight percent of the American population left the country, "carr[ying] their hatred—or fear—of the American Revolution to the extent of uprooting themselves from the land they loved and the property they owned."[29] Add to this the "overwhelmingly pro-British majority of blacks and the Indian population, [and] even by the admission of the revolutionary leaders nearly half the population was loyalist."[30]

Opposition to what the United States represented was so intense that it became a constitutive part of the national identity of Canada, the nation to which many Loyalists fled. Both French- and English-speaking Canadians recognized that "society required a high degree of law, and respect for a public conception of virtue. Both [groups] would grant the state much wider rights to control the individual than the libertarian American constitution."[31] Francophone Canadians were able to insulate themselves from the United States through language and a fierce loyalty to the Roman Catholic Church. Anglophone Canadians positioned themselves against their neighbors to the south by identifying culturally and politically with Britain well into the twentieth century, although that identification was not enough prevent George Grant's sapient *Lament* for his nation.

American scholars have also challenged the popular construction of the nation's establishment as a quest for freedom from tyranny. It is extremely important to air this historical work because there is now a pronounced tendency among many "conservative" public figures in the United States to cast this founding in a way that distorts the complex and often unpleasant realities of American nation building. For example, the Founders' original intent in constitutional interpretation takes on a very different meaning when we are more accurately situated in the socioeconomic and political realities of eighteenth-century England and its colonies. Drawing on historian David Hackett Fischer's seminal work in *Albion's Seed,* Walter McDougall has written that a noteworthy aspect of the English roots of U.S. colonial history was the strong influence of Cavaliers from southwest England in Virginia and Maryland, as well as the Scots-Irish in Appalachia and the inland South. The Cavaliers, or King's Men, had lost their estates in the English civil war, and many installed themselves as a new American aristocracy around Chesapeake Bay. They took inequality for granted and linked freedom for themselves to their ability to exercise authority over others.[32]

The Scots-Irish "were pure libertarians, for whom freedom meant the absence of any outside authority. They reckoned all who imposed or collected taxes and rents to be glorified thieves, and all who drew or enforced boundaries to be glorified jailers."[33] They embraced an "ecstatic evangelical" form of Christianity, and their spirit was embodied in men such as Patrick Henry, Daniel Boone, the Calhouns, and the Jacksons.[34] New England and Pennsylvania were dominated by the Puritan and Quaker cultures respectively, which existed in sharp tension with the other two, and this friction arguably set the stage for the nation's great civil war. Also significant in the development of the American colonies and early republic was a virulent anti-Catholicism and "the English notion of a racial hierarchy justifying expulsion or enslavement of lesser breeds who got in the way of expansion[, which] characterized American behavior even more than it did that of the British. 'White man's democracy,' tolerant or else fiercely supportive of slavery and Indian removal triumphed with Andrew Jackson in 1828." Indeed, the *bête noire* of the modern American Right is the elite culture that originated in the Northeast, and it is not at all surprising that the new electoral power base of the Republican Party lies in the South, Midwest, and inland West. Regional political tension has been a constant part of the American experience, and much of it has been rooted in cultural differences linked to religion. The American Right taps into strong currents of libertarianism, authoritarianism, and evangelical piety that have long been constituent parts of American identity.

Faith and Citizenship in a U.S.-Dominated World

Although Christians believe that their faith has access to universal truths, orthodox Christianity also teaches that those truths are accessible to all people regardless of culture and that no one political or economic system is completely consistent with a Christian worldview. Furthermore, Catholicism in particular has long instructed that true individual flourishing can occur only within the context of a web of human relationships. This culturally heterogeneous, situated understanding of human well-being is an accepted part of many political philosophies around the world, but it has typically been rejected in the United States in favor of contractarian understandings of rights, grounded in an idealized vision of individual autonomy—one that would have existed in a "state of nature." For Catholics, God is social, existing in the triune form of Father, Son, and Holy Spirit. The creation story inherited from the Hebrew Scriptures presents a story of man and woman in society with one another and with God. Traditional understandings of Christianity root human flourishing in community, and it is the communitarian aspect of Catholicism that creates a particularly jarring tension with American culture.

The central event of Catholic religious practice, the consecration of the Eucharist at the celebration of the Mass, is a communal recognition of the presence of Christ amid the assembled faithful. The Christian concept of incarnation—God taking human form—is the basis for the Catholic understanding of the sacredness of human life. The sacramental and cultural meaning of those ideas cannot be grasped apart from life in community with others. The integral engagement of the individual in community is the starting point for comprehending the individual in Catholic social teaching, and it links Catholic social teaching much more directly to the philosophical tradition of continental Europe than to Anglo-American analytic philosophy. Many of the political theorists whose work has most influenced Catholic social teaching have not come from the English-speaking world.[35] Although some of these thinkers have been translated into English, their work receives little attention in the United States outside of academia and rarely influences the development of American political theory.

If American law is any indication, the idea of moral obligation arising from life in community with other human beings is something increasingly foreign to American culture. A particularly telling example of this is the long-festering public debate over abortion in the United States. As legal scholar and theologian M. Cathleen Kaveny has noted, both sides in the abortion debate argue from a notion of law that sees as its main purpose the restraint of individuals or the state in order to protect a highly atomized understanding of individual rights.[36] Abortion foes fixate on the right to life of the fetus, a right that is violated by a woman who obtains an abortion. Yet, there is very little discussion of the real burdens women must bear to nurture a fetus to term or to raise a child to adulthood, nor is there any sustained discussion of responsibilities the broader community must assume in support of mothers and children.

Proponents of unrestricted access to abortion focus on the rights of pregnant women to be free from the coercive power of others—the state, men, parents—and on a woman's "right" to control what she does with her body. What about women's responsibilities to their communities as bearers of children? These perspectives on individual rights offer no language to discuss the common good or the rights and responsibilities that emerge from a life in community and solidarity with others. They have become so pervasive that U.S. law recognizes fewer and fewer duties that arise out of the existence of relationships, even those as intimate as those between parent and child. Kaveny has called this American perspective on legal relationships

> the marshal in the Old West view, [which] has long held sway in important aspects of American law. . . . Generally speaking, there is no obligation in tort or criminal law to help another person unless you have some well-defined personal or professional relationship with them. So, in the great majority of American states, if I hurry by a 2-year-old tipped over in a puddle, letting her drown rather than being five minutes late for my movie, I commit no legal wrong. Even in the few states where it is penalized, it is lightly penalized. What about the obligations of parents to their children? Well, I do have a legal obligation to fish my own toddler out of the puddle. But I do not have a legal obligation to give her a blood transfusion even if it is the only way to save her life and even if it is likely to cause only minimal inconvenience to me.[37]

In this environment, it is hardly surprising that the U.S. legal structures for the support of families, children, the poor, and the infirm are among the weakest in the industrialized world.

In the chapters that follow, I explore the current imperial direction of the American experiment and offer a critique that is rooted in Catholic social thought and the secular philosophical traditions that have influenced it, as well as an ecumenical, tradition-oriented approach to the challenge of Christian engagement in the modern world. I hope this work will spark a reexamination of the current direction of U.S. world leadership among people of goodwill from a variety of religious traditions. In particular, I hope to challenge attempts by key groups on the American political Right to claim a Christian mandate for their political agenda.

In response, I want to encourage Catholics and other sympathetic Christians in the United States to embrace the richness of their 2,000-year-old faith tradition and offer a more prophetic resistance to a false American civil religion that justifies and nurtures the distorted values of the American empire, notably libertarian freedom, consumerist materialism, and increasingly unrestrained free-market liberalism. To demonstrate how far U.S. law and public policy have drifted from traditional Christianity, I explore recent developments in key areas of those fields to demonstrate how individualist and market-based values undermine traditional Christian understandings of the essential components of human dignity.

I begin my critique with a look at the nation's political situation and its current domination by the Republican Party's agenda. Although one major justification for Republican electoral power is the consistency of the party's message with "traditional religious values," which are extremely important to large segments of the American public, I challenge this view by arguing that the religious vision that animates American "conservatism" is not orthodox Christian thinking, which respects scripture, tradition, and reason, but biblical fundamentalism and, among certain Roman Catholics, doctrinaire religious formalism rooted in romantic notions of pre-1960s' cohesive Western culture. These forces have aligned themselves with secular libertarians, free-market liberals, and the American money elite to offer a civil religion to the people that justifies the nation's wealth, power, and exceptionalism, while demanding little in terms of social solidarity, sacrifice, and sharing.

The burdens of this radical social and political model are shouldered by the weakest members of society. Poor people, the working class, children, single mothers, immigrants, and ethnic and racial minorities all bear the brunt of a political program that diverts resources to empire building and private wealth creation, while redirecting investment away from the public goods that enhance community life and serve a broad cross-section of the population. These people also become the guinea pigs for the legal changes pressed by those on the Religious Right who have become angry and disoriented by the last half-century of social change. Restrictive abortion laws, for example, tend to prevent primarily poorer, rural women in conservative states from getting abortions. Middle-class and wealthy women who have the means to travel and to pay have little trouble obtaining abortions, regardless of the laws in place. The insertion of certain religious ideas in the public school, such as mandated prayer or "intelligent design," is a controversy that does not affect the lives of those who can afford private schooling based on their preferred values or who live in the nation's wealthier and most academically rigorous public school districts, although affluence may no longer be the sanctuary it once was.[38]

In the second part of my analysis, I present an orthodox Christian response to the civil religion of the American political Right through the perspective of Catholic social thought and its philosophical underpinnings. Catholic social teaching and its secular philosophical companions reject the contractarian and libertarian political philosophy that drives U.S. law and public policy. I demonstrate how orthodox Christianity and Catholic social teaching bring to discussions of freedom, justice, or democracy radically different understandings of the human person in relationship to community. This insight has profound implications for what Christians should see as legitimate goals for economic, political, and social life in a pluralist democracy and, more profoundly, what is required to promote fundamental democratic values like human dignity.

One great failure of contractarian political philosophy in the United States is demonstrated by the ongoing battles over the role of African Americans in our society, exemplified most dramatically by the controversies that surround affirmative action. The Right has tended to deny or minimize the reality of race as an integral part of the American experience, while the Left has often allowed race to become a sine qua non of personal identity, the linchpin of a social welfare system that grants protections and privileges based on one's ability to claim membership in a victimized group. The approaches of both positions are in keeping with a long tradition of racism and racialism in the nation. The failure of American elites to construct a consistent vision of society that dignifies the unique burdens and contributions of African Americans and other minority groups, while at the same time calling upon members of these groups to assume the full duties and privileges of citizenship, demonstrates the inability of the American culture of autonomy to create a coherent social and narrative identity in a complex, multiethnic society. I argue that, through its concepts of solidarity and participation, Catholic social thought supports a vision of liberal pluralism that considers the needs of distinctive groups by means of cultural narratives that are meaningful within the nation's social and historical tradition. Indeed, the recognition of unique histories can help to create a more realistic national narrative around which a strong collective identity can evolve and deals more respectfully and honestly with the modern reality of cultural pluralism within democratic societies.

I look next at how the American society has struggled to give significant citizenship rights to immigrants and poor people. Of late, immigrants have become a scapegoat for the nation's fear of crime, social change, terrorism, and the implications of a global free-market economy. Immigration is one issue in which the internal inconsistencies of the Republican political coalition reveal themselves, and since most U.S. immigrants are brown-skinned, Catholic Mexicans and Central Americans, it brings to the fore the nativism and anti-Catholicism that have been recurring themes in American public life. The general indifference to and tolerance for poverty continue to set the nation apart from other wealthy countries. Furthermore, mounting economic difficulties faced by the middle and working class reveal the ugly underbelly of a free-market capitalism that is unchecked by a strong sense of social justice or solidarity and is nurtured by the privileged position that law and public policy accord to individual wealth creation and the protection of the assets of the rich. The insecurity and instability of the American family, as well as the precarious position of children in our society (all of which are profoundly related to the persistence of widespread poverty in the United States) cannot be understood apart from an economic system that preferences wealth-enhancement opportunities for the privileged—like tax cuts—over the creation of economic security for working people and the poor.

I conclude by offering a prescription for the public engagement of Catholics and other Christians in an American empire. Having assessed various areas of U.S. law and culture in the light of Catholic social thought and philosophical traditions that do not depend on contractarian concepts of rights, I ultimately reject the view that the American democracy is particularly sympathetic to Christianity or that the United States is a "Christian nation" in any compelling sense. Appeals by some American neoconservative intellectuals to natural law and the "true" intentions of the nation's Founders notwithstanding, the current state of our culture reveals a social and political order in which tradition-oriented Christian belief and Catholic social thought have little influence except in highly distorted forms. American Catholics and other sympathetic Christians would do well to recognize the United States for what it is, an economic republic structured to provide the greatest possible freedom for individuals and to maximize the material comfort of its citizens, particularly its wealthiest ones. As the nation's power has increased in the world, so too have its imperial tendencies, and those who govern the United States increasingly find unacceptable any competing visions of political and economic life that threaten the country's dominance of world affairs. Does that then mean that one cannot be a good Christian and a patriotic American? If being patriotic means that one cannot criticize or reject the central cultural and economic tenets of the American imperium, then yes, perhaps the two are completely inconsistent.

There is, however, another way for orthodox Christians to think about being American. Those who reject the premises of an American imperium can reimagine their role in American life by recognizing the universalism of Christian culture and by drawing on the strength of its multicultural influences to promote peace and human dignity around the world. They can see themselves as Christian cosmopolitans at a time when the significance of national borders has declined and the dangers of uncritical nationalism have become obvious. This means reassessing one's allegiance to an ideological concept of the American nation-state and rendering service to "Caesar" (as Jesus taught in the Gospels) by also rendering unto God what is God's through a commitment to peace and justice, as well as to human dignity and solidarity.

Christians who wish to deal with the modern world in unity with others, particularly the poor and the marginalized, and take seriously the implications of *imago Dei* should reject blind obedience to U.S. political and social values that are clearly inconsistent with the core values of a lived Christian tradition that has engaged with the world for 2,000 years. We should recognize that the diversity of human community and the imperfect nature of our worldly existence make a complete coalescence of religious and civic cultures impossible. Christians can and should continue to draw personal and group identity from history, language, and experience in a specific geographical place, but we cannot forget our moral obligations to the human community, both at home and abroad. When the empire demands our services, Christians must determine whether what we are being asked to do is consistent with a Christian understanding of the common good, and ultimately we must be willing in certain instances to reject the worldly benefits that an unquestioning identification with the American empire might offer.

I

Old-Time Religion in a Free-Market Empire

One important rationale for the American imperium is the promotion of a broad, self-referential notion of individual freedom that nurtures a constant expansion of consumer capitalism. The rhetoric of individual liberty and freedom is an ideal partner for the aggressive promotion of what French historian Immanuel Todd has called "individualist" Anglo-American capitalism, in which "one finds an economy in which the basic objective is the short-term maximization of corporate profits and in which the ideological justification is the satisfaction of the consumer.... Some essential consequences result from these priorities, such as the instability of organizational structures and the flexibility of the labor market ... a low savings rate, which demonstrates the preference for consumption, is also constitutive of this model[, as well as] a deficit in the balance of payments which simply demonstrates to the outside world the tendency of the system to consume more than it produces."[1]

In recent years, some of the defining aspects of the U.S. economic model have caused growing concern among economists and policymakers. In 2003 and 2004 the combined net savings rate of households, businesses, and government was only about 1 percent of gross national income, which gave the United States its lowest savings rate in 50 years.[2] Low savings have increased the demand for foreign capital, which now finances more than three-quarters of the nation's business investment.[3] Trade deficits broke records every year from 2001 through 2005, driven by soaring consumer demand for cheap imported merchandise and, in 2005, rapidly escalating oil prices, which hit record highs in 2006, and ultimately broke the psychological barrier of $100 per barrel in 2008.[4]

Moreover, America's relentless appetite for consumer goods has generally been encouraged by the Bush administration. After the 2001 terrorist attacks, President Bush exhorted citizens to spend the nation back into prosperity in order to demonstrate the superiority of the American way of life, and he and the Republican Party have made tax cuts an important part of their domestic political agenda.[5] Yet, the Bush administration is simply following a pattern of consumption-oriented economic growth that has become the American standard since World War II. Arguably, in the modern American incarnation of the free-market model, the purpose of government is to maximize individual freedom to choose in a marketplace that now embraces most aspects of everyday life, including decisions about everything from clothing to children.

In her book titled *A Consumers' Republic,* Lizabeth Cohen argues that in the post–World War II era, the identity of the American people as citizens began to merge with their role as consumer-actors in the marketplace. "Americans' identities as citizens and consumers are often presented as opposites. Citizens, individuals in a political relationship with government, are assumed to embrace a larger public interest. . . . Consumers, concerned with satisfying private material desires, are often denigrated for their personal indulgence, perhaps stemming from the word's original meaning, to 'devour, waste, and spend.'"[6] But by the mid-twentieth century, Cohen argues, those roles had become increasingly difficult to segregate, and after World War II "a new ideal emerged—the purchaser as citizen—as an alluring compromise. Now the consumer satisfying personal and material wants actually served the national interest, since economic recovery after a decade and a half of depression and war depended on a dynamic mass consumption economy. Most recently, during the last two decades, a new combined *consumer/citizen/taxpayer/voter* has gained influence in a *Consumerized Republic,* where self-interested citizens increasingly view government policies like other market transactions, judging them by how well served they feel personally."[7]

It is for the consumerized republic that our political leaders now govern. Market-oriented self-interest is a primary feature of public and private life in the United States: "Whereas from the 1930s to as late as the 1970s, to refer to the consumer interest was also to appeal to some larger public good beyond the individual's self-interest, the ubiquitous invocation of the consumer today—as patient, as parent, as social security recipient—often means satisfying the private interest of the paying customer, the combined citizen/consumer/taxpayer/voter whose greatest concern is, 'Am I getting my money's worth?'"[8]

There is nothing inherently wrong with a desire to raise living standards by improving the efficiency of the market for consumer goods and services, particularly when that desire helps to promote a more dignified human existence for all. It is certainly true that economic liberalization based on free-market reforms and consumer-oriented capitalism has enhanced living standards for millions of people around the world.[9] However, when does a quest for a better standard of living for the many become simply a clever way to justify the ongoing greed and self-indulgence of those already wealthy or powerful? When does the promotion of an economic system that is based on the satisfaction of transient needs become a threat to human dignity? Russia provides an excellent example of a nation where free-market reform threatens to re-create the nation's prerevolutionary extremes of income inequality, thereby fueling gangland-style violence, garish displays of wealth, political oppression, and vicious attacks on dark-skinned ethnic minorities who serve as easy scapegoats for the frustrations of those left behind in the nation's embrace of capitalism.[10]

However, Russia is simply a starker example of what is happening all over the world as the pursuit of wealth becomes the raison d'être of economic, political, and cultural life. In the United Kingdom, one of the world's wealthiest nations, income inequality has risen dramatically during the last decade, while many social indicators for the poor remain dismal. Among the nations of Western Europe, Great Britain has the highest rate of teenage pregnancy, an important predictor of poverty and state-funded aid dependency for women and children.[11] Parts of Scotland contain Western Europe's most deprived areas, with low life expectancies, high murder rates, and high rates of diseases like lung cancer.[12] Britain has embraced American-style free-market capitalism more willingly than any other Western European nation, so perhaps it is not particularly surprising that the nation tends to reflect American society when it comes to poverty-related social dysfunction.[13] On the other hand, an inability to reckon fully with the dominance of the U.S. economic model has caused social and political crisis in France and economic and political stagnation in Germany, two countries that have struggled to adapt free-market capitalism to their more communally oriented social traditions.[14]

In his encyclical titled *Sollicitudo rei socialis,* the late Pope John Paul II described the problems of an economic system that was obsessed with short-term profit and the promotion of materialism and consumerism: "Super-development, which consists in an excessive availability of every kind of material good for the benefit of certain social groups, easily makes people slaves of 'possession' and of immediate gratification, with no other horizon than the multiplication and continual replacement of the things already owned with others still better. This is the so-called civilization of 'consumption' or 'consumerism,' which involves so much 'throwing-away' and 'waste.' An object already owned but now superseded by something better is discarded, with no thought of its possible lasting value in itself, nor of some other human being who is poorer."[15]

A political community must be grounded in something more important than promises to raise living standards and to protect personal and economic freedom. What do those assurances mean for the majority of people, who will at best live their lives on modest incomes and tight budgets? No nation has the right to expect unlimited economic prosperity, and one that does will soon find itself poorly equipped to meet the inevitable economic, social, and political difficulties that all countries must face. Economic and political freedoms in a democracy are sustainable only when societies nurture countervailing duties and responsibilities that ensure respect and concern for others and allow and encourage people to pursue relationships and experiences that become distorted or destroyed when subjected to market-based assessments of their value.

Unfortunately, many American Christians, both Catholic and Protestant, appear unwilling to take a critical view of an economy and a political culture that not only promise easy prosperity at the cost of an increasingly dehumanizing—and profoundly anti-Christian—atomism but also offer simplistic answers to complex global economic and social problems. These same Christians have thrown their support to leaders who have demonstrated themselves incapable of demanding any kind of real communal work or sacrifice from the American people for the privileges and freedoms they enjoy. Instead, these Christians have devoted their energies to shoring up the culture of easy prosperity and unrestrained power. They have become apologists for an imperialist foreign policy that places heavy burdens on the poor and the working class, while at the same time they press for reactionary solutions to complex social problems like terrorism, abortion, homosexual unions, and immigration.

The Religious Right

To consolidate its power in what remains a fairly religious country, over the last quarter century the Republican Party has allowed its political vision of the relationship between religion and public life to be shaped increasingly by conservative evangelicals and traditionalist Roman Catholics. Catholics form the largest single religious denomination in the United States and were considered essential swing voters in the 2004 presidential election. During the last two decades, a tendency toward social conservatism among Catholics has revealed some common ground with evangelical Christians, thereby softening what has typically been a tense association. Furthermore, a common desire to overturn *Roe v. Wade* has allowed many Catholics and evangelicals to form close working partnerships and has revealed more religious common ground than was once assumed. An important milestone in the cooperation between evangelicals and Roman Catholics in the United States was reached in 1994 with the production of the statement "Evangelicals and Catholics Together."[16]

This move toward greater Christian unity is something to be celebrated, but, unfortunately, there is reason to suspect that the accord is directed more toward temporal political goals than to spiritual healing. Indeed, many evangelicals in particular remain skeptical of the substantive religious content of Catholic and evangelical cooperation because the theological differences between the two groups are so profound.[17] Richard John Neuhaus, editor of the influential journal *First Things* and one of the principals involved in the drafting of "Evangelicals and Catholics Together," was very much aware of the controversy generated by the document. In the year following its release he noted, "Many articles, several books, and a number of evangelical television and radio programs have attacked ["Evangelicals and Catholics Together"] vigorously, and sometimes venomously. . . . For most evangelicals, the Catholic Church has been understood as the enemy of the Gospel, and even as the Antichrist. In that view, it is the duty of Protestants to convert Catholics to the true faith and to work for extirpation of the papal system from the face of the earth."[18]

Despite continuing cooperation between Catholics and evangelicals in the following decade, most notably in matters political, evangelical suspicion of Catholicism has remained deeply entrenched. In 2005 a professor of medieval philosophy at Wheaton College, probably the premier evangelical center of higher learning in the United States, was fired after he converted to Roman Catholicism. Wheaton's president, Duane Litfin, could not see how a faithful Roman Catholic could in good conscience accept the faith statement required of all Wheaton faculty, which asserted the inerrancy of the Bible, and he noted during the controversy surrounding the firing that the core doctrinal issues separating Catholics and Protestants "have by no means gone away."[19]

In the end, the differences in opinion regarding the worthwhile nature of dialogue with Catholicism within the diverse community of American evangelicals point to a difficulty inherent in evangelical participation in public life generally. Who exactly are "evangelicals"? Apart from their emphasis on the authority of biblical text, opposition to the institutional authority of the church, and their belief in salvation through personal conversion, many evangelical Christians themselves cannot agree on any meaningful definition of "evangelicalism." Nonetheless, various scholars of evangelicalism in the United

States agree that an important aspect of the evangelical tradition, which is historically rooted in Protestant Christian fundamentalism, has been a reactionary impulse to social change:

> While evangelicals of the 1950s and 60s were breaking with fundamentalists by calling for a Christian social ethic, most renditions of "evangelical" ethics at the time tended to be both highly individualistic and socially conservative. Evangelical ethics, then, was characterized by an emphasis on a strict code of personal morality and a general tendency to oppose social change and progressive social movements.... The tendency toward a rigorous personal morality could be clearly grounded in Scripture, which remained central to Evangelicals, but opposition to social change was often more cultural than biblical, resulting in both victories for Christian fidelity (such as opposition to the sexual revolution) and grave defeats (such as resistance to racial integration and the civil rights movement).[20]

In recent years a growing number of evangelical movements have aligned themselves with progressive political issues like environmental protection and global poverty, and the years ahead may well witness a shift in the political emphases of a new generation of evangelical leaders.[21] In particular, evangelical leaders like Jim Wallis, president and executive director of *Sojourners* magazine, and theologian Tony Campolo have attempted to reevaluate the ways most evangelicals have participated in politics in recent years, and Wallis, most notably, has sought to redirect evangelicals from the political agenda of the Religious Right.[22] These attempts to broaden the focus of evangelical political action away from issues like abortion and homosexuality have not gone unchallenged, and in 2007 evangelical leaders like James Dobson and Gary Bauer urged the executive director of the American Association of Evangelicals, Rev. Richard Cizik, to stop speaking out on the issue of global warming.[23]

Indeed, in the latter part of the twentieth century, the emergence of the Moral Majority, the Christian Coalition, and a broad array of political action groups like Focus on the Family and the Family Research Council has underscored a strong association between evangelicals and the most socially conservative wing of the Republican Party.[24] Scholars of evangelicalism have also noted that a reaction to social changes in the 1960s and 1970s motivated evangelicals to enter the political arena: "What was especially striking about the exertion of evangelical influence in the American political arena [during the 1970s and 1980s] was the extent to which issues of gender—the proposed Equal Rights Amendment, the availability of abortion, private sexual morality—shaped their agenda. Evangelicals, especially those associated with the Religious Right, regularly attached the adjective 'anti-family' to policies and to politicians they regarded as inimical, and they have, curiously, paid singular attention to the issue of abortion."[25]

Social changes like the women's movement also produced a great deal of anxiety for many traditionalist Roman Catholics. Although the Catholic tradition has a complex history regarding women's roles in both lay culture and the church, Catholic societies have long struggled with unrealistic dichotomies related to the position of women. Popular Catholic culture has tended to glorify women in their domestic roles as mothers, wives, and daughters. Women who did not marry or have children were often able to take on traditional "male" roles as administrators of schools, hospitals, and other corporate bodies, but this would typically have been done as part of life in community with other women as a nun. Women who chose to pursue a vocation in the secular world without marital vows or the habit risked being seen as "fallen" or a threat to the sexual morality of the community primarily because their sexuality was not controlled or sanctified by an affiliation with either a religious community or a man. After the Second Vatican Council, these traditional constructs were challenged when thousands of nuns abandoned their vows (although not necessarily their lives of service to others), Catholic couples openly rejected the church's position on artificial birth control, more Catholic marriages ended in divorce, and abortion became legal in most of the wealthy countries of the industrialized world. For many traditionalist Catholics, these developments were signs of a culture and a church in free fall, and one common thread that connected the negative events was the "liberation" of women from their traditional roles.

Like many evangelicals, these Catholics failed to see that their vision of "appropriate" roles for women was rooted in romanticized, nineteenth-century notions of femininity that were popularized as middle-class ideals throughout Europe and the Americas. Christianity's relationship with women and women's roles has never been static, and even in the nineteenth and twentieth centuries, the lives of rural and working-class women (not to mention women of color in their roles as slaves and later as part of a racially segregated underclass) never reflected the idealized visions that controlled the lives of women in the dominant social groups. The social changes of the 1960s and 1970s not only allowed women from socially dominant groups to reassess their lives, which they did with gusto, but also allowed poor women, working-class women, and women of color to emerge from invisibility and add their experience to the understandings of women's roles in Western culture. However, the cultural changes that took place after World War II went beyond women. In the 1960s and 1970s the dominance of a prescriptive Western culture that rested on the authority of white men throughout much of the world was in obvious decline, bankrupted no doubt by two world wars and the end of European colonialism.

At the Second Vatican Council, the Catholic Church was able to respond to these events and emerge from a religious and intellectual mind-set rooted in mid-nineteenth-century Western Europe. Historian John McGreevy describes the "ultramontanist" Catholicism that existed prior to the council as a "shorthand for a cluster of shifts that included a Vatican-fostered move to Thomistic philosophy, a more intense experiential piety centered on miracles and Vatican-approved devotions such as that of the Sacred Heart, an international outlook suspicious of national variations within Catholicism, and a heightened respect for Church authorities ranging from the pope to parish priests."[26] Through documents such as *Gaudium et spes* and *Dignitatis humanae,* Vatican II moved Catholicism into a deeper understanding of itself as a world faith that responded to the new realities of the post–World War II era, such as a greater respect for individual conscience, support for human rights, a broader understanding of women's role in society, and a recognition of the importance of democracy, particularly to the non-European peoples emerging from colonialism.

For some American traditionalist Catholics, the loss of the cultural certainty and unquestioned obedience to the church they believed existed prior to Vatican II has been difficult to accept, even 40 years after the Second Vatican Council. Many have failed to realize that the pre–Vatican II Catholicism they see as normative was an American Catholicism distinctively shaped by ultramontanism from the mid-nineteenth century until the 1950s. Although that period occupies a significant portion of the Catholic experience in the United States, it was a relatively brief event within the 2,000-year history of the Catholic Church. Vatican II put an end to ultramontane Catholicism, but many people still see its full churches, mass religious devotions, and obedient laity as the most authentic expression of Catholic belief and religious practice.

In their distinctive responses to twentieth-century cultural and religious change, some traditionalist Catholics and conservative evangelicals have nurtured a reactionary civil religion in the United States, which has found its voice in politics through what is known as the "Religious Right." For the last 20 years or so, the Religious Right has provided the critical political base for the Republican Party. More than simply a marriage of convenience in an attempt to achieve certain political goals, the Catholic-evangelical partnership is driven by an intense belief in the religious truths underlying its reaction to late twentieth-century political and social change. Its partisans have become convinced that their task is to return America to the Christian "truth" of its founding and to undo many of the social changes of the last 40 years—particularly those related to women's roles and sexual mores. One example of the political power of the evangelical leaders in the Religious Right is James Dobson, the head of Focus on the Family. Dobson was probably the nation's most influential evangelical leader in terms of bringing evangelicals to the polls to vote for George Bush in 2004, and he has argued that "the First Amendment principle of church-state separation has been wielded by 'secular humanists' to strip the nation of its Christian identity."[27] Dobson is a relentless crusader for traditional marriage and has been active in efforts to curb abortions, ban gay marriage, and appoint more "conservative" judges to the federal courts.[28] Numerous commentators see these issues as critical to the aggressive political involvement of other evangelical leaders such as Gary Bauer, Ralph Reed, and Pat Robertson in Republican politics.[29]

The Religious Right has struggled for and achieved political dominance through the internal power dynamics of the Republican Party. Although traditionally known for the consistency of its message and the relative uniformity of the social makeup of its voters, in recent years the Republican Party has begun to look like the big, unruly tent of diverse agendas that was typically associated with the Democrats. Increasingly, small and mid-sized business interests, libertarians, white middle- and lower-middle-class suburbanites, and religious conservatives have all found a home in the party long dominated by WASP society, the money elites of Wall Street, and big business. As the influence of prescriptive WASP culture has declined in the United States, the values of public service and acting for the good of the nation traditionally associated with the Republican elite—noblesse oblige, if you will—have become less central to the power brokers of the newly "democratized" GOP. Indeed, names like Eisenhower, Rockefeller, Chafee, and Danforth no longer generate much admiration among the Republican faithful; thus any understanding of the Republican Party as a conservative organization in the Burkean sense—rooted not only in social hierarchies but also in a respect for public service, tradition, and community—no longer reflects reality, if indeed it ever did.

Today it is the Religious Right that gives the Republican Party its electoral strength at the polls, and religious conservatives are now generally seen as exerting significant control over the party. Former Missouri senator John C. Danforth—an Episcopal priest, former ambassador to the United Nations, and the key supporter in the U.S. Senate for the nomination of Justice Clarence Thomas to the Supreme Court—said as much when he recently accused the Republican Party of allowing itself to be transformed into the political arm of conservative Christians.[30] His remarks immediately drew attacks from the right-wing media and activist GOP regulars who, interestingly, did not necessarily disagree with the substance of Danforth's critique. Writing in the *American Spectator,* Patrick Hynes noted that "Danforth believes its relationship with the Religious Right will be bad for the Republican Party in the long run. It's hard to imagine how that can be. Indeed, it's hard to imagine a Republican Party at all without the Religious Right."[31]

Paul Weyrich, a key "movement conservative" and a Republican activist for decades, agreed, and he laid bare some of the class resentment and disdain for "liberal" Christianity that have helped reshaped the Republican Party into a political vehicle for American religious conservatism: "Danforth says the Republican Party has been taken over by zealots of the religious right and the party should return to the way it was before the religious right got involved. Mind you, values voters amount to a quarter of the entire GOP coalition. Danforth, who is an extremely wealthy member of the establishment, also is an Episcopal priest. No doubt he was chosen to say what has been on the minds of establishment types since the great unwashed were let into the GOP's inner sanctum."[32]

If there was any doubt about the power of the Religious Right, or "values voters," within the Republican Party, the reelection of George W. Bush in 2004 made their dominance quite clear. Bush was so completely dependent on this group for political legitimation that Harriet Miers, his first nomination to the Supreme Court to replace Justice Sandra Day O'Connor, was forced to withdraw her name from consideration after enduring withering and humiliating attacks, primarily from members of her own party. Because she could not demonstrate to the satisfaction of the Religious Right that she would forward their agenda for legal change, she had no chance of securing the necessary Republican support in Congress to survive the confirmation process.[33] The pressure of the Religious Right on the Republican Party apparatus is so extreme that party leaders have been willing—or forced—to turn on a dime and abandon long-held party principles in an effort to advance their agenda. The contentious debate surrounding the Terri Schiavo case was a prime example of this.

Terri Schiavo was a 41-year-old woman who in March 2005 had been in a vegetative state in a Florida hospice for many years, following brain injuries sustained in a stroke and a fall. Michael Schiavo, her husband and legal guardian, had successfully petitioned the Florida courts for an order that would allow him to remove the feeding and hydration tubes that were keeping his wife alive, claiming that she would have wished to suspend artificial means of life support if she became permanently incapacitated. Terri Schiavo's parents challenged Michael's attempts to end life support, contesting his claim that this would have been Terri's wish. The Florida courts, however, were unconvinced and found for Michael Schiavo at every stage of the litigation. Having lost in the courts, Terri Schiavo's parents turned to the state legislature, which passed an act that allowed Governor Jeb Bush to issue a stay that would prevent the withdrawal of Schiavo's feeding and hydration tubes. This was followed by an act of Congress, which President Bush returned from his Easter vacation expressly to sign, known as "Terri's law," which gave the federal courts jurisdiction over any claims related to the termination of her life-sustaining treatments. This transfer of jurisdiction by the Congress notwithstanding, the federal district court and the Eleventh Circuit Court both declined to hear the case on its merits. In March 2005 Terri Schiavo's feeding and hydration tubes were removed, and she died shortly thereafter.[34]

Strong support for federalism and the devolution of federal power to the states have long been cornerstones of the Republican political agenda, but in the Schiavo case, Republican congressional leaders refused to accept the results not only of the judicial process in the state of Florida but those of the federal judiciary as well. Guido Calabresi has argued powerfully for the view that Congress was basing its actions on a strong moral imperative to save an innocent life in a culture that has become increasingly coarsened by what Pope John Paul II called a "culture of death."[35] Given that a human life was at stake, many in Congress were no doubt moved by the gravity of the consequences of removing Terri Schiavo's feeding and hydration tubes. Nevertheless, thousands of American families were making the same decision under similar circumstances every year, and there seemed to be something grotesquely political and vulgarly partisan about the congressional response to this particular case. After Terri Schiavo's passing, then House majority leader Tom DeLay attacked the federal judiciary for its refusal to order the restoration of Schiavo's feeding tube, calling the federal judges "arrogant, out-of-control, and unaccountable." He then threatened the judges by asserting that they "would have to answer for their behavior."[36] DeLay and many of his allies on the Religious Right had long been engaged in a campaign to undermine public confidence in the "unelected" judiciary. Yet, despite all of the eleventh-hour political maneuvering, polls showed that 70–80 percent of the American public opposed congressional involvement in the Schiavo case.[37] Although he supported the actions of Congress in the Schiavo matter, Calabresi noted:

When I first glanced at the federal law Congress and President
Bush enacted to allow federal courts to take a second look at
Mrs. Schiavo's case, I must admit I was quite skeptical of its constitutionality. For thirty-five years, judicial conservatives like myself
have opposed broad federal court jurisdiction, favored broad res
judicata effect for state court judgments in federal court, favored

equitable doctrines of abstention, and opposed congressional power
to reopen final judgments in federal question cases. "Terri's Law"
flies in the face of all this, so it came to me as no surprise that even a
conservative, Republican-appointed judge like Judge Stanley F. Birch
on the Eleventh Circuit would determine that the law was uncon-
stitutional. As I read about the legal issues raised by the law in more
detail . . . I became increasingly skeptical of the arguments against
Terri's Law. One by one, each doctrine that judicial conservatives
invoked seemed to me to be more and more questionable as applied
to Mrs. Schiavo's case. Although it is a very close question, I finally
concluded that Terri's Law was constitutional, although it is not one
over which Tom DeLay should ever have threatened to impeach any
judges.[38]

After Schiavo's death, prominent Senate Republican Chuck Hegel called
the Schiavo bills "a mistake."[39] This did not, however, stop key voices on the
Religious Right from condemning President Bush and his brother, Florida
governor Jeb Bush, for their failure to speak out strongly against the removal of
Terri Schiavo's feeding tube, despite all of the political capital both had ex-
pended in removing the case from the Florida courts and supporting the
Republican Congress.[40] Indeed, it is difficult to separate the events of the
Schiavo case from the broader agenda of the Religious Right to undermine
the independence of the U.S. judiciary. The Schiavo case called for extremely
difficult choices and was a tragic situation that can strike any family. Theologians who had spent their careers thinking about end-of-life issues found
themselves unable to agree about what was "right" under the circumstances.[41]

That said, the Religious Right must be held responsible for the rhetoric
and tactics of people like Tom DeLay, for religious traditionalists formed the
bedrock of his political base. His was a politics that destroyed any chance of
meaningful dialogue among people who, despite their differences, sought
to build a healthy civil society around the treasured American institutions of
balanced government and a respect for the rule of law. In the end, the difficulty
America had coming up with an appropriate response to the Schiavo case is
best explained by an observation made by philosopher Alasdair MacIntyre in
Italy almost a decade before, in which he argued that, due to fundamental
disagreements about the ultimate ends of political and community life and
pervasive moral relativism, politics in modern, liberal democracies must isolate itself from moral and philosophical debates about fundamental questions
like the ones related to the beginning and end of life: "Political debate, whether
in electoral campaigns, in legislatures or in governmental bureaucracies, is

rarely systematic or in any depth. It is not directed by canons of enquiry or committed to following through the implications of arguments. It is instead sporadic, apt to be more responsive to the immediate concerns than to the longer term, carried through by those who are both swayed by and themselves make use of rhetorical modes of self-presentation, and open to the solicitations of the rich and the powerful. Political debate, that is, is generally the antithesis of serious intellectual enquiry."[42]

Shortly after announcing her retirement, former Supreme Court justice Sandra Day O'Connor said that the independence of the federal judiciary was under the greatest threat from Congress she had seen in her lifetime.[43] Republican political attacks on federal court judges continue to be relentless, particularly when the courts take any position against the Bush administration in the "war on terror." Former president Jimmy Carter has also expressed deep concern at the efforts of a broad range of "fundamentalist" political and religious groups to subjugate America's admirable tradition of an independent judiciary and open, collegial legislative debate: "Probing public debate on key legislative decisions is almost a thing of the past. Basic agreements are made between lobbyists and legislative leaders, often within closed party caucuses where rigid discipline is paramount. Even personal courtesies, which had been especially cherished in the US Senate are no longer considered to be sacrosanct. This deterioration in harmony, cooperation, and collegiality in the Congress is, at least in part, a result in the rise of fundamentalist tendencies and their religious and political impact."[44]

Like John Danforth, Carter blames much of the problem on the Religious Right and its mixing of religion and politics in an attempt to control the democratic process, to intervene in religious affairs, and to favor certain religious groups.[45] As a lifelong Southern Baptist who eventually felt it necessary to dissociate himself from the Southern Baptist Convention, Carter has deep personal knowledge of the battles with fundamentalist and politically reactionary tendencies within his own denomination. The significance of this break should not be underestimated. Jimmy Carter spent his political career as a Southern Baptist, made a successful run for the presidency, and enjoyed enormous popularity among African Americans. All of this he achieved despite being ridiculed for his faith by the nation's urban money and intellectual elites and despite his denomination's long-standing role as an apologist for racial segregation in the South. Under the traditional organization of the Southern Baptist Convention, however, Carter was able to live out his faith within the tradition and express more progressive views on racial and political issues.

Nevertheless, by 2000 this independence of conscience was no longer possible. Carter could no longer abide the convention's "departures from traditional Baptist beliefs, including the melding of religion and politics. . . . It became increasingly obvious that our convention leaders were in conflict with traditional or mainstream Christians. After much prayer and soul-searching, Rosalynn and I decided to sever our personal relationship with the Southern Baptist Convention, while retaining our time-honored Baptist customs and beliefs within our own local church."[46]

A broad cross-section of highly respected Americans have come to similar conclusions about the influence of the Religious Right on America's public life. Fundamentalism and dogmatism are inconsistent with democratic pluralism. Although many in the Religious Right believe that the issues for which they are fighting are nonnegotiable questions with black-or-white answers, the Terri Schiavo case demonstrates the fallacy of such a simplistic approach. If the polls have any meaning, most Americans do not believe that Terri Schiavo was murdered or euthanized, nor do they believe that the courts "ran amok" when they reviewed her case. Indeed, the public outrage the case generated was directed primarily at Congress, and for many Americans the judiciary demonstrated admirable sangfroid under political pressure from the legislature, the likes of which one might ordinarily associate with less-developed democratic political systems.

Libertarianism: The Binding Political Philosophy of the Right

The Religious Right's moral exhortations may motivate certain members of the electorate to vote Republican, but this bloc of voters alone would not win presidential or most congressional elections. Apart from religious conservatism, the other major issues that motivate Republican voters are strong commitments to individual autonomy, an unwavering faith in free-market liberalism, and a deep distrust of government. The key philosophical perspective that links these values is libertarianism, which is rooted in a hostility toward claims of community and proceeds from a foundational notion of a radical dissociation of human beings from one another. It is a philosophical worldview that is starkly inconsistent with the fundamentally communal orientation of orthodox Christianity but, in its most simplified constructs, has long found favor with a broad cross-section of the American people. Standard mantras of Republican political candidates like "the best government is as little government as possible" or "government is a necessary evil" owe much of their theoretical and rhetorical power to libertarian ideas.

In his essay "An Entitlement Theory of Justice," Robert Nozick has argued that "the minimal state is the most extensive state that can be justified. Any more extensive state violates people's rights."[47] This has become an article of faith for many Americans on the Right. Nozick's essay goes on to attack the idea of distributive justice, which, in many political systems, has served as a justification for a broader redistributive role for the state and is a cornerstone for the conceptions of justice in Catholic social thought:

> Whether it is done through taxation on wages or on wages over a certain amount, or through seizure of profits, or through there being a big *social pot* so that it's not clear what's coming from where and what's going to where, patterned principles of distributive justice involve appropriating the actions of other persons. Seizing the results of someone's labor is equivalent to seizing hours from him and directing him to carry on various activities. If people force you to do certain work, or unrewarded work, for a certain period of time, they decide what you are to do and what purposes your work is to serve apart from your decisions. This process whereby they take this decision from you makes them a *part-owner* of you; it gives them a property right in you. Just as having such partial control and the power of decision, by right, over an animal or inanimate object would be to have a property right in it.[48]

This is extremely powerful rhetoric, especially for an American audience, for it essentially compares the requirements of distributive justice to a form of slavery. In the United States, slaves (at least as a legal matter) were property, not people, and they were forced to labor without remuneration for those who owned them. No one has any legitimate claim to a property right in another person, and for Nozick and other libertarians, democratic liberalism must be grounded in the notion of human persons as full self-owners who control themselves much as humans exercise control over inanimate objects.

Friedrich von Hayek has given a particularly cogent presentation of the direct relationship between libertarian philosophical ideas and the global economic and political program of the Right. Hayek has demonstrated the complementarity that could be achieved between democratic pluralism and the aggressive promotion of free-market economics. He has argued that the "Great Society" would be a pluralist order in which no agreement existed about the members' respective ends. Like Alasdair MacIntyre, he recognized that a pluralist political and social order is easily destabilized when it becomes necessary to address core values in the political process: "What makes agreement and peace in such a society possible is that the individuals are not required to agree on ends but only on means that are capable of serving a great variety of purposes and which each hopes will assist him in the pursuit of his own purposes."[49]

The Great Society would come about spontaneously through the mechanism of the free market and the process of individuals satisfying their own needs: "Many people regard it as revolting that the Great Society has no common concrete purposes or, as we may say, that it is merely means-connected and not ends-connected. It is indeed true that the chief common purpose of all its members is the purely instrumental one of securing the formation of an abstract order which has no specific purposes but will enhance for all the prospects of achieving their respective purposes."[50] Thus the market order would be central to the sustenance of a free society because it would reconcile the competing ends of the members of a society that had no shared principles or values for the ordering of needs: "The task of all economic activity is to reconcile the competing ends by deciding for which of them the limited means are to be used. The market order reconciles the claims of the different non-economic ends by the only known process that benefits all. . . . The market is the only known method by which this can be achieved without an agreement on the relative importance of the different ultimate ends."[51]

Hayek linked individual liberty and freedom, as well as peace and prosperity for the entire society, to the unfettered functioning of the marketplace. A key role for the state would be the preservation of the market conditions that allow individuals and small groups to secure their own needs. Ordinarily, government intervention in the marketplace either proceeds from some ends-oriented conception of the societal good or is driven by the needs of some particular social group. Government action of this type limits the free functioning of a spontaneous order, thereby limiting the ability of individuals to make choices based on their own conception of what they want and need. Government intervention in the marketplace and, more generally, government provision of services risk thwarting the promotion of peace and prosperity for all. Services aimed at the general welfare, for example, are extremely difficult to provide because individuals tend not to perceive that they are especially benefited by them. Moreover, in a democracy, politicians recognize that they are more handsomely rewarded by directing the government's largess to special interests. Hayek pointed out that this favoring of special interests is frequently not in society's general interest and that the necessary services that the government provides are "services that must be fitted into that more comprehensive order of private efforts which government neither does nor can determine, and which ought to be rendered under the restrictions of the same rules of law to which the private efforts are subject."[52]

Nozick and Hayek helped to develop a modern libertarian philosophy that was successfully popularized and politicized in the post–World War II era by political leaders like Ronald Reagan and Margaret Thatcher. One sees in

Hayek's work in particular the foundation of the liberal, free-market paradigm that has dominated U.S. economic policy since the 1980s, particularly the moves to deregulate key industries and privatize public services. Hayek also provided the driving intellectual force behind Republican attacks on the government's efforts to redistribute resources downward from the wealthiest groups to the poorer ones. In its roles both as a force for the redistribution of wealth and as a promoter of social equality, the state became a new kind of slave master. In addition, the American and British experiments with more egalitarian social models (subsequent to Franklin Roosevelt's New Deal, for instance, which offered renewed emphasis on the common good through various systems of social welfare benefits) came to screeching halts. The 1980s ushered in an era of not only unparalleled economic expansion but also a return to a level of income inequality in the United States unseen since the 1920s. Libertarian philosophy is particularly hostile to communally oriented concepts like distributive justice and solidarity, which tend to underpin social welfare programs and economic regulation plans, as well as, notably, Catholic social doctrine.

As an Austrian, Hayek was very familiar with the centrality of distributive justice to Catholic social teaching and with the church's emphasis on social justice. He explicitly rejected both concepts. In Hayek's market order, the demand for social, or distributive, justice raised serious problems. First, Hayek rejected the notion of "society" for the purpose of determining whether market allocations have been "just" or "unjust": "Complaints about the market as unjust do not really assert that somebody has been unjust; and there is no answer to the question *who* has been unjust. Society has simply become the new deity to which we complain and clamour for redress if it does not fulfil the expectations it has created."[53]

Second, Hayek did not believe that a market order could be sustained if an authority motivated by specific ends attempted to establish a particular pattern of remuneration among individuals based on its assessment of performance or needs. The dependence of particular groups on the government would increase pressure upon the governmental authority to maintain a plan of distributive justice in which more and more individuals and groups would become subject to governmental control, thereby creating a process that would ultimately lead to totalitarianism.[54] Social justice undermined the personal freedom in which traditional moral values flourish, and the phrase

seems in particular to have been embraced by a large section of the clergy of all Christian denominations, who, while increasingly losing their faith in a supernatural revelation, appear to have sought a refuge and consolation in a new 'social' religion which substitutes a temporal for a celestial promise of justice and who hope they can thus continue their striving to do good. The Roman Catholic church especially has made the aim of social justice part of its official doctrine, but the ministers of most Christian denominations appear to vie with each other with such offers of more mundane aims—which also seem to provide the chief foundation for renewed ecumenical efforts.[55]

The money elites of the Republican Party and those from the middle classes who aspire to join them see the individual imbedded in community as an impediment to the individual liberty that fuels the expansion of free-market, consumer capitalism and the upward redistribution of wealth. Philosophically, they are libertarians in the mold of Nozick and Hayek who support an aggressive free market as the best arbiter of individual freedom and liberty in a pluralist democracy. These interests within the Republican Party are particularly sympathetic to the libertarian view that favors a minimalist state and disparages the modern welfare state as morally illegitimate.[56] The GOP is usually skeptical of or hostile to programs that transfer wealth from individuals and corporations for the purposes of funding public goods or ameliorating the material condition of the poor, the sick, or the elderly. More broadly problematic for the money elites in the Republican coalition is that persons with strong commitments to others tend to demand social accountability in the marketplace—distributive justice, if you will—which restricts the free movement of capital and labor and fetters wealth-creation opportunities for individuals and corporations.

Republican money elites are particularly concerned with organizing the apparatus of the state to promote and protect individual wealth accumulation. Thus, their political agenda attempts to provide the broadest possible sphere of operation for individuals within the marketplace. The libertarian link of this agenda to personal freedom provides a powerful connection to an American tradition of individualism and self-reliance, and this appeals to the American middle classes in two ways. First, it encourages and deepens a culturally conditioned belief that individuals are responsible for themselves and that we are as individuals primarily responsible for our own successes or failures in life. Second, it lessens any sense of guilt or shame about the circumstances of those on society's margins. As promoted by the libertarians and money elites of the GOP, the libertarian conception of freedom is based, at least theoretically, on personal responsibility, free access to wealth-creation opportunities, and limited state interference in the lives of individuals and corporate entities.

A libertarian mind-set is well suited to aggressive, short-term-focused, consumer-oriented, free-market capitalism, as well as a weak sense of communal responsibility for the poor and the weak both at home and abroad.

Of course, consistency with libertarian theory goes only so far. Although the Republicans are traditionally the party of limited government, big-business interests and Wall Street money elites have long been comfortable with government intervention in the marketplace when it protects the viability and profitability of large corporations for shareholders and shields key business sectors like agriculture, banking, automobile manufacturing, and air transportation from the negative results of free-market competition. This protectionist strategy meshes well with a vision of empire that seeks to maximize profitability from a global marketplace and to protect the elite interests that profit from it, much in the same way the British and French empires used their imperial dominance to promote and protect key business sectors in their domestic economies. The opening up of foreign markets requires the cooperation of a nation's political and military leaders if it is to be effective over the long term, and the recent controversies over the political influence peddling of companies like Halliburton and the "purchasing" of members of Congress by corporate lobbyists demonstrate that the symbiotic relationships between political and economic power are as important in the United States as they have been in other great powers throughout history.

Consistent with a political program oriented to the spontaneous workings of the free market unfettered by the false compassion of distributive justice, the last 20 years have witnessed major transfers of wealth from America's least affluent citizens to its wealthiest households.[57] Interestingly, the major domestic policy proposal of George Bush's second term was a plan to "privatize" the Social Security system, a federal government program that has been particularly successful in keeping huge numbers of America's elderly out of poverty. True to the libertarian and antistatist values of key groups in his core constituency, Bush wanted to divert public funds into private markets, thereby fundamentally changing a program based on a social insurance concept of mutual aid into one driven by the economic Darwinism of the marketplace. Inevitably, privatization would punish many investors (particularly those least knowledgeable about market volatility) and further enrich the money elite of the financial services industry, who would be charged with "advising" Americans on how to invest these funds, newly liberated from the government's illegitimate and inefficient control. Although the Iraq war and other events created a political climate inhospitable to Social Security reform, the Republican Party has managed to get a variety of tax "reform" legislation through the Congress that has helped ease the tax responsibility of the nation's wealthiest households. Of particular note has been the ongoing attempt to repeal the federal inheritance tax, which has often been recast as a "death tax" by the Right in an effort to distract voters from its role as a means of wealth redistribution.[58]

When it comes to libertarian individualism, however, the Democrats do not provide a particularly meaningful alternative to the pervasive libertarianism within the Republican Party. The Democrats have long pursued a domestic political agenda heavily reliant on extreme notions of individual autonomy, in which meaningful religious commitments and strong attachments to communal groups have been viewed as impediments to achieving a just society. The promotion of individual autonomy has been the Democrats' favored mode for liberating persons from discrimination and other negative forms of social control that are entrenched in "traditional society." Although this pattern is observed in Leftist politics throughout the Western world, in many other nations the Left has been much more heavily influenced by the communal orientations of Catholicism and the political ideologies that sprang from Marxism. Marxist philosophies have never formed serious political currents in the United States; consequently, many argue that there really is no "Left" in American politics. Thus, in the United States, the Left has never been closely linked to the social democratic or solidaristic traditions of Canada or Europe, and Left-leaning politics in the nation has nurtured a strong emphasis on personal autonomy. It is an emphasis that probably owes a great deal to the concept of "full self-ownership" in libertarian philosophy. Much of the modern political agenda of the Democratic Party is easily encompassed by what is known as "Left libertarianism."[59]

Left libertarians argue that natural resources are owned by all in some egalitarian manner. This ownership may take a variety of forms, but it rests on an independent, democratic assumption that is inconsistent with the generally antiegalitarian implications of libertarianism writ large. Left libertarians also stress the idea of complete liberty in the use and control of one's own person, which is quite consistent with the anti-interventionist views the American Left takes on divisive social issues like abortion and same-sex marriage. This concept of freedom grants individuals the right to do whatever they please "as long as they do not harm anyone else." Thus, American political liberals tend to be less concerned about certain "private" behaviors like drug use, gambling, consensual homosexual sex, and heterosexual sexual relations outside the bounds of marriage, assuming that these activities can be conducted in a way that does not impinge on others' liberties or rights to autonomous action.

In other words, the liberties connected to self-ownership operate freely to the extent that the exercise of this freedom does not conflict with the right to self-ownership that inheres in others. In essence, Left libertarianism is firmly linked with Right libertarianism on the issue of full self-ownership. By parting with Right libertarians on the issue of the ownership of natural resources, however, Left libertarians must admit the possibility of a morally justifiable role for the state in a more egalitarian distribution of those resources. In many ways, the promotion of equal rights for minorities, women, and homosexuals by the American Left is consistent with the liberal egalitarian commitments of Left libertarianism that would be expressed through redistributive policies related to natural resources.

The elites of the Democratic Party are dominated by highly educated professionals and managers who tend to see themselves as products of an educational meritocracy, which gives them a strong sense of their intellectual prowess and tends to weaken any sense of ancestral gratitude or noblesse oblige. They feel little need to abide by obligations inherited from the past, and in this view they are closely linked both to money elites now dominant in the Republican Party and to the highly individualist and antiegalitarian implications of Hayek's market order. The competing political views of the Right and the Left are joined in their dependence on the libertarian individual, and in the last several decades, a fairly extreme view of individual autonomy has come to define American culture and law. As a consequence, the American people have been wrenched from (or have voluntarily abandoned) the communal institutions and associations that are fundamental to cultivating the balanced, socially situated understanding of freedom that is essential to Catholic social thought and traditional Christianity.

In his classic, *The Person and the Common Good,* Jacques Maritain explained the significance of this situated notion of personhood:

> Animal groups or colonies are called societies only in an improper sense. They are collective wholes constituted of mere individuals. Society in the proper sense, human society, is a society of persons.... The social unit is the person. But why is it that the person, as person, seeks to live in society? It does so, first, because of its very perfection, as person, and its inner urge to the communications of knowledge and love which require relationship with other persons.... [U]nless it is integrated in a body of social communications, it cannot attain the fullness of its life and accomplishment. Society appears, therefore, to provide the human person with just those conditions of existence and development which it needs. It is not by itself alone that it reaches its plenitude, but by receiving essential goods from society.[60]

It does not seem unduly alarmist to suggest that an increasingly libertarian United States is struggling to retain the cultural and political unity forged during the Great Depression and in the hopeful decades following the Second World War. The right-wing political reaction that began in the 1980s and continues today indicates that the nation's mid-twentieth-century unity was probably more apparent than real, at least inasmuch as the nation's elites were concerned. Increasingly, Americans seem to have little real substantive agreement on the nature of their society and its values. Why do the people of the United States come together as a nation? Is it a shared desire for personal freedom and material wealth? Is it because Americans are God's chosen people? What values and shared histories give texture and meaning to membership in the American community?

Arguably, there are many divergent answers to these questions, and American politics has begun to represent a free-for-all of conflicting and increasingly hostile interests, thereby creating an environment of moral disagreement and emotivist argument, which Alasdair MacIntyre described in his classic work, *After Virtue*, as "rationally interminable."[61] As a product of these politics, U.S. law also suffers increasingly from an alienation from community-based values. To some degree, the American Left has robbed the society of the personal morality and social control that would have exercised some restraint on the current program of the American Right to empire-build and delegitimize social and moral checks on wealth accumulation and income inequality. This is the society that America's elites, particularly those on the political Right, want to export to other countries in the name of democracy and freedom. Is it any wonder that American hegemony is encountering increasingly stiff resistance abroad from friends and foes alike?

Faith Serving Power to Bless the American Empire

The American political and Religious Right have continued to cling to visions of nation and society that seem increasingly out of place among the global civilizations of the twenty-first century. The Right has laid claim to American nationalism and made love of country inseparable from a belief in the inevitability of U.S. military, economic, and cultural dominance of the world. James Q. Wilson, for example, has offered his voice as a spokesman for these views. He has written that the American people are probably as politically polarized today as they were in the nineteenth century immediately proceeding and following the Civil War. Wilson believes that this polarization is extremely problematic when it comes to foreign policy and military matters: "The United States, an unrivaled superpower with unparalleled responsibilities for protecting the peace and defeating terrorists, is now forced to do so with its own political house in disarray.... A divided America encourages our enemies, disheartens our allies, and saps our resolve—potentially to fatal effect. What General Giap once said of us is even truer today: America cannot be defeated on the battlefield, but it can be defeated at home. Polarization is a force that can defeat us."[62]

Arguably, the American people are polarized because, as was true in the nineteenth century, groups within the population have visions for the nation's future that are fundamentally inconsistent. Wilson's comments seem to assume that all Americans are duty bound to rally behind a foreign policy that empowers an imperial, war-oriented presidency and that they are obliged to fund morally and legally dubious military adventures in obedient silence. At least half of the "polarized" nation sees much of the Republican political project as inconsistent with American values. In fairness, another group within the population disagrees vehemently with this position, but given the low levels of participation by voters in elections, at best the Bush administration can claim the support of no more than half of the electorate, which is considerably less than half of the voting-age population. Nevertheless, Wilson uses nationalism and patriotism in an attempt to shame into silence legitimate critics who love their country but cannot support the direction in which the current political leadership is taking it. In asserting that opponents of the Right's imperialist foreign policy are undermining the nation, Wilson attempts to rekindle the baiting of those citizens who opposed the military conflict in Vietnam. Then, as now, those who supported peace were castigated for being disloyal and were marked as enemies of the nation who destroyed America's resolve and its will to fight.

Calling into question the loyalty and patriotism of those who oppose its views has become a hallmark of an increasingly aggressive "conservative movement" in the United States. Some of the movement's intellectual appeal is rooted in a nostalgia for a prescriptive, Anglo-American, Protestant culture. Unfortunately, this is impossible to separate from the nation's history of Native American removal and eradication, chattel slavery, and racism—aspects of the darker side of the American creed of individual freedom and personal prosperity. The Anglo-American intellectual tradition that fuels conservatism in the United States also developed primarily within a framework of English anti-Catholicism. Key thinkers such as Thomas Hobbes and John Locke, whose work is crucial to understanding libertarianism and free-market liberalism, proceeded in their consideration of the human person and human society from assumptions that are radically opposed to a Catholic vision of social and political life.

In Europe, much of the skepticism and suspicion among English conservatives today cannot be separated from a construction of English identity that defined itself against the Catholic threat from the Continent. Like their Tory counterparts in England, American conservatives tend to be intellectually "Europhobic," rooting their political philosophy in ideas that interpret the classical canon of Western thought through the cultural predilections of the English-speaking world and assuming, both implicitly and explicitly, the superiority of Anglo-American cultural, economic, and political institutions. One interesting aspect of this bias is that politically right-wing Catholics in the United States have taken pains to demonstrate, in the face of overwhelming counterevidence, the essential compatibility of Roman Catholicism, which is intellectually grounded in the continental European philosophical tradition, with a Republican-led "conservative" agenda intellectually dependent upon Anglo-American contractarian liberalism and libertarianism. Although the Republican Party has been successful in courting many Catholic voters based on its stances on particular issues such as abortion, key philosophical commitments like libertarianism, which are motivating Republican elites, are fundamentally hostile to Catholic social teaching. The tension between the American conservative movement and Catholicism becomes particularly apparent when one considers the role of the Religious Right in two of the most divisive aspects of the Republican agenda—militarism and abortion.

Religious conservatives in the Republican Party have become key apologists for an American quest to exert moral authority in the world by imposing American understandings of democracy, freedom, and human dignity around the globe. This muscular sense of the nation's confidence is in some respects a response to the tendency toward moral relativism and contrition for unpleasant events in the past that is associated with the political and cultural Left. For many on the Right, the United States is not simply a powerful member of the community of nations, blessed with an enviable democratic tradition, hardworking citizens, natural abundance, and relative peace over the last century; it is the greatest nation the world has ever known. The United States has nothing in its history to apologize for, and attempts to reconsider historical issues like slavery or Vietnam are signs of weakness and defeatism. It is a message that many people, tired of the challenges presented by an honest confrontation with the country's complex history and its ever-expanding cultural pluralism, are anxious to support. The threat to American peace and security posed by Islamic fundamentalism has provided the ideal rationale for a reassertion of national pride. Many religious conservatives have been happy to offer religious sanction to the fight against terrorism, which they have cloaked in the language of a Manichean struggle of good against evil, us versus them.

Another important link in the alliance of conservative Protestantism and traditionalist Catholicism within the Religious Right is the fight to outlaw abortion. More than any other issue, the existence of legal abortion on demand threatens the nation's moral integrity for many religious conservatives. Consider, for instance, this view from Joseph Bottum, an editor of *First Things:*

> Down somewhere in the deepest understanding of what America is for—something in the profound awareness of what it will take to reverse the nation's drift into social defeatism—there are reasons that one might link the rejection of abortion and the demand for a more active and moral foreign policy. . . . The opponents of abortion and euthanasia insist there are truths about human life and dignity that must not be compromised in domestic politics. The opponents of Islamofascism and rule by terror insist there are truths about human life and dignity that must not be compromised in international politics. . . . The desire to find intellectual and moral seriousness in one realm can breed the desire to find intellectual and moral seriousness in the other. . . . There may be several reasons to convince Americans to reject *Roe v. Wade*—but one of them is by remembering that the nation's founding ideals are *true* and worth defending against the enemies of freedom around the world.[63]

For those cultural and religious traditionalists who see the United States as a nation apart, President Bush's "war on terror" and the fight against legalized abortion have become key rallying points. A Christian-inspired foundation story promotes the "true" American values that will protect human dignity and freedom in the face of the killing of innocent children and the savagery of the Muslim terrorist threat. Thus the Republicans gained the necessary political support within their diverse coalition for an aggressive militarism that is an essential part of an imperial project, with an added bonus of a moral and patriotic cover that has made it difficult for critics of the policy to speak out without opening themselves to charges of weakness, immorality, and disloyalty. The depths to which some Republican politicians have been willing to sink to defend their increasingly indefensible military adventures were vividly revealed in November 2005, when Republican members of Congress impugned the bravery and patriotism of a congressional Democrat, John Murtha. Despite his status as retired Marine Corps colonel and Vietnam combat veteran, as well as his three decades of service in Congress, where he championed the needs of the armed services, Murtha dared suggest that it was time for the United States to withdraw its troops from Iraq.[64]

Christian voices who have attempted to challenge the use of Christian rhetoric by religious conservatives within the Republican Party have come under heavy attack as well, with particularly nasty battles being fought among American Catholics. As the Republican coalition has become more successful at the polls, some of its Catholic supporters, having been bestowed with prominence and power in a Republican-controlled government, have become deeply invested in the Republican political agenda. Thanks to appointments by Republican presidents, a majority of Supreme Court members are now Catholics, and prominent Catholics have offered vocal support for the Bush administration and its policies, including the Iraq war. When it became apparent that Catholic voters' ambivalence about the war and other parts of the Republican agenda could cost George Bush the 2004 election, groups of Republican Catholics, along with a small minority of U.S. Catholic bishops, began a furious effort to undermine John Kerry's presidential campaign by impugning his commitment to the Catholic Church. Some bishops, such as Raymond Burke of St. Louis and Charles Chaput of Denver, stated publicly that Kerry should be refused communion. Others, most notably Bishop Michael Sheridan of Colorado Springs, argued that Kerry's support for abortion rights would put any Catholic that voted for him in danger of excommunication.[65] Many of these same Republican Catholics, although not the bishops, had also suggested during the period immediately preceding the Iraq war that Catholics should leave the question of waging a preemptive or preventative war to the Bush administration's "prudential judgment."

The war in Iraq was a critical event for religious conservatives in the Republican coalition, for it brought to light important tensions between their vision of public Christianity and those drawn from creedal Christian theology. On the one hand, Saddam Hussein served as a perfect foil to the Republicans' imperial ambitions. Here was a corrupt Muslim dictator who was no longer useful to the United States and was easily linked by George Bush, albeit mendaciously, to the attacks of September 11 because the American public had little critical understanding of or interest in the Arab world. It was a perfect rallying point for an aggressive, yet moral, foreign policy that used the explanation of a "just war" to control the spread of "Islamofascism" and to promote American values of democracy and freedom in the Middle East. Republican traditionalist Catholics in particular provided useful interpretations of Catholic just-war theory to make the case that a morally driven American nation would have to fight wars like that in Iraq from time to time in order to demonstrate a meaningful commitment to freedom and human dignity worldwide.

Michael Novak and George Weigel were key intellectual architects of the strategy to convince Catholics that the Iraq war was "just." In 2003 President

Bush sent Novak, a fellow of the American Enterprise Institute, to Rome in an effort to convince the pope and Vatican officials that an American-led war in Iraq would be consistent with just-war principles.[66] At the same time, Weigel attacked the notion that Christians should approach the decision to go to war from a presumption that war was a failure to maintain a commitment to peace, although this was the position of the Vatican and most orthodox Christian theologians.[67] What was particularly striking about Weigel's support for the war was his underlying premise that, because so many religious leaders began with incorrect assumptions about war, "The claim that a 'presumption against violence' is at the root of the just war tradition cannot be sustained historically, methodologically, or theologically. If the just war tradition is a tradition of statecraft, and if the crucial distinction that undergirds it is the distinction between *bellum* and *duellum,* then the just war tradition cannot be reduced, as too many religious leaders reduce it today, to a series of means tests that begins with a 'presumption against violence.'"[68]

Weigel went on to argue that a proper understanding of just-war theory required a readiness to engage in war to preserve global peace:

> International terrorism of the sort we have seen since the late 1960s, and of which we had a direct national experience on September 11, 2001, is a deliberate assault, through the murder of innocents, on the very possibility of order in world affairs. That is why the terror networks must be dismantled or destroyed. The peace of order is also under grave threat when vicious, aggressive regimes acquire weapons of mass destruction—weapons that we must assume, on the basis of their treatment of their own citizens, these regimes will not hesitate to use against others. That is why there is a moral *obligation* to ensure that this lethal combination of irrational and aggressive regimes, weapons of mass destruction, and credible delivery systems does not go unchallenged. That is why there is a moral *obligation* to rid the world of this threat to the peace and security of all. Peace, rightly understood, demands it.[69]

The U.S. government does not operate in a cultural framework in which one religious tradition is dominant; thus defining the "moral responsibilities of government" is a complex and highly contested matter. Most Americans believe that George Bush draws his political authority from the people, not from God. In a democracy, religious values and institutions should act as mediating structures that are meant to influence and check elected power, but in a pluralist society they do not necessarily provide a universal moral standard for assessing a government's decision to go to war. Since the Second World War, democratically elected governments around the world have come to increasing consensus about the appropriate uses of force in international affairs, a consensus that is remarkably consistent with most orthodox Christian theological thinking on the application of just-war theory. In Weigel's view, it was for the Bush administration alone to decide whether the decision to go to war was based on "morally worthy political ends" and whether the Iraq war was a "moral" one that used proportionate and discriminate force to "defend the innocent." Weigel dismissed attempts by religious leaders to link just-war theory to the strong pacifist tradition deep within the Gospels as meddlesome and politically motivated. His message seemed to be that Catholics who were loyal and moral Americans should follow their president, not their church, for the just-war tradition was designed to serve the president. Serious theologians were nevertheless quick to challenge Weigel's assumptions. For example, the archbishop of Canterbury, Rowan Williams, defended the presumption against violence: "Weigel's claim that there is no presumption against violence in classical just-war theory needs a good deal of refining. The ruler who administers the law may use coercion for the sake of the common good in domestic policing and in international affairs. But such coercion will always need publicly available justification in terms of the common good, since otherwise it will appear as an arbitrary infringement of natural justice. The whole point is that there is precisely a presumption against violence, which can be overcome only by a very clear account of the needs of the common good and of what constitutes a 'natural' life for human beings."[70]

Catholic theologian William Cavanaugh, who questions the ability of the modern nation-state to promote the common good, has noted how Weigel's view effectively sidelines the church from any real ability to critique state-sanctioned violence through its moral authority over Christians separate from the state:

> In regarding the nation-state as responsible for the common good, the Church's voice in such crucial matters as war becomes muted, pushed to the margins. Just war reasoning becomes a tool of statecraft, most commonly used by the state to justify war, rather than a moral discipline for the Church to grapple with questions of violence. The Church itself becomes one more withering "intermediate association," whose moral reasoning and moral formation are increasingly colonized by the nation-state and the market. To resist, the Church must at the very least reclaim its authority to judge if and when Christians can kill, and not abdicate that authority to the nation-state.[71]

The language of moral war and justifiable violence is extremely important to the Religious Right, and it has been employed liberally in reference to the conflict over abortion. Downplaying core messages of the New Testament, the Religious Right is often tied to a notion of "righteous" warfare rooted in the Hebrew scriptures. Anglican theologian Michael Northcott sees a direct relationship between this evangelical pietism and the lack of critical social and political engagement of a highly privatized, twentieth-century American Protestantism:

> The contiguity between conservative evangelicalism and civil religion indicates the roots of American civil religion in Protestant Christianity. But the dogmas of civil religion are sufficiently different from orthodox Christianity, neglecting as they do Trinitarian belief, and in particular the Incarnation of Jesus Christ, who resisted evil nonviolently and was put to death at the hands of Empire. It stresses instead a Deist account of a distant creator God who sets the world in motion, and whose divine purpose for human history, and in particular American history, are revealed as a kind of latent providence. This God is only encountered directly through individual religious piety. . . . But in the public world, America's God is a divine Father of the nation who prospers the nation and fights with her against her enemies. . . . America's God is a God who acts on the world *in* and *through* America, and through America's military.[72]

Political scientist James Kurth has also argued that U.S. foreign policy is shaped by the nation's Protestant origins, but he sees the current understanding of Protestantism as a heresy that is the result of a declension from the original religion. Kurth notes that Protestantism is probably "unique among the world's religious traditions in its criticism of hierarchy and community and of the traditions and customs that go with them."[73] Despite a wide range of hierarchical structures within Protestant churches, from the more hierarchical Anglicans and Lutherans down to the Congregationalists, Baptists, and various nondenominational sects of American evangelicalism, "at the level of fundamental theology and doctrine, Protestantism denies that hierarchy and community are of fundamental importance."[74]

> By the beginning of the nineteenth century, the Protestant rejection of hierarchy and community spread to important areas of temporal and secular life. This was especially true in the new United States. In the economic arena, the elimination of hierarchy (monopoly or oligopoly) and community (guilds or trade associations) meant the establishment of the free market. In the political arena, the

elimination of hierarchy (monarchy or aristocracy) and community (traditions and customs) meant the establishment of liberal
democracy.... However, the free market could not become so free, nor
liberal democracy so liberal, that they degenerated into anarchy...
they had to be ordered by something. That something reflected the
Protestant emphasis on the written word and was a version of the
written covenant among individual Protestant believers. In the economic arena, this was the written contract; in the political arena it
was the written constitution.... The Protestant reformation was giving
birth to what would become the American Creed. The fundamental
elements of that secular creed—liberal democracy, free markets, con-
stitutionalism, and the role of law—were already fully in place in the
United States of the early nineteenth century.[75]

Kurth argues that the various Protestant creeds in the United States were
ultimately replaced by an American creed, whose elements were free markets
and equal opportunity, free elections and liberal democracy, and constitu-
tionalism and the rule of law. "The American creed definitely did not include
as elements hierarchy, community, tradition, and custom. Although the
American creed was not itself Protestant, it was clearly the product of a Protestant culture and was a sort of secularized version of Protestantism."[76] Since
the 1970s, the American creed has been universalized into a universalist
conception of human rights, and with the collapse of communism and the
stagnation of alternative models of European and Asian capitalism, some in
the United States have begun to see the American creed as "a new world
religion." As such, this creed places itself in competition with other world
religions. If Kurth is correct in his description of its disdain for hierarchy,
community, custom, and tradition, this ideology and its ongoing promotion
certainly present a direct challenge to orthodox Christianity, most notably
Catholicism. This challenge is something that the Vatican has long been aware
of, and John Allen, the Vatican correspondent for the *National Catholic Reporter*, summarized long-held Vatican concerns about the United States in his
book *All the Pope's Men: The Inside Story of How the Vatican Really Thinks*:

Key Vatican officials, especially Europeans from traditional Catholic
countries, have long worried about aspects of American society—
its exaggerated individualism, its hyperconsumer spirit, its relegation of religion to the private sphere, its Calvinist ethos. A fortiori,
they worry about a world in which America is in an unfettered position to impose this set of cultural values on everyone else. The
Calvinist concepts of the total depravity of the damned, the uncon-

ditional election of God's favored, and the manifestation of election through earthly success, all seem to them to play a powerful role in shaping American cultural psychology. The Iraq episode confirmed Vatican officials in these convictions. When Vatican officials hear Bush talk about the evil of terrorism and the American mission to destroy that evil, they sometimes perceive a worrying kind of dualism. The language can suggest a sense of election, combined with the perversity of America's enemies, that appears to justify unrelenting conflict.[77]

Although Kurth and the Vatican may think that the American creed is heresy, it is obvious that millions of churchgoing Americans disagree. At churches throughout the United States on any given Sunday, the U.S. flag is given pride of place upon the altar. This is particularly true in many Protestant fundamentalist and evangelical congregations, where patriotic songs and demonstrations are often included as part of the worship service, but flags are hardly unknown on the altars of Catholic churches in the United States as well. Americans who are regular churchgoers are much more likely to express their political views through the Religious Right and the Republican Party.[78] Yet, rather than offering an authentic Christian witness to warn of the corruptions of power, the Religious Right works diligently not only to infuse the American creed with religious meaning but also to support its bellicose nationalism and imperial pretensions.

Those who dissent from the vision of a world dominated by U.S. military power and from a Christianity perverted by the American creed are attacked as unpatriotic and bad Christians. Effectively, orthodox American Christians who seek a global and national politics rooted in a more social democratic vision of community, who seek peace through greater international cooperation and understanding, and who question an Americanist co-opting of Christian faith can expect to be castigated for being weak in the clash of civilizations represented by the "Islamic threat." Even the Vatican is not immune from attack for being diffident in this regard. When a Danish newspaper published cartoons offensive to Muslims, the Vatican issued a statement that maintained that the action exhibited a "lack of human sensitivity and may constitute in some cases an inadmissible provocation."[79] Joseph Bottum responded to this with the following in First Things: "Despite the murder of a Catholic priest in Turkey, apparently because of these cartoons, the Vatican issued a statement in which obtuseness seemed caught in a death struggle with inanity. It's not nice to tease our backward brothers or hold them to the same standard we might hold Danish newspaper editors. . . . This is infamous and offensive."[80]

Both the U.S. State Department and the British foreign secretary issued statements that were similar in substance to the Vatican's.[81] Bottum attributed the statements of both the Vatican and the State Department to political correctness, and he was enraged that a *Boston Globe* editorial that offered similar views was, to his mind, more concerned about protecting Muslim sensibilities than respecting those of Christians at home when similar issues of "respect" arose.[82] Despite its control of the presidency and, until recently, the Congress, the American Right has been engaged in a ceaseless campaign of demonizing the Muslim "other" in the hopes of generating enough fear and hate to support a military crusade against the Islamic world, while at the same time it continues to nurse decades-old grievances about how they are treated by the "liberals" at home. Shockingly, Bottum is unwilling even to assume the Vatican's good faith and respect for the Gospels, and he is dismayed that the Holy See refused to take the bait that an act of senseless violence offers for an escalation of the rhetoric of hatred.

Heinrich Schneider has argued that, in the Western world, nationalism is a particularization of certain elements of the Christian faith and that it actually operates as "a substitute religious construct."[83] He distinguishes nationalism from the classical virtue and duty of patriotism. Whereas patriotism, rightly understood, comprehends a love of one's country and an acceptance of the political and social duties that come with membership in the community, nationalism results when patriotism becomes extreme.[84] On the one hand, "a political community needs a force to give it unity and to preserve that unity. It is not enough for the ruling order to be regarded as legitimate and certainly not enough that it and the decisions made within its framework should be accepted on the assessments of interests and calculation."[85] Ultimately, what is the force that keeps the political community together, particularly when the citizenry does not necessarily share the traditional attributes of culture and identity, such as language, religion, or history? One force is the identification of a common enemy: "Nothing creates and strengthens group identity so much as a common enemy, a 'wholly other' adversary; so that quite often, hostile stereotypes are conjured up to stabilize identities. National identity is often defined by reference to counter identities."[86]

If James Q. Wilson is correct in seeing the current era in American life as one of extreme polarization (and there is much to suggest that this is indeed the case[87]), one can begin to see a powerful rationale for the pseudoreligious nationalism of the Right. Earlier I discussed the deep social discord within the United States during the 1990s. Despite an excellent economy, the nation was riven by social and political crises, such as the Oklahoma City terrorist bombing, riots in Los Angeles, and the Columbine shootings. Issues like affirmative action and welfare reform generated deep anger and hostility, and civility in Congress evaporated. What was particularly noteworthy about this time (and also takes us back to Schneider's thesis) is that, in 1989, the United States lost its primary external enemy, the Soviet Union. Almost immediately thereafter it seemed as if the nation had turned in upon itself.

Then, in 2001, the tragedy of the Twin Towers provided the common enemy that Americans had lacked for more than a decade, thereby offering a much-needed excuse for the nation's political elites to turn away from the United States' festering internal divisions. Suddenly the country seemed remarkably unified once again. Much was made of the renewed spirit of American cooperation and patriotism in the wake of the terrorist attacks. Yet, truth be told, America's divisions might simply be a permanent part of the national condition, unresolved at the nation's inception, brutally put down by the Civil War, and reopened in the 1960s and the culture wars of the late twentieth century. Perhaps those on the Right have recognized the fragile state of the nation's unity and seized upon the "Islamic threat" as a means of providing the American people with the glue for their political community that common institutions alone cannot deliver. For good measure, the Religious Right has offered an extra dose of religious justification necessary to make the conflict with Islam an epic clash of warring worldviews similar to America's monumental battle with communism.

Key groups in the Religious Right have collapsed Christianity into a nationalistic civil religion that places the United States in the role of Israel in the Hebrew scriptures. This role justifies U.S. militarism and a unilateralist approach to international affairs since the United States, like Israel in the Old Testament, answers directly only to God. State-sanctioned violence is legitimate if the state is moral and the cause is just. Thus, it becomes extremely important to purify the polity of unjust practices like legalized abortion in order to preserve the nation's moral integrity. During the Clinton administration, in despair over the legal status of abortion and fearing that they might not ever control the entire apparatus of government, religious conservatives were taking a much less triumphant stance toward the nation. Some commentators came remarkably close to saying that the state had lost its legitimacy and that Americans who opposed abortion could no longer accept the immoral policies imposed by a "tyrant state."[88] Once the Republicans gained power, a purification of the state began, and unquestioned loyalty to executive authority was demanded from all citizens. Dissent, even when it was rooted in a shared commitment to the Incarnation and the Gospels, was not tolerated. Thus became the role of "Christianity" in the right-wing power apparatus of the American empire.

2

Combining Faith and Reason in the Modern World through Catholic Social Teaching

The coupling of Protestant evangelicalism and fundamentalism with traditionalist Catholicism has nourished an American civil religion on the political Right that claims the title "Christian" for itself but often bears only a passing relationship to orthodox Christianity. Under the current circumstances, in which this vision of public Christianity reigns supreme in the nation's public life, it is hardly surprising that large numbers of Americans of deep Christian faith have retreated from an engagement with politics, recoiling from the idea of being identified with or bullied by the Religious Right. Regardless of the speakers' faith tradition, Christian discourse in the United States has become increasingly "fundamentalist" in its tone, rooted in a Manichean approach to Christian ethics that proffers black-or-white responses to a range of complex political and religious questions like abortion, prayer in public schools, homosexuality, and war. This leaves little room for a dialogue that respects context, complexity, or nuance, and it repels people of goodwill who are committed to a vision of human dignity rooted in democratic pluralism. As Jimmy Carter has noted, this fundamentalist tendency has spread to encompass public discourse more generally and contributed to a serious debasement of political life in the United States.

One can indeed live out authentic Christian belief in the modern world on the basis of respect and compassion for other human beings, and Christians can engage in civic life and meaningful political dialogue with those who do not share their religious beliefs. For more than a century, the Catholic Church has been developing its social teaching in recognition of the challenges and opportunities presented to people of faith as a result of the social, political, and economic upheavals that have become inseparable from life in the modern world. Begun initially as a purely Catholic reaction to the problems raised by the collapse of the ancien régime in Europe, Catholic social teaching has evolved to become a comprehensive embrace of the challenges of living out Christian faith in modern conditions. Defining Catholic social teaching precisely is somewhat complex, but here I rely on a vision of the tradition provided by theologian Johann Verstraeten:

> The Catholic social tradition can be interpreted as a tradition which comprises a particular set of shared understandings about the human person, social goods, and their distributive arrangements. This particular understanding is grounded in a living relation to the constitutive narratives provided by the Bible, integrated in a theoretical framework which makes it possible for the Catholic understanding to remain open to rational explanation and public debate. A distinctive "cultural" feature is its connection to sacramental and liturgical practices. . . . It is a continuous learning process of interpretation and re-interpretation of the meaning of the human person as a social being and of the shared understandings within the Catholic community . . . about social, economic, and political goods and their distribution.[1]

This view of Catholic social teaching goes beyond a more traditional definition that emphasizes key authoritative texts in the encyclical letters of various popes. These texts are essential, and I discuss many of them here. But as Verstraeten has argued, it is important not to see Catholic social teaching in a way that is too rigidly doctrinal. One reason for this is that "doctrine" is at times susceptible to ideological misuse.[2] Another is that "the limitation of Catholic social thought to the texts of the magisterium is by no means uncontested or uncontestable within the Church and has not always been the view of either scholars or activists in the field of the Church's social mission. If nothing else, a glance at the quantity of letters from Bishops' conferences in different countries on the economy and development and contemporary social issues is enough to persuade us that even the scope of the official teaching is wider."[3] Thus, I use the terms *Catholic social teaching* and *Catholic social thought* interchangeably to describe this tradition in a way that not only communicates its dynamism and its reliance on a wide range of sources but also emphasizes its ability to foster dialogue across the Christian traditions and among all people of goodwill.

Although Catholicism has always been an international and universalist religion, the Second Vatican Council propelled the church to embrace its global role in a fundamentally different way. After the council, Roman Catholicism truly became a "world church" for the modern age, as Robert Ellsberg described it: "It was only at Vatican II that there arose a consciousness that the church was not essentially European. To be truly catholic the church must do more than seek a geographical extension; it must become incarnate in the cultures, the hopes, and the struggles of the entire human race."[4] In the wake of the council, the church addressed its social teaching to "all people of goodwill."[5] Moreover, it has attempted to confront global challenges like economic inequality, military conflict, human rights, family life, and the environment while maintaining a deep and unwavering respect for universal human dignity. The result has been that, more than any other Christian faith, Catholicism has developed a thickly layered social teaching that is deeply embedded in the traditions of Christian orthodoxy and humanism and reflects the lived experience of Christianity around the world.

Catholic social teaching relies on biblical exegesis, tradition, and intellectual argument drawn from the global reach of Catholic Christianity. Given its deep theological and intellectual roots and the growing influence of Asian, Latin American, and African theologians on its development, it resonates not only with people across the Christian traditions but also among people of other faiths. Furthermore, because it engages in an intellectual, as well as a religious, discourse, Catholic social teaching is not limited to religiously observant people. Avoiding the emotivism, dogmatism, and fundamentalism that have become prevalent in modern American public life and much of the nation's public religious discourse, Catholic social teaching uses rational argument to create an intellectual platform for discussion of global social questions, thereby allowing for meaningful dialogue even when there is sharp disagreement in principle.

An excellent example of this process occurred in 1995 at the United Nations Fourth World Conference on Women. Delegates representing the Vatican were able to negotiate across religious and philosophical boundaries and promoted positions on key issues rooted in Catholic social teaching that ultimately affected significant aspects of the final documents.[6] More recently, in 2004, then Cardinal Joseph Ratzinger engaged in a discussion with secular German philosopher Jürgen Habermas concerning the latter's essay on the moral foundations of democratic politics. Although Habermas was wary of the conviction of religious believers that their religion alone provides the route to salvation (something he has termed "theological narcissism"), he agreed with Ratzinger (and, indeed, has long argued) that Judeo-Christian precepts have formed the basis of secular precepts such as equality, fairness, and the intrinsic worth of all persons. Habermas was not convinced that the secular concepts dependent upon these religious ideas could be sustained if the religious sources of morality and justice were allowed to atrophy.[7]

Catholic social teaching indeed finds many points of agreement with secular constructions of liberalism, particularly those that relate to human dignity and human rights. On the other hand, the foundational principles of Catholic social teaching exist in sharp tension with certain features of American society (and, to a greater or lesser extent, modern Western culture in general) that tend both implicitly and explicitly to glorify individualism.[8] Whereas Catholic social teaching relies heavily on understandings of liberalism drawn from the political theory of modern continental European philosophy, American political theory and public argument are heavily dependent on the autonomous individual of free-market liberalism or the social contract theories of Rawlsian liberalism, positivism, and libertarianism.

Catholic social thought, however, proceeds from completely different premises about the theoretical preconditions for stable human political and moral community. Theologically, Catholicism sees the human person as formed in the image and likeness of God—the *imago Dei*—and at the same time views the person as inherently social, created to live in community with others, and flourishing only in that context. Not only does Catholic social teaching reject as a theological matter any understanding of a "state of nature" in which humans were solitary beings without any relational commitments, voluntarily ceding rights and assuming duties in order to establish community, it has also been heavily influenced by secular philosophical ideas that reject these presumptions. These philosophical views presume that human dignity and justice are inseparable from the selfless behavior toward others that is a requirement of life in community, and they build on a philosophical vision championed by G. W. F. Hegel that views true freedom as a product of life in an ethical community whose members accord one another recognition and respect.

Brief Historical Background of Catholic Social Teaching

Modern Catholic social teaching is generally seen as having begun in 1891, when Pope Leo XIII issued the encyclical *Rerum novarum*. The antecedents of the social teaching, however, can be traced back to the eighteenth century. In the decades preceding the release of *Rerum novarum,* a number of Catholic thinkers, most notably in Germany and France, had begun to consider the growing tensions between the traditional understandings of Catholic social philosophy, which stressed an organic, hierarchical community, and the egalitarian individualism of postrevolutionary Europe. Although some of this work was often used to identify the errors of "liberalism" and further entrenched the church on the side of reactionary voices against democratic change, many of these thinkers also drew increasing attention to the growing misery of the rapidly expanding urban working class.

As industrialization and democratization spread throughout Europe in the mid-nineteenth century, the appalling living conditions of the increasingly urbanized poor and their growing alienation from Christianity became issues of great importance to the church. One of the most notable figures that arose during this era was Wilhelm von Ketteler, bishop of Mainz. To respond to the inequities and dehumanizing conditions of the early industrial era, Ketteler formed a critique that combined aspects of Catholic and German ideas of an organic social order with an appreciation for and an embrace of key democratic and economic reforms. He argued for self-governing worker organizations as a way of ethically restructuring society and was acknowledged by Leo XIII as a key inspiration in the drafting of *Rerum novarum.*[9] Thus, historically, Catholic social teaching arose in an era of profound political, social, and economic change, one that ultimately produced the American and French revolutions, democracy, industrialization, free-market capitalism, and communism: "Modern Catholic social thought emerged from an effort to confront transforming historical events with a reaffirmation of divine purpose and human responsibility. During the eighteenth and nineteenth centuries basic social, economic, and political changes in Western Europe undermined the whole system of Christian civilization on which traditional religious identification depended. Industrialization, nationalism, political and cultural freedom, and a bewildering variety of pluralisms were bound to influence most severely the Catholic church, which in the aftermath of the Reformation had linked its fortunes closely with the old order."[10]

In many ways, *Rerum novarum* was a revolutionary document. Pope Leo was extremely critical of the social costs exacted by industrial capitalism, and he announced some "radical" ideas to protect working people, such as a living wage, the regulation of child labor, and guaranteed Sunday rest. He also denounced socialism, which was making significant inroads among the working classes, often to the detriment of the church:

In a remarkably evenhanded manner, the pope laid anathemas both on liberal capitalism, which released the individual from social and moral constraints, and socialism, which subordinated individual well-being without respect for human rights or religious welfare.... Leo insisted that wages be determined not by economic considerations alone, but by taking into account the basic needs of the individual. Property, too, was subject to social and moral restraints; while all had a right to possess private property, none had the right to use that property without reference to the needs of the community. Leo insisted that the moral law—based on a rational understanding of human nature supplemented by revelation—had to [have] part of every economic system and indeed of every economic transaction.[11]

At its core, however, early Catholic social teaching was rooted in an understanding of social hierarchy and a role for the church that took a nostalgic view of prerevolutionary Europe. Pope Leo argued for an orderly society modeled on an idealized vision of medieval unity, with relations between classes ordered by strict adherence to principles of justice and friendship.[12] In 1891 at least, the church was still a somewhat unwilling participant in the modern age.

Forty years later, when Pope Pius XI wrote *Quadragesimo anno*, the international situation had changed dramatically. Europe had endured the Great War, and the world economy was gripped by the Great Depression. Communism was triumphant in Russia, and, given the desperate worldwide economic situation, socialist ideas had gained increasing legitimacy and were even generating interest among Christians across the social classes. After World War I, the old order was unquestionably finished, but the alternatives for the future offered little cause for hope. Both capitalism and its Marxist response had ravaged the societies of Europe.

Quadragesimo anno is often remembered for its failed attempt to offer a "third way" between capitalism and communism through a corporatist model of state-controlled syndical organizations for workers and employers. Unfortunately, Pius's vision became entangled in the rise of fascism in Italy and other authoritarian regimes in Catholic countries such as Spain and Portugal. But *Quadragesimo anno* also left an important intellectual legacy. It was unstinting in its criticism of both socialism and capitalism, and it attacked the notion that the "laws" of the marketplace were somehow natural in their operation and consequences. Indeed, the criticism of individualism and capitalism was particularly scathing.[13] It also introduced some important new ideas into the body of Catholic social teaching, namely the principle of subsidiarity and the concept of social justice and its relationship to the common good.

More than any other event, however, it was the Second Vatican Council that propelled the Catholic Church into the modern age. The council put an end to the vision of the church as a fortress standing in opposition to a hostile post-Enlightenment modernity. At the same time, in opening itself to modern ideas and allowing for a greater level of participation by the laity, the church lost some of the authority it had wielded in the precouncil era, which was characterized by a strong Catholic identity tied to a rich array of institutions and highly ritualized religious practice rooted in duty and obedience. Up to this point, Catholic social teaching had been "first and foremost a papal doctrine, forged and proclaimed by popes themselves in encyclical letters."[14]

Prior to Vatican II, the major focus of Catholic social teaching was what was generically called "the social question." Simply put, the social question involved the changing class structures of European societies that emerged with industrialization and the conflict that resulted, particularly that between labor and capital. After World War II, the social question (as it had been traditionally understood in Europe) resolved itself as the European nations developed into wealthy, modern welfare states.[15] Thus, by the early 1960s, when Pope John XXIII called the Second Vatican Council, the church's attentions had shifted to the worldwide implications of the social question, particularly in Latin America, Africa, and Asia. In Second Vatican Council documents such as *Lumen gentium, Gaudium et spes,* and *Dignitatis humanae,* the church embraced key concepts of liberal democracy, thereby repositioning itself as a zealous advocate of democracy and human rights in the postcolonial states of the developing world. Greater comfort with democratic values also affected the role of the laity. As part of an active engagement with a lived Christian faith, they were now called to be much more active participants in ecclesial life and encouraged to apply their gifts and talents to the betterment of humanity: "By their competence in secular disciplines and by their activity which grace elevates from within, let [the laity] do all in their power to ensure that through human labor, technical skill, and civil culture the goods of creation may be developed for the benefit of everyone without exception, according to the plan of the creator and the light of his word, that these goods may be more equitably distributed among all men and women and may make their own contribution to universal progress in human and Christian liberty."[16]

Although it is impossible to condense the stunning magnitude of the change that Vatican II wrought on the Roman Catholic Church, for the purposes of Catholic social teaching, new emphases on the dignity of the individual and on individual action and conscience became extremely important for the teaching's modern development. For example, moved by the experience of the United States and the work of John Courtney Murray, the council embraced the liberal democratic concept of religious freedom in *Dignitatis humanae*. More broadly, the church announced its concern for the dignity of all men and women and its commitment to their essential humanity at a time when discrimination of every type was endemic throughout the world, including the United States:

> Any kind of social or cultural discrimination in basic personal rights on the grounds of sex, race, color, social conditions, language, or religion must be curbed and eradicated as incompatible with God's design. It is deeply to be deplored that these basic personal rights are not yet being respected everywhere.... Furthermore, while there are just differences between people, their equal dignity as persons demands we strive for fairer and more humane conditions. Excessive economic and social disparity between individuals and peoples of the one human race is a source of scandal and militates against social justice, equity, human dignity, as well as social and international peace.[17]

With Vatican II, the aims of Catholic social teaching and the Catholic Church itself became truly global, and the social question taken up by *Rerum novarum* became worldwide. David Hollenbach provides an excellent description of the council's effect on the understanding of Catholicism as a global faith in the modern world:

> The Council's consideration of the Church's relation to the modern world was influenced in a special way by the extraordinary participation of bishops from virtually every corner of the world. This was an ecumenical council unlike any other in history in that its participants came from countries around the world and from societies where all the great world religions play significant roles. Thus the Council's experience of the challenges facing the Church were strongly shaped by the way voices within it spoke in the language and accents of many peoples of the world. This experience was one of the most fundamental influences of Vatican II on the Church's understanding of its role in society.[18]

After Vatican II, Catholic social teaching began a sustained critique of an unrestrained, global free-market order and began to call attention to the growing economic divide between the global north and the global south. The point of analysis for the responsibilities of the wealthy toward the poor was shifted from the domestic context within nation-states to the international context among nation-states. In his 1967 encyclical *Populorum progressio*, Pope Paul VI called attention to the duties of social justice and human solidarity that should define the relations between the rich and poor nations of the world:

> It is not just a matter of eliminating hunger, or even of reducing poverty. The struggle against destitution, though urgent and neces-sary, is not enough. It is a question, rather, of building a world where every man, no matter what his race, religion, or nationality, can live a fully human life, freed from servitude imposed on him by other men or by natural forces over which he has no control. . . . This de-mands great generosity, much sacrifice, and unceasing effort on the part of the rich man. . . . Is he prepared to support out of his own pocket works and undertakings in favor of the most destitute? Is he ready to pay higher taxes so that the public authorities can inten-sify their efforts in favor of development? Is he ready to pay a higher price for imported goods so that the producer may be more justly rewarded? Or leave his country, if necessary and he is young, in order to assist in this development of the young nations?[19]

Pope Paul reminded the rich nations of the world that the church's long-standing position was one of special solicitation for the poor.[20] This was an early indication of what eventually became known as *liberation theology*, one of whose key contributions was the development of the theological concept of the "preferential option for the poor." Father Gustavo Gutiérrez, who is generally acknowledged as the creator of liberation theology, has defined this idea in Catholic theology as "preference to the poorest and most needy sectors and to those segregated for any cause whatsoever. The very word 'preference' denies all exclusiveness and seeks to call attention to those who are the first—though not the only ones—with whom we should be in solidarity."[21]

Twenty years later Pope John Paul II reaffirmed the teaching of *Populorum progressio* in his encyclical *Sollicitudo rei socialis*. Although the intervening years had witnessed some tension between Rome and various interpreters of liber-ation theology, John Paul II wholeheartedly embraced the preferential option for the poor and located it firmly within the church's tradition: "The option or love of preference for the poor . . . is an option, or a special form of primacy in the exercise of Christian charity, to which the whole tradition of the Church bears witness. It affects the life of each Christian inasmuch as he or she seeks to imitate the life of Christ, but it applies equally to our social responsibilities and hence to our manner of living, and to the logical decisions to be made concerning the ownership and use of goods."[22] This principle provides an important insight into a core commitment of Catholic social thought and has dramatic implications for Christians in the wealthy nations of the world. The poor have a special claim to our attention, particularly as we consider the consequences of the global economic system.

Core Themes of Catholic Social Teaching

In 2005 the Pontifical Council for Justice and Peace produced the *Compendium of the Social Doctrine of the Church*. One advantage of the compendium is that it presents Catholic social teaching as a unified doctrinal corpus from which to begin a consideration of the breadth and depth of Catholic social teaching. It highlights four key "permanent" principles of Catholic social teaching—human dignity, the common good, subsidiarity, and solidarity—and states that these principles "must be appreciated in their unity, interrelatedness, and articulation. . . . Examining each of these principles individually must not lead to using them only in part or in an erroneous manner, which would be the case if they were invoked in a disjointed and unconnected way."[23] Moreover:

> The principles of the social doctrine, in their entirety, constitute that primary articulation of the truth of society by which every conscience is challenged and invited to interact with every other conscience in truth, in responsibility shared fully with all people and also regarding all people. In fact, man cannot avoid the question of freedom and the meaning of life in society, since society is a reality that is neither external nor foreign to his being. These principles have a profoundly moral significance because they refer to the ultimate and organizational foundations of life in society. To understand them completely, it is necessary to act in accordance with them, following the path of development that they indicate for a life worthy of man.[24]

In its root principles, Catholic social teaching sees the life of a Christian as grounded intrinsically in the life of society. In direct confrontation with the dismissive attitudes of libertarianism and economic neoliberalism toward community, Catholic social teaching sees the interrelatedness of human persons in the social order as a moral matter of profound importance. This relational view of human beings is evident in the principles that are fundamental to Catholic social thought, so it is worthwhile to consider them and some of their most important implications in turn.

This review of the core principles also demonstrates the relationship of modern Catholic social teaching to important developments in post–World

War II European political philosophy, particularly ideas about the moral imperative of the individual's relationship to others in any attempt to build just institutions and societies. I highlight the work of two modern European philosophers who have been influential in Catholic theology since Vatican II: Emmanuel Lévinas and Paul Ricoeur. Although both of these men were religious believers, neither was Catholic. Lévinas was a Jew and Ricoeur, a Protestant, and both were completely immersed in the secular philosophical dialogue of the twentieth century. Their work helps to demonstrate the ability of Catholic social teaching to engage an ecumenical audience and to promote dialogue across intellectual and religious traditions. In addition, like the conversation between Ratzinger and Habermas (noted earlier), their writings provide important insight into the way in which the interrelatedness of human beings creates moral imperatives that are vital supports to core democratic and liberal values.

Human Dignity

Catholic social teaching flows out of profound respect for human dignity. "The church sees in men and women, in every person, the living image of God himself."[25] This concept of *imago Dei* is fundamental to our understanding of the goals and priorities of the social teaching. "Men and women, in the concrete circumstances of history, represent the heart and soul of Catholic social thought. The whole of the Church's social doctrine, in fact, develops from the principle that affirms the inviolable dignity of the human person."[26] Inseparable from the inherent dignity of people, who are created in God's image, is the understanding that we are social beings: "Linked to the dignity of human life is our understanding of the social nature of the person. As the creation narratives tell us, we are made in the image of a Triune God and we are created in relationship to God and to each other. Our inherently social nature means that the structures of social, political, and economic life must reflect basic respect for the dignity of every human person as well as a commitment to the common good."[27]

This socially rooted concept of human dignity has important moral and theological implications, for Catholic social teaching is based on the claim that people always exist in a web of social relationships. God is social, human beings are social, and, ultimately, salvation is social. To understand what it means to say that "salvation is social," we must remember that the orthodox Christian image of God is triune—Father, Son, and Holy Spirit. Thus, our understanding of God involves interrelationship and association of different parts that form a whole, and any attempt to understand the implications of *imago Dei* must take this into account. One imperative of our social nature is that it implies moral and even legal obligations of mutual assistance.[28] This imperative is developed in the other key principles of the social teaching, particularly through the common good and solidarity.

Fundamentally, then, Catholic social teaching offers a framework for engagement with the modern world that proceeds from the principle that human beings are sacred and social. This sacred nature is not limited to Christians or to those who have announced themselves "saved" but extends to all men and women on the planet. Promoting human dignity is the goal of all social activity. Rights and duties come to us not because of a social contract but because of our origin in God's image.[29] Men, women, and the communities they form, such as families, do not come into being because of the state; rather, they precede the state. An essential responsibility of the state is to preserve human dignity by respecting the sacred nature of human beings, as well as organizations and institutions formed as a result of our social nature.[30]

Catholic social teaching is not alone in the importance it places on the relationship between human dignity and responsibility to others. Many philosophical critiques exist of those understandings of liberalism that consistently privilege the individual over the community. In the English-speaking world this challenge has been taken up by philosophers of the communitarian school like Michael Sandel and Charles Taylor, as well as by scholars of a more Aristotelian perspective, particularly Alasdair MacIntyre. In Europe there has long been resistance to an understanding of liberalism that leaves little room for moral claims of community that might impede individual action, and these philosophical traditions have been particularly influential in modern Catholic social teaching. Indeed, an arguable failing of modern Anglo-American political philosophy is its growing unwillingness to engage non-English sources of modern thought.

Charles Taylor, a Canadian with deep roots in both the English- and French-speaking communities of Quebec, has noted that being a product of two distinct cultures has made a deep impression on his work as a philosopher, and his French influences have drawn him to expressivist theories of language and selfhood:

> My attraction to [eighteenth-century German philosopher Johann
> Gottfried von] Herder was prepared long ago by my situation in
> Quebec, where two philosophies, as well as two philosophies of
> language, came face to face: while English speakers considered lan-
> guage as an instrument and did not understand why someone would
> refuse to adopt the most widely used instrument . . . for French

speakers language constitutes a way of being in the world. Having belonged to a mixed family for several generations, it always seemed obvious to me that language was more than an instrument, that each language carries with it its own sense of humor, conception of the world, etc. Hence my interest for language and for the Romantic philosophy of language, which criticized the instrumentalist philosophy of Hobbes, Locke, or Condillac.[31]

Taylor has become known for elaborating a theory of the "situated self" in Anglo-American philosophy, and his experience is noteworthy because, as a North American, his "communitarianism" exists in strong tension with a more dominant, Anglo-American libertarianism, positivism, and individualism, all heavily dependent on the instrumentalist philosophies of Hobbes and Locke. Like Taylor, Catholic social teaching draws heavily on the French and German philosophy that has produced the hermeneutics and phenomenology of philosophers such as Hans-Georg Gadamer and Paul Ricoeur, both of whom have profoundly influenced orthodox Christian theology since the Second World War. Ricoeur argued through his hermeneutics, which he defined as the process of discovering indirect meaning, that we understand our existence as a "self" not simply as an autonomous entity but also as a being that develops through the "linguistic mediation of signs and symbols, stories and ideologies, metaphors and myths. The self returns to itself after numerous hermeneutic detours through the language of others, to find itself enlarged and enriched by the journey."[32]

Much of Ricoeur's work, however, has not been translated into English. Agnès Poirier, London correspondent for the French news daily *Libération*, has noted that many in the English-speaking world have retreated proudly into a monolingualism in which they can fantasize that everyone in the world speaks their language, but "to argue that the English language now rules our global culture is misleading. First of all, it induces the blind assumption that everything significant in the world—in politics, the arts, business, academe—is done in English. It is also pernicious: what kind of English are we talking about? We're not referring to Shakespeare, but rather to the how-to-use guide sold with the latest software. Nothing to boast about, nothing to anchor a new global culture."[33] In 2003, only 25 percent of U.S. colleges and universities required foreign language study in secondary school as a prerequisite for admission, and the vast majority of American students who study foreign language learn only one—Spanish.[34] A recent study, "States Prepare for the Global Age," which looked at the international competitiveness of the United States, found students' knowledge of other nations and cultures "weak and increasingly dangerous."[35] All of this underlines the difficulty of communicating a Catholic social doctrine formed by an international and multilingual dialogue across cultures to an American audience rooted in a political and cultural milieu that has remained linguistically and intellectually parochial.

Not only is the Catholic concept of human dignity the product of a multicultural and multilingual religious tradition; it is also engaged with philosophical ideas that are not exclusive to one linguistic or religious community. One example is the relationship between the concept of human dignity in Catholic social teaching and that in the work of Emmanuel Lévinas, a man of four cultures—Jewish, Russian, German, and French. In *Alterity and Transcendence*, Lévinas offers nonreligious, philosophical arguments for the existence of the transcendent—not in the traditional sense of a great, unknowable beyond or an afterlife but an ethical transcendence that comes through our relationship with others. He explores the "I-you" relationship and seeks a meaning beyond a circumstance in which some kind of reciprocity is sought because "the moment one is generous in hopes of reciprocity, that relation no longer involves generosity but the commercial relation, the exchange of good behavior. In the relation to the other, the other appears to me as one to whom I owe something. Toward whom I have a responsibility. Hence the asymmetry of the I-you relation and the radical inequality between the I and the you, for all relation to the other is a relation to a being toward whom I have obligations. I insist therefore on the meaning of that gratuitousness of the 'for the other,' resting on the responsibility that is already there in a dormant state."[36]

Lévinas's thought deepens the inquiry about what "love thy neighbor" really means and therefore links us to a Christian concept of human dignity inseparable from our associations with others. Loving one's neighbor is not simply loving those who love us or an opportunistic engagement of the other in hopes of reciprocity. The challenge of loving our neighbor is in embracing the humanity of a person who is truly "other"—a person with whom I may have no natural affinity. Lévinas uses the French word *altérité*, which is typically translated as "otherness," to describe a sense of profound difference. Thus, this may be an association "in radical contradiction of [the other's] alterity, that place from which, for an insufficiently mature soul, hatred flows naturally or is deduced with infallible logic. One must deliberately abstain from the convenience of 'historical rights,' 'rights of enrootedness,' 'undeniable principles' and the 'inalienable human condition.' One must refuse to get caught up in the tangle of abstractions, whose principles are often evident, but whose dialectic, be it ever so rigorous, is murderous and criminal."[37]

What we achieve when we embrace the others in all of their alterity is an ethical transcendence that takes us beyond our "social totality." In other words, we can escape the biases, prejudices, and hatreds that give us a rationale to dehumanize the other, and we are able to rise to a new ethical plane that recognizes their profound humanity. Lévinas takes these ideas and links them to a concept of justice that flows from this radical recognition of the other in which "sociality is . . . the best of the human. It is the good. . . . Sociality is the alterity of the face, of the for-the-other that calls out to me, a voice that rises within me, in the mortality of the I, from the depths of my weakness. That voice is an order. I have to answer for the life of the other person. I do not have the right to leave him alone to his death."[38] But does not this obligation impose an unsustainable burden or at the very least set out some type of utopian ideal of social responsibility? Lévinas addresses this concern as well: "When you have encountered a human being, you cannot drop him. Most often we do so, saying 'I have done all I could!' We haven't done anything! It is this feeling, this consciousness of having done nothing that gives us the status of hostage with the responsibility of one who is not guilty, who is innocent. . . . The other involves us in a situation in which we are obligated without guilt, but our obligation is no less for that. At the same time it is a burden, it is heavy, and if you like, that is what goodness is. The trace of the infinite is inscribed in my obligation toward the other."[39]

We do not abandon the call to love our neighbor because, logically, it is impossible or, practically, unbearable. In our relationship to the divine, we strive for the perfection that it represents. From a Christian perspective, Lévinas offers a remarkable analysis that explains the struggle to live out a Christian vocation. We are created as God, not to be God but to seek God through our lives with others. On the surface, this concept of human dignity in Catholic social teaching and in Lévinas seems consistent with the respect one finds for the human person in liberal democracy. The idea that "all men are created equal" and that "they are endowed by the Creator with certain unalienable rights" from the Declaration of Independence suggests an inherent, God-given dignity for humankind. Certainly, Western liberal democracy and Christianity share a common intellectual and cultural heritage that has long commanded respect for this dignity, and, despite the church's resistance to liberalism in the nineteenth century, Vatican II represented something of a rapprochement between Catholicism and certain core liberal values. Since that time, however, liberalism in the wealthy countries of the West has increasingly distanced itself from an understanding of human dignity rooted in commitments to others and relied instead on a respect for individual autonomy and personal freedom: "If we consider contemporary western society, we find an individualism elevated and legitimated by free-will, a reassertion of rights over responsibilities, an established tendency to privilege the procedural to the detriment of the substantive through an unwillingness to transmit any principal truths. The individual of late modernity is the source of his own definition of the good, having just replaced the 'good' with 'values' that are subjective . . . his responsibilities vis à vis others, close or distant, do not come into being except through his own decision and cease when he is no longer willing to bear them."[40]

More and more, the concept of the human person in the liberal state has become disconnected from any notion of responsibility to others, be they close or distant, and human relationships are defined by whether they meet the personal needs or desires of those involved. Thus, neither the deeply reciprocal model of society in Catholic social teaching, in which rights are always balanced with responsibilities and relationships with others are not only necessary but also desirable, nor the profound link of one's own dignity to that of the other, as expounded by Lévinas and Ricoeur, has resonated strongly in the United States. Ours is a culture that places a premium on autonomy, personal liberty, and independence from obligations imposed by others, and culture here has become the standard-bearer of the radically autonomous self to the rest of the world.

The Common Good

Defining the common good can be a challenge. On the one hand, it flows quite logically from an understanding of human dignity rooted in relationships with others. *Gaudium et spes,* for example, defines it as "the sum total of social conditions which allow people, either as groups or individuals, to reach their fulfilment more fully and more easily.[41] The bishops of southern Africa have offered their own straightforward rendering of the concept:

> Throughout history people have been bound together in community with each other. We depend on each other for our well-being and development. It is impossible for any of us to live fully human lives as isolated individuals. We therefore have duties and responsibilities towards each other. We should order our lives in such a way that we advance not only our own interests, but also recognise and promote the community's interests—in other words, the common good. We should therefore avoid those choices which, while they may appear to be to our individual advantage, are not favourable to the good of the community as a whole—to all the children, women, and men with whom we share life. "The Common Good" means thinking for each other.[42]

An understanding of the human person rooted in social-contract theory makes the common good even more difficult to understand. In Catholic thought, one cannot come to the "table" of society with a complete notion of one's personal good apart from the community. A person is never purely autonomous. Therefore, the idea that the common good could be a collection of the needs and desires of individuals inasmuch as they do not conflict with those of others is inconsistent with Catholic social teaching. Since our dignity as individuals is entwined with our relationships with others from the start, we cannot understand our own good without reference to the needs of others. For example, in his 1991 encyclical *Centesimus annus,* which commemorated the one-hundredth anniversary of *Rerum novarum,* Pope John Paul II devoted an entire section to "private property and the universal destination of material goods." While reaffirming the church's long-standing support for the right to private-property ownership, John Paul noted immediately thereafter that this right has always been subject to important limits.[43] These limits are rooted in the Christian understanding of the earth as God's gift to "the whole human race for the sustenance of all its members, without excluding or favoring anyone."[44] Likewise, in *Gaudium et spes,* the council linked property ownership directly to the common good: "The state has the duty to prevent people from abusing their private property to the detriment of the common good. By its nature private property has a social dimension which is based on the law of the common destination of earthly goods. Whenever the social aspect is forgotten, ownership can often become the object of greed and a source of serious disorder."[45]

It is easy to see how this vision of private property would create tension with a market order driven by competition and self-interest and with another cornerstone of the common good in the Catholic tradition—justice. Catholic teaching has historically understood justice in three ways. *Commutative justice* encompasses the idea of fundamental fairness in exchanges between individuals and among private groups within society. *Distributive justice* addresses the allocation of basic goods and insists that these allocations be evaluated in light of the existence of individuals whose basic needs are unmet. Finally, *social justice* grants individuals the right and the responsibility to participate actively in the life of the community. It also imposes a duty on the larger society to make this participation possible for everyone. This multifaceted understanding of justice in Catholic teaching imposes responsibilities on members of the community that must be considered in tandem with concomitant rights:[46]

> If any section of the population is in fact excluded from participation
> in the life of the community, even at a minimal level, then that is
> a contradiction to the concept of the common good and calls for

rectification. If that exclusion comes about from poverty, even if only "relative poverty," then that poverty demands attention. Governments cannot be satisfied with provision for poor people designed only to prevent absolute poverty, such as actual starvation or physical homelessness. What level of social security provision is adequate to meet the criteria of the common good is a political judgment, and may indeed involve trial and error. But there must come a point at which the scale of the gap between the very wealthy and those at the bottom of the range of income begins to undermine the common good. This is the point at which society starts to be run for the benefit of the rich, not for all its members.[47]

The promotion of the common good in Catholic social teaching thus creates an important role for the state in the promotion of human dignity and justice. Right-wing political thought in the United States strongly tends to situate state power in opposition to human dignity—understood primarily as personal freedom—in a manner that undermines the legitimacy of the use of state power to address destabilizing economic and social inequalities. Consider, for example, this statement from the 2004 Republican Party platform, which supported the Republicans' efforts to reduce taxes: "We believe that good government is based on a system of limited taxes and spending. Furthermore, we believe that the federal government should be limited and restricted to the functions mandated by the United States Constitution. The taxation system should not be used to redistribute wealth or fund ever-increasing entitlements and social programs. Many Democrats, however, believe the government has the right to claim the money earned by working Americans."[48]

Putting aside for the moment what exactly it is that "many Democrats believe," as well the question of how a modern state is meant to restrict its actions to the relatively general terms of a document more than 200 years old, Catholic social teaching has some fairly explicit views about the state's role as it relates to the common good. The responsibility for the promotion of the common good belongs to individuals and to the state, "since the common good is the reason that the political authority exists. The State, in fact, must guarantee the coherency, unity, and organization of the civil society of which it is an expression, in order that the common good may be attained with the contribution of every citizen. The individual person, the family, or intermediate groups are not able to achieve their full development by themselves for living a truly human life."[49]

Catholic social teaching sees the state and the political authority as a natural extension of our life in community. The state is not a power imposed upon the community; rather, its power springs from the community and must be directed to appropriate ends. The common good is promoted and supported when the power of the state is employed to ensure "the sublime dignity of all human persons ... who ought, therefore, to have ready access to all that is necessary for living a genuinely human life: for example, food, clothing, housing, the right to freely choose their state of life and set up a family, the right to education, work, to their good name, to respect, to proper knowledge, the right to act according to the dictates of conscience and to safeguard their privacy, and rightful freedom, including freedom of religion."[50] This promotion of human dignity and the common good cannot happen by itself, and Catholic social teaching explicitly endorses the use of taxes as a means to this end.[51]

In their 1986 pastoral letter, *Economic Justice for All*, which draws directly from the documents of the Second Vatican Council and subsequent papal encyclicals, the Catholic bishops of the United States made it clear that social and economic rights, along with civil and political rights, were both encompassed by Catholic social teaching as essential to the promotion of the common good. Furthermore, what may be required to implement and protect certain social and economic rights may be different from what has been used to secure civil and political rights:

> These fundamental personal rights—civil and political as well as social and economic—state the minimum conditions for social institutions that respect human dignity, social solidarity, and justice. They are all essential to human dignity and to the integral development of both individuals and society and are thus moral issues. Any denial of these rights harms persons and wounds the human community.... Both kinds of rights call for positive action to create social and political institutions that enable all persons to become active members of society.... In seeking to secure the full range of social and economic rights today, a similar effort to shape new economic arrangements will be necessary. The first step in such an effort is the development of a new cultural consensus that the basic economic conditions of human welfare are essential to human dignity and are due persons by right. Second, the securing of these rights will make demands on *all* members of society, on all private sector institutions, and on government.[52]

Although much more might be said about the common good in Catholic social teaching, a discussion of its modern implications would be incomplete without some mention of its global repercussions. Apart from its broader positioning into an international context as discussed earlier, Catholic social teaching has considered the wide-reaching ramifications more specifically through its rejection of a purely economic conception of human development. These ideas were launched by Pope Paul VI in his 1967 encyclical titled *Populorum progressio,* through what theologian Donal Dorr has called a "heuristic" concept of development that attempts to take into account the entire human person: "*Populorum progressio* does not give a privileged place to the economic dimension of human development any more than to the cultural, psychological, political, ecological, or religious dimensions. Rather, it challenges Christians to take full account of the non-economic elements—for instance, to recognise the value of different cultures and basic human rights."[53] Thus, Paul was able to craft an understanding of development that saw it as a movement from "less human" to "more human" conditions, one that took account of the need to nurture "higher values" like love and friendship, acknowledged the debilitating effects of unjust social structures and exploitation, and argued for a minimal standard of material comfort.[54] Thus, according to Dorr, *Populorum progressio*

> provides the basis for integrating personal development with community development and reconciling national development with global development. . . . The pope believes that a human being can be fulfilled personally by a willingness to cooperate with others, even when this imposes a personal cost on the individual; therefore, self-interest is not opposed to concern for others. . . . Equally significantly, the pope sees frugality not as a limitation to personal development, but as a positive element within it. This means that development can be reconciled with ecological restraint. It also opens the way to reconciling genuine human development with a relinquishment by the wealthy of waste and excess in order to allow the poor a fair share of the resources of the earth.[55]

From this point, Catholic social teaching has been able to engage with the modern global conversation around human rights and human development; notably, the important literature has developed in secular thought that emphasizes the need to nurture people's "capabilities."[56] In the 1980s and 1990s Pope John Paul II made remarkable strides in the contribution of Catholic social thought to the international discourse about human dignity that challenged the prevailing economic and materialist rendering of the value of human existence. The two other core principles of Catholic social teaching, solidarity and subsidiarity, have done important intellectual work for Catholic social teaching in this area, and John Paul II was extremely influential in the modern development of these principles.

Solidarity

From the use of the word *solidarity* in everyday language alone, it should by now be clear that Catholic Christianity is a solidaristic tradition that interprets the message of the Hebrew scriptures and the Gospels with an emphasis on the essential nature of human social connections and the ways in which they reflect humanity's intimate connections to God. During the past century, the term *solidarity* was used in documents associated with the social teaching. It was, nevertheless, Pope John Paul II who offered the most comprehensive treatment of the concept of solidarity. In reflecting upon Pope Paul VI's call for a more human understanding of the urgent need for development in *Populorum progressio*, John Paul II urges the readers of *Sollicitudo rei socialis*, his 1987 encyclical celebrating the twentieth anniversary of *Populorum progressio*, to appreciate the demands of solidarity in an interdependent world:

> It is already possible to point to the positive and moral value of
> the growing awareness of interdependence among individuals and
> nations. . . . It is above all a question of interdependence, sensed as a
> system determining relationships in the contemporary world, in its
> economic, cultural, political, and religious elements, and accepted as a
> moral category. . . . The correlative response as a moral and social at-
> titude, as a virtue, is solidarity. This then is not a vague compassion or
> shallow distress at the misfortunes of so many people, both near and
> far. On the contrary, it is a firm and persevering determination to
> commit oneself to the common good; that is to say the good of all and
> of each individual, because we are all really responsible for all. This
> determination is based on the solid conviction that what is hindering
> full development is that desire for profit and . . . thirst for power. These
> attitudes and "structures of sin" are only conquered . . . by a diamet-
> rically opposed attitude: a commitment to the good of one's neighbor
> with the readiness, in the gospel sense, to lose oneself for the sake
> of the other instead of exploiting him, and to serve him instead of
> oppressing him for one's own advantage.[57]

In this one paragraph, John Paul II advanced Catholic social teaching in three significant ways. First, he placed renewed emphasis on the essential connection between the social teaching and global interdependence and the global common good. Second, he alerted Catholics in particular to the idea of solidarity as a virtue that exerted responsibilities upon them as believers to commit themselves to the good of others. Third, he announced a new theological idea that results from the failure of the cultivation of the virtue of solidarity—the existence of "structures of sin." John Paul's vision of solidarity draws fairly obviously on the philosophical concepts of Ricoeur and Lévinas. In this respect, John Paul II is making an association between Catholic social teaching and phenomenological philosophy in an effort to underscore both the broad applicability of his vision of solidarity in an interdependent world and the general effort since Vatican II to direct the social teaching to all people of goodwill.[58] Solidarity is a concept that is broadly understood, and for John Paul II, it is "a fundamental concept that all humankind and Christians should agree upon and put into practice. Solidarity should influence the lives of persons, nations, and the world in general."[59]

The "structures of sin" describes "institutional realities, such as colonialism and imperialism, that create an unjust distribution of wealth, power, and recognition and thus push a section of the population to the margin of society where their well-being or even their life is in danger.... Sinful structures are rooted in personal sin, and thus always linked to the concrete acts of individuals who introduce these structures, consolidate them, and make them difficult to remove."[60] The emphasis on structures in the social teaching offers a more sophisticated way of understanding how and why human beings make choices, particularly in circumstances where there is little opportunity for a meaningful exercise of freedom of action. John Paul II's experience under communism obviously influenced his understanding of how structures shape, constrain, and distort individual choice, but he is careful not to dismiss the role of individual responsibility, which, indeed, is vital if sinful structures are to be removed or reformed. Solidarity offers a way to combat structures of sin by moving people toward a virtue that must be embraced individually in an effort to promote the common good.

Theologian Gregory Baum asks, "Does the social sin in which we live implicate us in guilt and culpability? And correspondingly, must the conversion of which we seek include repentance? ... Following traditional theological principles, we have to say that we are guilty to the extent that we knowingly support and defend the structures of evil, and we are not guilty to the extent we are blinded by ideology and unaware of what is going on, except possibly for having been unmoved by the misery of others and for not having tried harder to get a better grasp of the situation. Guilt increases, I suppose, in proportion to one's closeness to the decision-making elite."[61] Baum suggests, however, that guilt may not be the best way to respond to our awareness of structures of sin, as many of us are caught up in inherited structures and their "legitimating ideologies."[62] He offers a twofold theological response that would move both individuals and the social order toward a process of conversion. The first would be mourning, which would unite the middle classes with society's victims, who also mourn, albeit for different reasons: "The process of conversion in the face of social sin includes mourning. The Bible speaks of lamentation. We lament before God over the great suffering inflicted upon us, and more especially upon those with whom we are in solidarity."[63] The second way is through a meaningful recognition of the imperative of solidarity in all of its breadth.

What does solidarity mean in practical sense for life in a wealthy democratic society like the United States? Perhaps it means that Catholics there should work more diligently to cultivate an ethical disposition that takes the values of the social teaching seriously and demonstrates a meaningful understanding of what those values require. Of course, solidarity with the weak, the poor, and the marginalized may make Catholics less popular with America's power elites, who might well reject both the premises and the implications of solidarity. Solidaristic Roman Catholicism has struggled to adapt to an American cultural milieu dominated by more individualistic forms of Protestant Christianity, particularly as one moves away from the mainline churches and into its more evangelical and fundamentalist movements. This cultural context has had a profound influence on how American Catholics understand their faith.

Moreover, their assimilation into the mainstream has affected their ability to provide critical assessments of U.S. economic, political, and social structures that are firmly rooted in the cultural and intellectual life of their faith tradition. That Catholicism might suggest a different outlook regarding capitalism, for instance, has long been argued. The seminal work in this area was *The Protestant Ethic and the Spirit of Capitalism,* by Max Weber, which is noteworthy in particular for its argument that Protestantism encouraged an ethos in the societies in which it was dominant that was particularly suited to the successful development of a capitalist market economy.[64] Sociologist John Tropman has developed an argument for a countervailing "Catholic" ethic, one that embraced Weber's basic interpretive paradigm but sought to draw out the implications of certain discernible Catholic values in the United States. In *The Catholic Ethic and the Spirit of Community,* Tropman demonstrates how a Catholic ethic, rooted in solidarity, produces very different perspectives on the merits of various types of social assistance, particularly government assistance to the poor.[65]

Tropman defines an "ethic" in a sociological sense as "thoughts about conduct, rationalizations for conduct, justifications for conduct, ideas about situations, and guides for action that characterize a people or groups of people."[66] He sees a number of ways in which a Catholic ethic distinguishes itself. One example that offers particular insights into how an active embrace of solidarity in Catholic social teaching would create tension with more dominant, individualistic ideas in U.S. culture is his statement that solidaristic Catholicism translates into an ethic that often values "community help" over "self-help." Catholicism tends to foster a "helping culture," which emphasizes (1) sympathy toward people in need, with a special concern for the poor; (2) a willingness to provide concrete aid; (3) a desire to make the aid both programmatic and personal; (4) support for the role of government in helping; and (5) a sense of some collective responsibility for social conditions.[67]

The helping culture demonstrates how a Catholic ethic draws on the principle of solidarity in Catholic social teaching. In addressing the Catholic sense of "collective responsibility" in particular, Tropman offers a practical understanding of how these values might be more conducive to the development of theological concepts like the structures of sin: "Collective responsibility obtains with respect to efforts at remediation, but it also is present with respect to causation. Although community helping concern will not set aside individual responsibility completely, there is still a sense that a variety of forces, other than one's own efforts (or lack thereof) account for one's position in life.... This view naturally decreases the blame that poor people have to endure for their poverty; it also questions the wisdom and special talents that well-to-do people may claim as the cause of—and hence justification for—their wealth."[68]

Subsidiarity

Michael Schuck describes Catholic social teaching as springing from traditionalist, cosmopolitan, and transformational impulses within Roman Catholicism that can be traced to the early Christian church.[69] The principle of subsidiarity has its earliest origins in what Schuck identifies as a politico-economic cosmopolitanism in Catholicism during the nineteenth century that connected economic reform to a "spirit of Catholic republicanism."[70] A central figure who embodied this outlook at that time was Wilhelm Emmanuel von Ketteler, bishop of Mainz, Germany. His work (described earlier) and that of German Jesuits Heinrich Pesch and Oswald von Nell-Breuning created the foundations of the modern principle of subsidiarity. Pesch, an economist, and Nell-Breuning, who drew heavily on Pesch's work through his association with Pesch's student, political economist Gustav Gundlach, studied the labor situation in Britain and Germany during the late nineteenth and early twentieth centuries based on Ketteler's idea of "an ethical reconstruction of society for the benefit of workers on the basis of cooperative, self-governing work organizations."[71] From this work, Nell-Breuning developed the concept of subsidiarity as "helpful assistance" that offers support to those who cannot help themselves past a certain degree. To interfere where the person would otherwise have the chance to act and thereby develop would be an injury. Where the working person is capable of exercising his or her own powers, there the community must refrain from interference. Where individuals face the limits of inability, there ought the community to provide aid, as service to those who need. Furthermore, where persons are capable of acting but where their powers are insufficient, there the community ought to offer that support which is sufficient to fill the deficiencies in its members' capacities. The service to those at the limits applies not only to needy individuals but also to smaller, needy groups which can be served in their limitations by a larger community.[72]

The ideas of Ketteler, Pesch, and Nell-Breuning found their way into the 1931 papal encyclical titled *Quadragesimo anno*, key portions of which were written by Nell-Breuning.[73] In this document we find the first "official" enunciation of the principle of subsidiarity in Catholic social teaching: "It is a fundamental principle of social philosophy, fixed and unchangeable, that one should not withdraw from individuals and commit to the community what they can accomplish by their own enterprise and industry. So, too, it is an injustice and at the same time a grave evil and a disturbance of right order to transfer to the larger and higher collectivity functions which can be performed and provided for by lesser and subordinate bodies. Inasmuch as every social activity should, by its very nature, prove a help to members of the body social, it should never destroy or absorb them."[74] In the 1930s, Pius XI was particularly concerned about the increasing strength of the all-encompassing state power of communism in Europe. At the same time, by 1931 both World War I and the Great Depression had demonstrated important failings of liberal nationalism and unrestrained free markets, and fascist movements on the Right were rising, glorifying the power of the state from the right wing of the political spectrum.

With fascism discredited in Western Europe in the wake of World War II, the principle of subsidiarity continued to be seen as offering important insight on how to confront the dehumanizing aspects of communism, but in the postwar era it also provided a way to emphasize human dignity in the face of the ever-expanding, all-encompassing, modern welfare state. Paolo Carozza describes how the subsidiarity principle, which after World War II had also been given a secular role as part of the Basic Law of the Federal Republic of Germany, moved from these relatively narrow confines to the broader platform of the European Community: "Throughout the 1970s and 1980s [subsidiarity] became increasingly visible and began to make its way into European Community documents, with the particularly strong support of Jacques Delors while he was president of the European Commission. The principle finally found a central juridical place in the European Union in 1991, as part of the [Maastricht Treaty]."[75]

Carozza's work emphasizes the importance of subsidiarity as a principle that can be employed in secular and theological contexts, but he emphasizes that it is rooted in a Catholic understanding of the human person that presupposes an organic relationship of individuals and the organizations they create within the social order. Thus, it respects one's inherent dignity without succumbing to the radical individual autonomy of libertarian or utilitarian philosophies, and it does not "derive its force from an instrumental concern for social efficiency or a need for political compromise."[76] With regard to the state's role in particular, subsidiarity "is a somewhat paradoxical principle. It limits the state, yet empowers and justifies it. It limits intervention, yet requires it. It expresses both a positive and a negative version of the role of the state with respect to society and the individual."[77]

Carozza sees an important role for the subsidiarity principle in the area of international human rights, and his analysis offers important insights as to how the deep respect for human dignity in Catholic social thought offers a natural link to the broader global dialogue around human rights. Not only does subsidiarity provide a community ideal that appreciates the critical link between human diversity and human dignity, but it also offers important theoretical support for pluralism: "Subsidiarity's affirmation of the value of diversity in society, although not as commonly appreciated as other implications of the principle, is strong. The premises emphasize the integration of all forms of human association and the ultimate unity of their ends in the service of individual human dignity and the common good."[78] The subsidiarity principle is also an excellent basis upon which to envision a more cosmopolitan presence of Christians in global affairs, thereby allowing them to articulate a respect for the fundamental importance of particularity, while at the same time emphasizing the core value of human solidarity.

A respect for pluralism and human diversity is ultimately linked to a regard for human freedom. Freedom is the ability to choose, and the Catholic Church made tremendous strides in recognizing important modern implications of an authentic respect for freedom when it embraced religious freedom and democracy in the documents of Vatican II. Nonetheless, freedom is not personal license, and in his 1991 encyclical Centesimus annus, John Paul II offered some powerful reflections on what freedom means for an individual situated in social relationships, time, place, and culture:

> The manner in which the individual exercises his freedom is conditioned [in] innumerable ways. While these certainly have an influence on freedom, they do not determine it; they make the manner in which the individual exercises his freedom more difficult or less difficult, but they cannot destroy it. Not only is it wrong from the ethical point of view to disregard human nature, which is made for freedom, but in practice it is impossible to do so. Where society is so organized to reduce arbitrarily or even suppress the sphere in which freedom is legitimately exercised, the result is that the life of society becomes progressively disorganized and goes into decline. Moreover, man, who was created for freedom, bears within himself the wound of original sin, which constantly draws him toward evil and puts him in need of redemption. . . . Man tends toward good, but he is also capable of evil. He can transcend his immediate interest and still remain bound to it. The social order will be all the more stable the more it takes this fact into account and does not place in opposition personal interest and the interests of society as a whole, but rather seeks ways to bring them into fruitful harmony. . . . When people think they posses the secret of a perfect social organization which makes evil impossible, they also think that they can use any means, including violence and deceit, in order to bring that organization into being. Politics then becomes a secular religion which operates under the illusion of creating paradise in this world.[79]

These words resonate most obviously in response to the excesses of any number of totalitarian ideologies the world has witnessed, particularly during the twentieth century. Indeed, John Paul II's observations were specifically directed to the 1989 fall of communism in Europe. But his words should also speak to those of us who have long had the privilege of living in democratic societies. When the leaders of any society purport to have discovered the "ideal" system of political, economic, and social organization and become convinced that the system must be extended worldwide for the good of the nation and of those on whom they wish to impose it, the use of violence to achieve those ends begins to seem necessary, even reasonable, to them. The illusion of a civil religion, be it secular or the distortion of a traditional faith, is rooted in the human weaknesses of pride and hubris, sins hardly limited to the leaders of totalitarian regimes.

Catholicism Glossed for the American Imperium

In Catholic social teaching, the heavy emphasis on communal concepts like the common good and solidarity and the wariness with which it has viewed the free market sent the teaching on a collision course with key American elites in the decades following the Second Vatican Council. The 1970s witnessed the beginning of the end of the political consensus around the New Deal and the Great Society in the United States, programs that had brought millions of Americans out of poverty and social marginalization. As a vibrant economy that had been expanding since World War II lurched into the crises of the Arab oil embargo, inflation, and recession, strong reactionary political and cultural impulses began to build against the progressive social movements of the 1950s and 1960s. By the late 1970s, the political Right had begun to rally around an economic vision that promoted aggressive free markets, deregulation, and an essential link between liberal capitalism and political freedom. This latter idea, rooted in the libertarian political philosophy of Nozick and Hayek, found new power in the growing influence of economic thinkers like Milton Friedman:

> So long as effective freedom of exchange is maintained, the central feature of the market organization of economic activity is that it prevents one person from interfering with another in respect of most of his activities. The consumer is protected from coercion by the seller because of the presence of other sellers with whom he can deal. The seller is protected from coercion by the consumer because of other consumers to whom he can sell.... And the market does this impersonally and without centralized authority. Indeed, a major source of objection to a free economy is precisely that it does this task so well. It gives people what they want instead of what a particular group thinks they ought to want. Underlying most of the arguments against the free market is a lack of belief in freedom itself.[80]

Although Friedman's ideas became influential during the Carter administration in matters such as the deregulation of the airline and financial services industries, the Reagan presidency is generally seen as the defining political moment for the triumph of his economic model, which ultimately transformed the U.S. economy and has become a driving force behind the current expansion of global free-market capitalism.

The 1970s also witnessed the ascendancy of new Catholic voices that were eager to embrace the logic supporting a nexus between free markets and individual freedom. In theological matters, these thinkers were increasingly repelled by what they saw as an uncritical acceptance of leftist critiques of the free market by the mostly continental European Roman Catholic theological establishment, and they resented the support given to these views by the arbiters of Catholic opinion in the United States. At base, these Catholic neoconservatives began questioning whether many Catholic thinkers appreciated the genius of the "American experiment." Increasingly, they saw critiques of free-market capitalism as leftist intellectual hostility toward the United States and the success of its democratic tradition. For them, the dynamic nature of American society had more than a little to do with the nation's aggressive embrace of the free-market economic model.

In 1984 Michael Novak argued for "a profound consonance (although not identity) between the Catholic vision of social justice and the liberal institutions which, in this poor and broken world, have better than others allowed the human spirit to flourish."[81] Novak then considered the long-standing anticapitalism among Catholic thinkers and the Catholic association between free-market liberalism and the destruction of communal bonds and responsibilities. Although he acknowledged the condemnation of both socialism and capitalism within the key documents of Catholic social thinking, he was moved to ask the following:

> If Catholic social teaching condemns both capitalism and
> socialism . . . what vision of political economy does it put in their
> place? Here is where the term social justice becomes a catch-all. It is
> true that individual Catholics have social and political obligations, as
> citizens, in addition to their personal, individual ones. The term social justice reminds them of these obligations. . . . But without a vision
> of particular political, economic, and moral cultural institutions—
> without a worked-out vision of a functioning political economy—
> social justice remains a vague and partly gnostic phrase, disembodied
> and merely idealistic.[82]

The vision of political economy that Novak offered was the liberal, free-market economy as embodied in the experience of the United States: "I hold that the liberal society, among known workable present and future societies, best serves Catholic social thought: best uplifts the poor, institutionalizes the dignity of the human person, makes possible the growth and manifold activities of human associations of every sort, and conspires to establish a more voluntary and open and communitarian form of life than any society of the past, present, or foreseeable future."[83] Novak praised the American bishops for the work they had initiated in the pastoral letter "Economic Justice for All" as an important step in harmonizing free-market economics with Catholic belief and practice. Yet, despite his early hopes, he was ultimately disappointed with the bishops' final product.[84]

Novak correctly interpreted much of the political theory underlying the corpus of Catholic social teaching prior to Vatican II as being drawn from the solidaristic social traditions of France and Germany, and he noted that this tradition tended to react harshly to the individualism and weakening of traditional social connections that Catholics in Europe associated with nineteenth-century Anglo-American liberalism.[85] In Novak's view, British and American forms of liberalism were not less supportive of social connections and social virtue, just different in the way they nurtured these values: "Social life in Britain and America...appears to be rooted less in primordial connections and traditions of shared purpose and more in voluntariness. This difference does not make Americans less gregarious, open, and accessible, or more socially obdurate and impenetrable; on the contrary, Americans exhibit a social spirit, a range of social virtues and an instinct for sociality which compares quite favorably with that of the Germans."[86]

Novak's assessment of Catholic social teaching since the Second Vatican Council, however, deserves particular attention. On the positive side, Novak saw the papacy of John XXIII as turning away from what heretofore had been an intellectual disdain for liberalism and free-market capitalism. At Vatican II the Catholic Church ended its battle with liberalism, particularly in the area of political and civil rights, and embraced many liberal insights. Still, what it did not do was embrace market capitalism as coterminous with the liberal state's protection of human dignity and freedom, which proved deeply troubling for Novak. Throughout the 1960s and 1970s, the church remained critical of what it viewed as the excesses of free-market capitalism, and the social teaching developed a growing sympathy with the plight of the peoples and nations of the developing world. Novak saw the social encyclicals of this era as captured by a Catholic intelligentsia still in thrall to Marxist ideology and economic analysis:

> The Catholic Church under Paul the VI attempted to do two things at once. It wished to protect the human rights of individuals, families and intermediate institutions as Marxism does not desire to do, but some in it also wished to accept the Marxist analysis of economic imperialism and to claim that dominant elites had become rich through oppressing others and were unconscionable beneficiaries of the misery of others. Such heady brew is unstable. Its fruit is the schizophrenia felt most acutely in Catholic nations, between terrified defenders of the status quo on the one side and righteous revolutionaries on the other. Its fundamental defect is the empirically

flawed "theory of dependency" and its failure to grasp how wealth is actually created.... In a stagnant society one can have justice and peace. One can have justice and peace, of a sort, even in a totalitarian society. Yet justice and peace are not, even on the premises put forth by John XXIII and Paul VI, sufficient ideals for Catholic social thought. Justice and Peace alone will not lead to economic development or protect human rights. Until Justice and Peace becomes *Freedom,* Justice, and Peace, Catholic social thought cannot achieve the ends it has set for itself.[87]

Although Catholic social teaching had by this time developed a rich understanding of the human person, it had rooted that respect in community, the common good, and, less explicitly, solidarity. This quote reveals the heart of Novak's neoconservative critique of post–Vatican II Catholic social teaching: The teaching was insufficiently appreciative of the importance of individual freedom to human dignity. This freedom was nurtured in both political and economic life, but the communal orientation of Catholic social teaching, which emphasizes concepts like the universal destination of goods in tandem with private property, as well as social and economic rights, made aspects of the U.S. economic model appear inconsistent with Catholic principles. This was particularly true in the 1980s, when certain political and economic elites tied primarily to the Republican Party were taking the nation in a more explicitly libertarian direction, a movement that would certainly be more difficult if American Catholics heard their church question its morality. Catholic neoconservatives hoped to demonstrate that the church should hold up political liberalism and capitalism in the United States as an example for the world because it properly supported the individual freedom necessary for human dignity. In order to make this argument, Novak had to de-emphasize key aspects of U.S. history that had (consistent with the critique in post–Vatican II theology) allowed certain individuals to flourish in tandem with the aggressive marginalization of other members of the society.

Although not a major colonial power, the United States did engage in pseudocolonial activities in Latin America in particular, and Americans of European descent were the primary beneficiaries of an aggressive suppression and elimination of the Native American tribes that promoted the nation's westward expansion. Merchants were key participants in the "triangle trade," and great fortunes were amassed because of the maintenance of slavery throughout much of the nineteenth century. Slavery was then followed by a repressive system of de jure and de facto racial segregation, the legal aspects of which were still in place during the Second Vatican Council. It is thus difficult for the United States to claim moral high ground relative to the European relationship with the former colonies of Africa and Asia, and it was perhaps somewhat disingenuous for Catholic neoconservatives to argue that America's economic success was not to some extent rooted in the very sorts of global economic and social injustices that received greater attention in Catholic social teaching following Vatican II.

How could John XXIII and Paul VI, writing in the 1960s, ignore the dramatic evidence of colonial-era atrocities in places like the Belgian Congo, Algeria, and other parts of Africa when considering the witness of African Catholics in crafting the social teaching's approach to development in the Third World? Were not the Latin American bishops and theologians best placed to consider the complex intermingling of history, culture, and politics that created the deep disparities of wealth and power in their nations? Was it simply a fascination with Marxist analysis that moved Gustavo Gutiérrez to articulate and develop the "preferential option for the poor," or might his insight have resulted from a deepening awareness that the dehumanizing effects of poverty and racism in Latin America were not conditions that Christians should willingly accept? It is of course true that certain theologians were unduly captured by Marxist analysis, particularly as it related to the theology of liberation.[88] The same, however, cannot be said of the bishops of the Second Vatican Council.

The American experience of capitalism and free markets is in many ways unique, and, by way of positive examples, it offers much insight into how free markets and democratic freedom can work together to build a stable, affluent society. Yet, despite the material success it evidences, capitalism in the United States also demonstrates the self-absorbed consumerism and atomism that many have argued characterizes free markets when they are not property tethered to communal cultural values. Certainly, given the explosive growth of the Catholic Church in the developing world, the American experience with free markets is not the only one that should inform Catholic social teaching on these matters. In the twenty-first century, Asia's or Africa's experience might resonate more forcefully.

Another important American critic of mainstream theological views of Catholic social teaching is neoconservative George Weigel. Responding to a 1986 comment by then cardinal Joseph Ratzinger, who described post–Vatican II theological dissent in the United States as an expression of "bourgeois Christianity," Weigel noted that many Catholic theologians seemed to hold that the United States was:

a republic, not in the classic sense of a community of virtue, but in the distinctively modern sense of a non–tradition bound, accidental collectivity in which, so as to pursue their own private interests, men agreed to basically leave each other alone. The "common good" in such a "bourgeois republic" would not reflect universal moral norms; it would not be pursued by civic virtue. Rather, the common good in a Lockean republic of radical individualism would be a utilitarian, least common denominator arrangement in which the pursuit of various private (usually commercial) interests would become a centrifugal, rather than a centripetal force. In such a bourgeois republic the temptation to reduce liberty to licence would be severe indeed.[89]

Weigel then argued that the framers of the Constitution were well aware of and concerned with public virtue as an essential part of the apparatus necessary to preserve liberty in the new republic. Moreover, he maintained that historians who have argued for an "economic reductionist" view of the nation's founding, rooted in self-serving commercial interests, have simply got the evidence wrong.[90]

Since the 1980s, Weigel has emerged among Catholic intellectuals as a key apologist for American social, political, and economic institutions from a politically right-wing perspective rooted in what might be called "virtue theory." Along with Michael Novak and Richard John Neuhaus, he has been extremely influential in proffering an interpretation of Catholic social teaching that lessens the sting of questions about the consistency of the nation's economic and social model with many of the teaching's core principles. In the same way that Novak sees the American experience with capitalism as strong evidence that the church should embrace the neoliberal economic model, Weigel sees the founding of the American republic as rooted in natural law principles and a Judeo-Christian ethical framework that is, when properly connected to the nurturing of key virtues within American society, consistent with the Catholic natural law tradition. Weigel interprets the country's current leadership in the world community as important evidence of the "rightness" of the American project in Christian terms and therefore fundamentally consistent with core Christian values and beliefs, at least as traditionally understood. The need for a return to these core truths in an effort to redirect the American project away from misguided postmodern distortions like abortion rights, gay marriage, and pacifism has set the stage for a "Catholic moment" in U.S. history that has the potential of renewing democracy and strengthening the nation's role as a promoter of democracy and freedom worldwide:

The ultimate test of rightness or wrongness of public policy in the United States is not whether a proposition manages to gain majority support. Some things, in these United States, are not up for a vote. The most fundamental "oughts" in American public life derive, not from counting votes, but from a view of the human person that is derived from transcendent moral norms. . . . The pursuit of freedom, and the right ordering of political community according to norms that transcend that community, go together in the American experiment. Or, at any rate, they should. Whether Catholicism in the United States is capable of leadership in bringing those norms to bear for the renewal of American democracy is, indeed, a basic test of the vitality of the American Church.[91]

Most Christians would share Weigel's view that a political community that viewed people in a way consistent with Christian moral truths would be worth supporting. There is, nevertheless, a great deal of disagreement about whether the American republic was founded on such an understanding. Even if it had been, it is clear that the preservation of a democratic consensus about the nature of the republic today is not rooted in a shared religious understanding of the transcendent moral truths or the maintenance of a "community of virtue." Whether such community would be desirable is a separate question altogether and one that cannot be answered here. In any event, it is hard to find much evidence of its existence currently. As I have already described, the United States is in many ways the very accidental collectivity that Weigel rejects, and whether it is or is not, this view is much closer to the truth of the condition in which the republic currently functions than any concept of community rooted in shared moral truths would be.

Certainly there are core values that all Americans who respect the nation's democratic traditions share, but they come to these values from a wide range of perspectives—be they religious or purely utilitarian. The "economic reductionalist" view of U.S. history that Weigel challenges may or may not describe the perspective of the framers of the Constitution, but it comes close to describing the neoliberal and libertarian economic and social vision that in recent decades has been embraced by most American elites and, truth be told, by a broad cross-section of the American public. The resonance of this vision is due in no small part to acceptance of value pluralism as an unavoidable and in many instances beneficial part of modern Western democracy and to the aggressive dismantling of social democratic systems of mutual aid and public provision in favor of the promotion of a free-market money culture.

Citing sociologist Peter Berger, Weigel has recognized that modern liberal capitalism needs strong social and communal institutions like the family and religion to balance the atomizing effects of the free market, particularly in the current era of rapid technological change, and he is convinced that capitalist economic systems are better at nurturing these institutions than socialist ones.[92] What the last 30 years has demonstrated, however, is that whatever harm socialism and communism did to these institutions from the Left (and few would argue that the harm was not significant), these same social and communal institutions have also been undermined by libertarian visions of freedom and neoliberal global economic theory from the Right.[93]

Furthermore, the United States has been at the forefront of resisting market-taming measures proposed by other free-market nations with more communal traditions—Germany, France, and Japan, for instance—because these measures are seen as harming the "free" functioning of the marketplace, limiting wealth creation, and giving too much power to the state or international organizations. This has occurred despite the fact that they might provide a countervailing force to social atomization in an era when traditional structures like the family, the church, and the labor union are changing or fading away. Weigel and Novak have been strong supporters of the Republican Party and the Bush administration, and neither has offered any sustained criticism of a Republican neoliberal and libertarian global economic agenda that has arguably accelerated the United States' transformation into an ever-more individualist, commercial republic.

Weigel, Neuhaus, and Novak have all argued that the papacy of Pope John Paul II marked a significant break with the leftist, Marxist-influenced theology within Catholic social teaching that was in evidence during the 1960s and 1970s. Neuhaus wrote that "*Centesimus Annus* must surely prompt a careful, and perhaps painful, rethinking of conventional wisdom about Catholic social teaching. It may be, for instance, that controlling assumptions of the American bishops' 1986 pastoral letter, *Economic Justice for All*, must now be recognized as unrepresentative of the Church's authoritative teaching."[94] Signaling earlier neoconservative disapproval of the adoption of a broad collection of economic, social, and political rights in Catholic social teaching typically advanced by a more activist state (as opposed to the more limited American model of political rights designed to defend the individual from state power), George Weigel noted that "the human rights language is a bit more muted in *Centesimus Annus* than in John Paul's earlier encyclicals—and far more muted than it was in Pope John XXIII's *Pacem in Terris*. The pope has not lost any interest in the problems of human rights. Rather, he now seems determined to deepen (and, in some respects, to discipline) the debate over 'rights' by linking rights to obligations and truth."[95] Finally, Michael Novak found in *Centesimus annus* the realization of the church's acceptance of the relationship between the neoliberal economic model and authentic human freedom:

The encyclical *Centesimus Annus* does what may of us had long hoped some church authority would do: it captures the spirit and essence of the American experiment in political economy. The pope showed an extraordinary grasp of American ideas, achievements, and points of view. His vision of a free economy, within a culture moral and religious to its core, guided and energized by a democratic polity, is American in spirit and definition. Thus Pope John Paul II has brought economic liberty (plus democracy) into Catholic social teaching, just as Vatican II brought in religious liberty. In both cases, these are predominantly American contributions to the church universal.[96]

Not everyone saw *Centesimus annus* as such a fundamental change from prior encyclicals. Theologians deeply immersed in the social tradition have offered a much more balanced view of the encyclical, one that situates it more properly in the broad corpus of the social teaching. Daniel Finn has written a particularly thoughtful review that provides important context to the neoconservatives' attempt to "claim" *Centesimus annus* for their particular agenda:

How, then, should one interpret the various claims and counterclaims as to whether John Paul has indeed endorsed "capitalism" or "some form of capitalism"? The best way to answer this question is to step back and ask what this is all about. If what is at stake is the difference between the economic system of the United States and the former Soviet Union, there is little doubt that the former is far less objectionable to John Paul than the latter. Much talk about the difference between capitalism and socialism in the United States has construed the debate as exactly this difference.... The real debates that occur within the United States and other industrialized nations concern differences of opinion across a much narrower range of the ideological spectrum.... Thus the differences really at stake might be characterized as ranging from U.S. democratic capitalism to Swedish democratic socialism. While John Paul's assertion of various balancing principles clearly exclude Soviet communism and North American libertarianism, they leave him open to allowing for a variety of structures as long as each nation attends to its obligations.... In any case, it is clear from both [*Centesimus annus*] and John Paul's later writings that he has not given a blanket approval to the U.S. economy as it exists, and it will be an ongoing challenge to moral theologians and social ethicists, from across the political spectrum, to work out what his vision means for changes in government and society.[97]

Indeed, the important question is, What does the vision of Catholic social teaching (prior to and including the important contributions of John Paul II) mean for changes in government and society in the United States? The legal system provides us with an excellent vehicle for considering the ways in which the social teaching might offer Christians a means for assessing the nation's direction. Are Christians to be one-issue voters, pulling the Republican lever on the basis of the party's facial commitment to a pro-life position on abortion, yet ignoring the party's inconsistent support of life issues more broadly defined? What about the party's promotion of an economic program for the nation and the world that is clearly rooted in a North American libertarianism that Catholic social teaching excludes? On the other hand, can Christians support a Democratic agenda that is marked by the exaltation of the atomized individual in the social order and seems hostile to the role that families, traditions, and communities of memory and meaning might play in the shaping of an individual conscience? At the very least, it appears that an informed Christian would need to confront U.S. politics with critical distance and could not assume that matters political in the nation necessarily reflect a coherent Christian worldview. Nor could the Christian assume, given the close relationship between law and politics in a democracy, that Christian moral commitments can be effectively communicated in every case through the civil law.

Catholic social teaching offers a means by which Christians might consider the overall direction of our political and cultural life in a modern, pluralist, democratic environment. Drawing on the work of important Catholic thinkers like Cathleen Kaveny, Michael Perry, J. Bryan Hehir, and John Courtney Murray, Gregory Kalscheur has offered a number of axioms that "might inform our vision of the proper relationship between religious values, the objective moral order, and civil law and public discourse in the context of contemporary American pluralism."[98] Two that are of particular relevance to the analysis of law and Catholic social teaching that I discuss in later chapters are the following:

1. Any evaluation of the degree to which the civil law conforms to the moral law should consider the legal framework in its entirety.
2. The church as a mediating institution has a crucial role to play in bringing moral and religious critique of law and public policy into public conversation. The primary context for this role is in the realm of society and culture.[99]

With respect to the first axiom, Kalscheur notes that "the legal system as a whole reflects a set of moral judgments. Rather than simply looking to see whether or not offenses against public morality are prohibited by criminal law, the desire to ensure that the civil law not be divorced from the moral law requires a further line of inquiry. What sort of society are we becoming through the entire range of legal policies we advocate and enact?"[100] In elaborating on the second axiom, Kalscheur reminds us of the church's important role as a mediating institution in a pluralist society: "Religious and moral critique of civil law and social policy within the institutions of society and culture helps to ensure that the law and democracy do not become idols to which we unthinkingly submit."[101] Thus it is not the role of Catholic social teaching to validate the social and economic system in which we currently live.

Rather, it gives us the tools to assess the entire framework of our law and public policy and to measure its consistency with Christian principles. Additionally, if we embrace democratic values that nurture and seek to protect pluralism, Catholic social teaching enables us to engage in a dialogue with those with whom we disagree in a manner that proceeds from a position of both a respect and a need for the other. Real engagement with disagreeing (and perhaps even disagreeable) others is a necessity for Christians if we are ever to begin to comprehend the transcendent nature of God's love for us. Democratic pluralism provides us with a shared space for dialogue that respects the dignity of others and at its best offers a nonreligious, commensurable way to realize humanity's diverse commitment to what Lévinas would describe as the "transcendent dignity of the face." Our goal as Christians is not to command or to coerce; our goal is to transform. We seek to transform the societies in which we live so they might be a better reflection of the divine plan, but all Christians should also seek for themselves the radical transformation that comes from loving their neighbor.

3

Justice, Community, and Solidarity in the American Battle over Affirmative Action

In an essay in the *Michigan Law Review*, James Boyd White argued that there "was something awry in the way we in the law talk both about race in general and about affirmative action in particular, something simply missing, or misrepresented."[1] White continues:

> I think the line we maintain between white and black has the effect of corroding or disabling our democracy in another way, for it divides people where other interests would seem to unite them—interest in good public schools, in sensible penal policies and humane penal institutions, in rules concerning drug use that focus on education and rehabilitation instead of incarceration, in a decent public health system, in adequate transportation, in sensible controls on spreading suburbs, and so on. In every one of these issues, I believe, one can see at work the cancer of racism, and its effect is to distort democracy at the most basic level by preventing the formation of effective political majorities that would otherwise exist.[2]

I believe he is quite correct, and this chapter expands on his "intuition" that the way U.S. law approaches race and affirmative action is deeply flawed. Not only has this "misrepresentation" contributed to the relentless Sturm und Drang over issues of race in American life, but it has also made it impossible for the law to deal honestly and effectively with any number of legal and public policy issues rooted in the nation's experience of race.

Using the problem of affirmative action as a reference point and limiting myself for the purposes of this chapter to the American notion of "black and white," I argue that the construction of liberalism now dominant in U.S. law inappropriately directs the legal system toward the creation of "neutral" legal principles and arguments ill suited to dealing with a culturally particularized and communal racial problem, one rooted in the system of race-based chattel slavery.[3] I also challenge a basic assumption of Anglo-American liberalism: that human dignity is most effectively advanced through the promotion of individual freedom and autonomy.[4] This view of the human person neglects the role of culture and community in imparting dignity and meaning to human existence and ultimately dehumanizes politics, the legal system, and civic life.

Because U.S. law increasingly defines individual well-being in terms of personal autonomy, its legal language and argument tend to fall short when addressing problems rooted in communal understandings of identity and suffering, as well as privilege and power. This type of "misrepresentation," to use James Boyd White's term once again, works to limit the full participation and flourishing of many groups of people within American society, particularly African Americans, because the reality of their lives cannot be explained in the radically autonomous language of an American liberalism fixated on individual rights. Some of the nation's harshest critics of affirmative action, such as Clint Bolick of the libertarian Cato Institute, have relied on historical renderings of civil and natural rights that tie them to the nation's founding and emphasizes its libertarian philosophical underpinnings:

> First, civil rights are inherently *individual* rights, defined essentially
> as the right to life, liberty and the pursuit of happiness. Second, these
> rights are held *equally* under law. Third, these rights are *universal*,
> belonging to every individual. Fourth, these rights consist not of
> material entitlements, but essential *liberties*, that is, freedom from
> coercion. The classical liberal vision of civil rights traces its roots to
> the fertile soil of the American Revolution. The foundations of the
> new republic were built on the philosophy of 'natural rights.' . . .
> Natural rights are the rights that individuals possess in a state of
> nature before creating governments. In a society with no govern-
> ment, individuals possess complete autonomy, which is bounded
> only by the equal autonomy possessed by other individuals.[5]

I then consider the American experience of race and the contentious debate over affirmative action in the midst of this type of legal and cultural environment. African Americans bear an almost impossible burden in public discourse when they attempt to articulate their experience of group victimization in a legal system that wants to restrict itself to neutral legal principles designed to promote fairness by focusing on individual justice and striving to treat everyone the same. Not only does this bias toward neutrality and individualism disadvantage claims grounded in a history of repression based on membership in a group, but it also makes it difficult to discuss the common benefits that white Americans received as a group from the nation's culture of racism, regardless of whether they were directly involved in acts or institutions of racial oppression.[6]

Finally, I use Catholic social thought to argue for a change in the way U.S. law views people based on a richer understanding of human dignity and the idea that we are social beings whose potential can be fully realized only when situated in culture and in community with others. After demonstrating why Catholic understandings of the human person ought to be admissible in public life, I show how a legal discourse that draws from Catholic social thought (particularly the concept of solidarity) would produce much more convincing rationales for public policies designed to confront and remedy a legacy of slavery and racism in the United States. Ultimately, an ethic of solidarity might provide a much more powerful justification for affirmative action programs in the United States and create the groundwork for more meaningful notions of equality.

Situated versus Autonomous Selves in the Procedural State

The Canadian philosopher Charles Taylor has described the dominance of a particular construction of liberal political theory in the Anglo-American world, particularly the United States:

> There is a family of liberal theories now very popular, not to say dominant, in the English speaking world, which I will call "procedural." It sees society as an association of individuals, each of whom has a conception of a good or worthwhile life and correspondingly, a life plan. The function of society ought to be to facilitate these life plans, as much as possible and following some principle of equality. That is, the facilitation ought not to be discriminatory, although there is obviously some room for serious question as to exactly what this means: whether the facilitation ought to aim at equality of results, resources, opportunities, capacities, or whatever.[7]

Taylor's understanding of procedural liberalism draws on a more detailed critique developed by Michael Sandel. In *Democracy's Discontent*, Sandel has argued that the public philosophy that dominates legal discourse in the United States is an outgrowth of "the liberal resolve that government be neutral on moral and religious questions, that matters of policy and law be debated and decided without reference to any particular conception of the good life. But we are beginning to find that a politics that brackets morality and religion too completely soon generates its own disenchantment. A procedural republic cannot contain the moral energies of a vital democratic life. It creates a moral void that opens the way for narrow, intolerant moralisms. And it fails to cultivate the qualities of character that equip citizens for self-rule."[8]

Both Sandel and Taylor argue that this conception of liberalism, grounded in the philosophical works of Immanuel Kant and John Rawls, is dependent on the idea of the unencumbered self, which requires us to "respect the dignity of all persons, but beyond this, we owe only what we agree to owe. Liberal justice requires that we respect people's rights (as defined by the neutral framework), not that we advance their good. Whether we must concern ourselves with other people's good depends on whether, and with whom, and on what terms, we have agreed to do so."[9] The unencumbered self fails to recognize the power and meaning of loyalties and relationships that may not be assumed voluntarily. This raises a number of problems. Sandel argues that the unencumbered self cannot "capture those loyalties and responsibilities whose moral force consists partly in the fact that living by them is inseparable from understanding ourselves as the particular persons we are—as members of this family, or city, or nation, or people, as bearers of that history, as members of this republic."[10]

Taylor develops this point further by noting that the existence and survival of a distinct community (he uses the example of Quebec within Canada) cannot be squared with this conception of liberalism. In order to flourish, these communities must by definition choose and promote some collective notion of the good held by the majority of citizens. By necessity, this choice will be at the exclusion or diminution of concepts of the good that a minority may prefer. In the case of Quebec, this good is the French language. Taylor believes that choosing such a good does not make a society illiberal, but one must move beyond the Anglo-American procedural construct in order to recognize this possibility:

> So Quebeckers, and those who give similar importance to this kind of collective goal, tend to opt for a rather different model of liberal society. On their view, a society can be organized around a definition

of the good life, without this being seen as a depreciation of those who do not personally share this definition. Where the nature of the good requires that it be sought in common, this is a reason for its being a matter of public policy. . . . One has to distinguish the fundamental liberties, those that should never be infringed and therefore ought to be unassailably entrenched, from privileges and immunities that are important but can be revoked or restricted for reasons of public policy—although one would need a strong reason to do this. A society with strong collective goals can be liberal, on this view, provided it is also capable of respecting diversity, especially when dealing with those who do not share its common goals, and provided it can offer adequate safeguards for fundamental rights.[11]

Another Canadian, political philosopher Will Kymlicka, makes a similar argument, but he rejects Taylor's critique of liberalism inasmuch as it is grounded in a challenge to an atomized individualism that gives insufficient attention to claims of community and culture. Kymlicka is a strong supporter of the primacy of individual freedom and autonomy who does not find the communitarian critique of liberal individualism compelling, but he agrees with Taylor that groups like the Québécois are entitled to protection in a liberal state. He does not see group rights that assist disadvantaged or oppressed minorities as necessarily inconsistent with a strong respect for individual autonomy. By describing group rights as supplemental to individual rights and as opposed to a restriction of them, Kymlicka develops a theory of group rights that is designed to stabilize certain groups that are threatened by the larger society, through what he calls "external protections," which are designed to promote equality by recognizing particular vulnerabilities of minorities:

External protections . . . can be entirely consistent with liberal norms. Many groups seek to protect their distinct identity by limiting their vulnerability to the decisions of the larger society. . . . Guaranteeing representation for a minority on advisory or legislative bodies reduces the chance that the group will be outvoted on decisions that affect the community. Devolving power to local levels enables the group to make certain decisions on its own. These sorts of external protections are not inconsistent with liberal democracy and may indeed promote justice. They may help put the different groups in a society on a more equal footing, by reducing the extent to which minorities are vulnerable to the larger society. . . . In most cases, the minority has no ability or desire to dominate larger groups. The external protections they seek would not deprive other groups of their fair share of economic resources, political power, or language rights. As a rule, minorities simply seek to ensure that the majority cannot use its superior numbers and wealth to deprive the minority of the resources and institutions needed to sustain their community. And that is, I think, a legitimate demand.[12]

Despite apparent differences at the level of core theory, both Kymlicka's and Taylor's models of liberal society share much in terms of the implications they have for the way *any* society might understand itself, particularly if that society is to be more than simply a collection of individuals linked by the most general of ideals. Indeed, if as Michael Perry has said, "we are all liberals now,"[13] and if membership in a community or a distinctive cultural or minority group is to have real meaning, the conception of the liberal state needs to allow for constitutive understandings of community identity that might preclude the freest possible exercise of all individual liberties.[14] Certain societies and individuals within societies may owe "special responsibilities" to specific members or to "members of those communities with which they have some morally relevant history, such as the morally burdened relations of Germans to Jews, of American whites to American blacks, or of England and France to their former colonies."[15] Indeed, Kymlicka has argued that the situation of African Americans is sui generis, confounding attempts to place their experience in the United States into the standard models of minority groups and therefore offering a particularly compelling case for unique approaches to problems of inequality and exclusion:

> African Americans do not fit the voluntary immigrant pattern, not only because they were brought to America involuntarily as slaves, but also because they were prevented (rather than encouraged) from integrating into the institutions of the majority culture (e.g. through racial segregation, laws against miscegenation, and the teaching of literacy). Nor do they fit the national minority pattern, since they do not have a traditional homeland in America in which they are a majority or a language that distinguishes them from the majority. . . . The situation of African Americans, therefore, is virtually unique, although the use of "race" to define subordinate groups is certainly more common. Given their distinctive situation, it is widely accepted that they will also have distinctive demands.[16]

Public discourse in the United States and the recent jurisprudence of the Supreme Court on affirmative action often show little recognition of the existence of a morally burdened history shared by Americans both white and black.

Certainly, a great deal of resistance remains to any acknowledgment of the African American experience as a unique component of and commentary on the American experience and identity. Arguably, that history calls for public acknowledgment of its implications on current views of justice and fairness within American society. Yet, because of its dependence on procedural understandings of liberal justice, U.S. law treats race and affirmative action in a way that places primary emphasis on the protection and promotion of the fullest possible exercise of individual autonomy. Thus, the Court has felt compelled to confine the use of race to the narrowest of circumstances because it believes that racial categories are offensive to notions of individual dignity and, when used by the state to assign benefits and burdens, promote the good of certain individuals at the expense of others. As Kymlicka has noted, attention to the special needs of African Americans is seen as restricting the individual rights of others and threatening the conception of liberal democratic values.[17]

Grutter v. Bollinger and the Language of Neutrality and Autonomy in U.S. Law

Affirmative action is a source of great contention in the United States. On the one hand, incessant attacks on the practice, particularly during the last 25 years, have had a politically polarizing effect on civic life and delayed the healing of many African Americans' sense of grievance about the nation's racist past. For them, affirmative action is the closest the nation has come to any collective acknowledgment of its ongoing battle with racism, a struggle that is integral to their lives and identities.[18] On the other hand, many Americans cannot understand why African Americans continue to feel burdened by racism and the historical legacy of slavery. They see waves of immigrants from around the world succeeding in the United States and wonder why African Americans cannot seize the opportunities provided by the freedom and openness of American culture. Although most recognize the evils of slavery and racism, they view these things as historical wrongs that have been eliminated and wonder why these burdens are qualitatively different from the political and social oppression that many immigrants have fled from and ultimately transcended.[19]

The general unwillingness of Americans to take collective ownership for anything they view as beyond the scope of their individual responsibility has meant that the nation has failed to embrace a shared narrative about the past that privileges African Americans' unique role in the nation's story. This allows certain groups within the society to pretend that African slavery (and the racism bound up with it) was only a minor distraction in the development of U.S. law and culture, thereby creating the false impression that democratic values and institutions lack the historical baggage of other democratic societies. Take, for example, this quote from Michael Novak's extremely laudatory exposition of the American founding as it relates to a Catholic understanding of the common good: "Behind America's evident energy and enterprise lay liberty and social union, the protection of the rights of each, and the multiplication of opportunities for each (the population of Southern slaves, alas, excepted) had resulted, exactly as the framers had expected, in the growth of the wealth and the opportunity of all."[20]

Note how slavery becomes a parenthetical and an unfortunate regional problem. Yet, we know as a historical matter that slavery existed throughout the colonies for most of the eighteenth century and that, during the nineteenth century, tremendous wealth was created in the North through direct and indirect participation in Southern slavery and the slave trade. The accommodation of slavery and the nurturing of racism throughout the nineteenth and early twentieth centuries in U.S. law and politics are fundamental parts of American social and legal history; it is simply dishonest (though hardly unusual) to deal with them parenthetically. In the same text, however, Novak condemns the social structures of Europe at the time of the American founding: "When men lack liberty, when their station is fixed for life, and when opportunity for self-advancement is lacking, how can the social order in which they live not seem to be an enemy, even if they allow for its necessity. . . . Such a social order is also their enemy, because the yeast embedded in their natural liberty is neutralized against its natural rising."[21] African Americans could make similar statements about the United States well into the mid-twentieth century.

Justice Antonin Scalia, himself a descendent of Italian immigrants, has long been known for pressing the view that "under our Constitution, there can be no such thing as a creditor or debtor race. That concept is alien to the Constitution's focus upon the individual and its rejection of dispositions based on race or blood. To pursue the concept of racial entitlement—even for the most admirable or benign of purposes—is to reinforce and preserve for future mischief the way of thinking that produced race slavery, race privilege, and race hatred. In the eyes of the government, we are just one race here. It is American."[22] Yet, when we know as a matter of fact that "black and white" still drive the public perception of any number of issues, how can the legal system in a color-conscious society promote justice through a commitment to a color-blind Constitution? Can the legal system be fair or just when it refuses to recognize the racial distinctions that operate every day in citizens' lives? Catholic thought, for example, understands that this type of "neutrality" simply favors the current social, political, and economic arrangements and does not move societies toward real social change. Justice, properly understood, is compatible with partiality to certain groups in certain cases, particularly when the rights of those groups are imperiled or have ordinarily not been respected.[23]

In the United States, the inability of legal argument to produce rationales for special assistance to African Americans that enjoy broad-based citizen support can be explained at least partially by the absence of a common understanding of key events in U.S. history. Another by-product of a culture of individual autonomy is the lack of any sense of collective memory. This absence of a common historical and cultural framework presents special problems for legal discourse, particularly when it must struggle with concepts like justice and fairness in relationship to race. James Boyd White has offered a strong critique of the narrowness of judicial opinions in this regard, and he has argued for "integration and transformation [of legal discourse]; the attempt to put parts of our culture and corresponding parts of ourselves together, in ways that will make new languages, voices, and discourses possible."[24] White's idea of creating a holistic discourse that unites both the disparate voices within a community, as well as the often warring aspects of the human personality, also provides a natural theoretical link to Sandel's and Taylor's communitarian philosophical perspectives and to Kymlicka's liberalism. White links legal language to richer understandings of human community without undermining liberal respect for the individual. One way White suggests for a reader to approach a judicial opinion in this context is to consider the "ideal reader" it addresses:

> Who, we can ask, is the Ideal Reader defined by the Constitution, or by this statute or contract? This a question every judicial opinion can be said to address, whether its author knows it or not; and a question that every judicial opinion invites for itself, for it too claims to speak with authority.
>
> . . .
>
> In every opinion, a court not only resolves a particular dispute one way or another, it validates or authorizes one form of life—one kind of reasoning, one kind of response to argument, one way of looking at the world and at its own authority—or another. Whether or not the process is conscious, the judge seeks to persuade her reader not only to the rightness of the result reached and the propriety of the analysis used, but to her understanding of what the judge—and the law, the lawyer, and the citizen—are and should be, in short, to her conception of the kind of conversation that does and should constitute us.[25]

In her majority opinion in *Grutter v. Bollinger*, Justice Sandra Day O'Connor considered the affirmative action policies of the University of Michigan Law School. Although her statement upheld the law school's use of affirmative action, the way Justice O'Connor spoke to her ideal reader says more about how U.S. law and society view race and affirmative action than does the actual decision. The analysis in the majority opinion began with a consideration of the Court's landmark decision in *Regents of California v. Bakke*. This 1978 opinion had been the Supreme Court's most significant statement on the subject of affirmative action for the past 25 years. In that case, a splintered court upheld the use of race as a factor in university admissions. Since that time, Justice Powell's opinion had served as the primary reference for the understanding of affirmative action's constitutionality in university admissions, and Justice O'Connor examined that ruling in some detail.

O'Connor's analysis of the *Bakke* precedent revealed a great deal about how racial questions are conceived in U.S. public law. In her initial examination of Justice Powell's opinion, O'Connor noted that Powell "rejected an interest in remedying societal discrimination because such measures would risk placing unnecessary burdens on innocent third parties 'who bear no responsibility for whatever harm the beneficiaries of special admissions programs are thought to have suffered.'"[26] Indeed, "Justice Powell approved the University's use of race to further only one interest: 'the attainment of a diverse student body,' with the important proviso that 'constitutional limitations protecting individual rights may not be disregarded.'"[27] Before going on to endorse Powell's views on the compelling nature of a university's interest in student diversity, she noted with approval Powell's view that race should be only one element in a range of factors that ought to be considered when attempting to create student diversity.

In reaching her decision in *Grutter*, O'Connor discussed those "constitutional limitations protecting individual rights" by reviewing the protections afforded individuals under the Equal Protection Clause: "Because the Fourteenth Amendment protects persons, not groups, all governmental action based on race—a group classification long recognized as in most circumstances irrelevant and therefore prohibited—should be subjected to detailed judicial inquiry to ensure that the personal right to equal protection of the laws has not been infringed."[28] Without such an inquiry, there would be no way to determine "what classifications are 'benign' or 'remedial' and what classifications are in fact motivated by illegitimate notions of racial inferiority or simple racial politics."[29]

O'Connor then noted that the Court was to apply strict scrutiny in order to "'smoke out' illegitimate uses of race."[30] Thus, before a racial classification would be constitutionally acceptable, it needed to pass a strict scrutiny test; that is, it had to be "narrowly tailored to further compelling governmental interests."[31] Applying strict scrutiny to the University of Michigan Law School's admissions policy, O'Connor accepted the idea that furthering the "educational benefits that flow from a diverse student body"[32] was sufficient justification to pass the compelling governmental interest portion of the strict scrutiny test.[33] Having determined that the admissions policy furthered a compelling government interest, O'Connor considered whether the policy was narrowly tailored to achieve that end. She concluded that it was not an impermissible quota system that would have fixed a "number or proportion of opportunities... reserved exclusively for certain minority groups."[34] Rather, the Michigan law school admission policy used race only as a "plus" factor in the otherwise equal selection of candidates.[35]

O'Connor's emphasis on the importance of the individualized character of the law school's admission policy also found its way into the next step of her analysis. She noted that, even if the policy did not require quotas, it could not pass a strict scrutiny analysis if the program did not "remain flexible enough to ensure that each applicant is evaluated as an individual and not in any way that makes an applicant's race or ethnicity the defining feature of his or her application."[36] Examining the law school's admission policy, O'Connor concluded that the program was a "highly individualized, holistic review of each applicant's file, giving serious consideration to all of the ways an applicant might contribute to a diverse educational environment."[37] Perhaps more important, the law school did not limit the application of this process to members of minority groups but rather "afford[ed] this individualized consideration to applicants of all races."[38] Thus, O'Connor focused on the individualized treatment of candidates and furthered the Court's long-standing refusal to accept affirmative action programs that would give special deference to members of a particular group based on a unique history of social exclusion and discrimination.

Is this a reasonable way to understand the Equal Protection Clause? Is justice enhanced or fairness promoted when we draw neutral principles from these provisions of the Constitution without situating them properly in the history from which they sprang? At the very least, it is ahistorical for U.S. legal institutions to attempt a racially neutral discourse, particularly when discussing the Fourteenth Amendment, which has everything to do with slavery, racism, and the bloody crucible of the American Civil War: "The first step might be to think of the Civil War Amendments less as an effort to create neutral and universal rules of law, to be applied by the work of a universal reason... than as an effort to address the greatest single social and political issue the nation has ever faced: human slavery and its consequences, particularly the denial of full citizenship to the descendants of slaves. . . . This is a way of conceiving of the amendments as designed to achieve something specific in the world, not just as articulations of general or political philosophical principles to be applied to all alike."[39]

Not only is the Fourteenth Amendment a product of a society that almost collapsed over the issue of the maintenance and extension of race-based slavery, but it also arose from the political system of a society that moved from slavery into a particularly virulent and dehumanizing form of racism that continues to burden people of African descent in the United States today. The construction of racial "blackness" was designed to maintain a permanent underclass based on traceable African ancestry. What the nation was unable to accomplish through the preservation of a legal regime of slavery, it achieved through legal and de facto racial segregation designed to marginalize any individual that could be linked to Africa and, by extension, to the status of a chattel slave. In 2006 Brown University completed an extensive scholarly report that explored the institution's relationship to the slave trade, which, despite its location in Providence, Rhode Island, was extensive. In laying out the importance of slavery to the formation of the nation and the significant contribution the "peculiar institution" made to its wealth, the authors noted some particular aspects of slavery in the United States:

> The dishonor and degradation associated with enslavement gave rise to contempt for the people who were enslaved. Though the particulars differ, slaves throughout history have been stigmatized as inferior, uncivilized, bestial. Few if any societies in history carried this logic further than the United States, where people of African descent came to be regarded as a distinct "race" of persons, fashioned by nature for hard labor. . . . This process of dehumanization was abetted by developments in American law. In contrast to the plantation colonies of Spain and Portugal, which inherited legal definitions of slavery through the Catholic Church and the tradition of Roman-Dutch law, settlers in mainland North America were left to fashion their own slave codes. And the laws they fashioned . . . were historically unprecedented in their complete denial of the legal personality of the enslaved. Slaves in North America were chattel. . . . The North American colonies were also highly unusual in tracing slave descent through the maternal rather than the paternal line, a system that ensured, in practice, that most children of mixed ancestry would themselves be enslaved. . . . If American slavery has any claims to

being historically "peculiar," its peculiarity lay in its rigid racialism, the systematic way in which racial ideas were used to demean and deny the humanity of people of even partial African descent. This historical legacy would make the process of incorporating the formerly enslaved as citizens far more problematic in the United States than in other New World slave societies.[40]

The virulence of racism in the United States and the extraordinary lengths to which American society went in order to maintain a racial underclass reveal deeply disturbing aspects of the nation's character throughout its history. Despite the essential role of Africans in the formation of an American social, political, and cultural consciousness, slavery encouraged a cult of "whiteness" in the United States that viewed black people as less than human. These traits have led some critical race scholars to theorize that the most appropriate way to understand race in American life is as something akin to property. As Cheryl Harris noted in her seminal article, "Whiteness as Property," "Slavery produced a peculiar, mixed category of property and humanity—a hybrid with inherent instabilities that were reflected in its treatment and ratification by the law."[41] The implications of the conflation of slaves with property in a culture that has long been grounded in an aggressive pursuit of individual freedom and personal wealth were enormous:

> Because the "presumption of freedom [arose] from color [white]" and the "black color of the race [raised] the presumption of slavery," whiteness became a shield from slavery, a highly volatile and unstable form of property. In the form adopted in the United States, slavery made human beings market-alienable and in so doing, subjected human life and personhood—that which is most valuable—to the ultimate devaluation. Because whites could not be enslaved or held as slaves, the racial line between white and black was extremely critical; it became a line of protection and demarcation from the potential threat of commodification. . . . White identity and whiteness were sources of privilege and protection; their absence meant being the object of property.[42]

In the United States, race relations reveal the centrality of materialism, personal autonomy, and self-aggrandizement to our culture. In such a society, nothing could be worse than to have been "owned" by another. It was, however, the presence of slaves that fed the creation of the cult of individual freedom within the white population and provided the key point of juxtaposition for an idealized rendering of rights in a kind of all-or-nothing format: slavery or freedom, men or animals, black or white.[43] Drawing on the work of Jacques Derrida, Kimberlé Crenshaw has demonstrated that the tendency of Western thought to create positive and negative polarities manifested itself in the American ideology of race: "Laws and customs helped to create 'races' out of a broad range of human traits. In the process of creating races, the categories came to be filled with meaning: whites were characterized one way and associated with normally positive characteristics, whereas blacks were characterized another way and became associated with the subordinate, even aberrational characteristics."[44] This understanding of the nature of American racism caused Derrick Bell to make the following attack on the reasoning of *Bakke:* "Relying heavily on the formalistic language of the Fourteenth Amendment and utterly ignoring social questions about which race in fact has power and advantages and which race has for centuries been denied entry into academia, the court held that an affirmative action policy may not unseat white candidates on the basis of their race. By introducing an artificial and inappropriate parity in its reasoning, the court effectively made a choice to ignore historical patterns, to ignore contemporary statistics, and to ignore flexible reasoning. . . . Bakke serves as an example of how formalists can use abstract concepts, such as equality, to mask policy choices and value judgments."[45]

The ideal readers of the *Grutter* opinion, which is steeped in such neutrality and formalism, most likely are not African American, nor are they people who might question the ongoing legitimacy of the current social, political, and economic arrangements in American society. The language and assumptions of the opinion suggest that it is directed to someone who has not been burdened by or does not see the complexities of the nation's history of racism. The ideal reader is encouraged when history and situated understandings of identity are eliminated from legal discourse. The *Grutter* opinion also says that race is a negative, an irrelevance that the state should acknowledge only in the most limited of circumstances. This legal construct implicitly rejects the idea of a moral imperative to give positive recognition to race based on a collective understanding of a difficult history or as a way of acknowledging the special responsibilities that flow from a uniquely American experience of slavery and segregation.[46] It also leaves no room for the possibility of a positive embrace of the African aspects of American identity for blacks and whites alike. Most African Americans cannot understand themselves in these terms. How can a society engage important questions of racial justice and healing when the legal system is unwilling to situate current discussions of affirmative action in the nation's history of racism, slavery, and segregation? Ultimately, who benefits from "neutral" readings of the Civil War amendments? If African Americans are not among the ideal readers of an opinion upholding affirmative action, under what circumstances can they hope to receive real recognition and acknowledgment from their fellow citizens, from the legal system, and from the state?

Rethinking Affirmative Action through a Catholic Ethic of Solidarity

The concept of solidarity as understood in Catholic social teaching might help move American law and society toward a vision of community in which constitutional rights and the principles in which they are grounded are seen as part of a broader cultural framework in a quest to deepen the nation's commitment to justice and human dignity and become the tools for enriching our lives in common. Rather than further isolating us from one another, solidarity would allow all Americans to come to terms with the racist ideology that was an integral part of the nation's past by promoting a real engagement with those who have been most directly harmed by it. The ultimate result of this encounter with one another might be a clearer understanding of the strengths and weaknesses of our social structures and ultimately a richer and more bonded sense of community that is rooted in a deeper commitment to those among us who have been oppressed and excluded. As the U.S. Conference of Catholic Bishops noted in its pastoral letter on racism in 1979:

> The structures of our society are subtly racist, for these structures reflect the values which society upholds. They are geared to the success of the majority and the failure of the minority. Members of both groups give unwitting approval by accepting things as they are. Perhaps no single individual is to blame. The sinfulness is often anonymous but nonetheless real. The sin is social in nature in that each of us, in varying degrees, is responsible. The absence of personal fault for an evil does not absolve one of all responsibility. We must seek to resist and undo injustices that we have not caused, lest we become bystanders who tacitly endorse evil and so share in guilt in it."[47]

Why Catholic Social Thinking Is a Legitimate Part of the Discussion in a Pluralist American Society

Michael Perry has written that the "foundational moral commitment of every liberal democracy is to the true and full humanity of *every* person, without regard to race, sex, religion, and so on. This commitment is axiomatic for liberal democracy."[48] Yet, what is the conceptual framework that gives this idea of the humanity of all persons its real power? Perry has argued that its source is religious: "There is no intelligible (much less persuasive) secular version of the conviction that every human being is sacred; the only intelligible versions are religious."[49] The essential link between Catholic social teaching and conversations about law and public policy in a liberal democracy is that the former is rooted in the idea of the sacredness of human beings. Drawing from the creation story in Genesis, people are seen as created in the image and likeness of God: "Human dignity comes from God's free gift; it does not depend on human effort, work, or accomplishments. All human beings have a fundamental, equal dignity because all share the generous gift of creation and redemption from God.... Consequently, all human beings have the same fundamental dignity, whether they are brown, black, red, or white; rich or poor; young or old; male or female; healthy or sick."[50] In this way, Catholic social teaching announces its commitment to the most basic norm of modern social and political life. Additionally, Catholic teaching offers two thousand years of reflection on human society. "It expresses for our times the reflection of the Church on social realities, assessing them in the light of the Gospels and offering guidelines for practical behavior in society. It is basically an application of theology, and especially moral theology, to the ethical questions raised by human societies."[51]

The other foundational pillar for understanding the human being in Catholic social teaching is that we are inherently social:

> Catholic social teaching recognizes that the whole of the Catholic tradition testifies to the social nature of human beings. Through creation we are all brothers and sisters who have the same God as our Creator.... The twofold commandment of love of God and neighbor illustrates the fact that we are brothers and sisters who belong to the same human family, with moral obligations toward one another.... Catholic social teaching alludes to the Catholic philosophical tradition's insistence on the social nature of human beings. Thomas Aquinas—who was shaped by the Christian tradition and Aristotelian philosophy—insisted that the human being is social and political by nature. By our God-given nature we are called to live in political society with one another. The state is natural and necessary for human beings.[52]

This idea demonstrates how Catholic social teaching shares a basic presumption with the communitarian vision of liberalism in the secular philosophical works of Sandel and Taylor. Indeed, this emphasis on our inherently social nature diverges radically from the underlying anthropology of much of U.S. law and affirmative action jurisprudence in particular. Radical personal autonomy, equality grounded in neutral principles that make no effort to define what is good or true about human existence, and distrust of government— so evident in the affirmative action opinions of both Justice Powell and Justice O'Connor—are not consistent with the church's understanding of a Christian conception of human social and political life. Yet, Catholic social teaching is grounded in premises that are in no way inconsistent with the fundamental values of liberal democracy, and a true commitment to liberal pluralism suggests that these ideas should be part of conversations about the direction of law and public policy in the United States rather than excluded from them.

The Catholic Ideal of Solidarity and a New Rationale for Affirmative Action

In Catholic social teaching, the core concepts of our dignity and social nature also provide a framework for the concept of solidarity. Based on the recognition of human sacredness and interdependence, solidarity recognizes the moral imperative of individual commitment to the common good: "The exercise of solidarity *within each society* is valid when its members recognize one another as persons. Those who are more influential, because they have a greater share of goods and common services, should feel responsible for the weaker and be ready to share with them all they possess. Those who are weaker, for their part, in the same spirit of solidarity, should not adopt a purely passive attitude or one that is destructive of the social fabric, but, while claiming their legitimate rights, should do what they can for the good of all."[53]

Solidarity recognizes that human dignity suffers when those who have more do not recognize their obligations to those with less, particularly when the latter cannot fully participate in society. Solidarity does not, however, see those in a weaker position simply as victims. It also acknowledges their reciprocal duties to work toward the common good as best they can. Those excluded from full participation should not become a destructive force in society but should seek integration into civic and cultural life. The themes of responsibility and reciprocity are also an important part of solidarity and signal the relationship of human dignity to God and to the fundamental human need for life in community: "In the light of faith, solidarity seeks to go beyond itself, to take on the *specifically Christian* dimension of total gratuity, forgiveness, and reconciliation. One's neighbor is then not only a human being with his or her own rights and a fundamental equality with everyone else, but becomes the *living image* of God the Father."[54]

Reciprocity, gratuity, and reconciliation are also themes sounded by James Boyd White, who argues for a more holistic understanding of legal discourse that is rooted in a fuller range of human intellect, experience, and emotion.[55] Conceptually, solidarity offers a potentially powerful basis for meaningful social and political change. Pope John Paul II recognized this by viewing it as "a firm and persevering determination to commit oneself to the common good; that is to say to the good of all and each individual, because we are *all* really responsible for all. This determination is based on the solid conviction that what is hindering full development is the desire for profit and the thirst for power.... These attitudes and 'structures of sin' are only conquered— presupposing the help of divine grace—by a diametrically opposed attitude: a commitment to the good of one's neighbor with the readiness, in the gospel sense, to 'lose oneself' for the sake of the other instead of exploiting him, and to 'serve him' instead of oppressing him for one's own advantage."[56]

If one considers the structures of American society and the "American way of life" throughout our history, one can easily see how the nation's racist ethos has been linked to quests for money and power. Racism was a way to guarantee a subordinate laboring class in the United States, and it also created internal divisions among the nation's poorest citizens that were effective in preventing these people from forming strong social and political coalitions throughout much of U.S. history. Unspoken racial demons continue to exercise power in our social, political, and economic life: Pandering to racial fears is still an integral part of politics in the United States, and issues as diverse as public education, crime, and urban sprawl all turn in some degree on how we perceive race. Although significant strides have been made to move the nation beyond this history and its legacy, much of this progress has been accomplished by appealing to a notion of tolerance grounded in autonomy and individualism.

In his book titled *The Common Good and Christian Ethics*, David Hollenbach has demonstrated that a lack of any substantive notion of the common good in the United States prevents Americans from appreciating structures that consistently exclude certain members of the society from full participation in the nation's common life and that this failure is an ethical and moral problem for our society.[57] In particular, he notes that the growth of a liberal notion of tolerance, which he believes is an important part of the explanation of the decline in racism among American whites, may not be enough to get to the root of many of the problems intertwined with that racism: "Tolerance means *acceptance* of difference, perhaps even a kind of acquiescence in such differences. When such acceptance of difference leads to inclusion of those who have been excluded by a long history of racist attitudes and actions, tolerance makes very important contributions to the creation of community. But when barriers are the result of economic inequalities that are deeply ingrained and institutionalized in the class structures of society, more than an attitude of tolerance is needed."[58]

Solidarity requires more. It demands that all Americans recognize the unique burdens that have been placed on African Americans throughout U.S. history. Hollenbach suggests that solidarity requires dialogue across boundaries in order to create an "intellectual solidarity" in which we learn from both listening and speaking to one another: "Christian love calls for the building up of the bonds of solidarity among all persons, and such solidarity requires efforts to understand those who are different, to learn from them, and to contribute to their understanding of the good life as well. Intellectual solidarity with them forges a bond that goes beyond tolerance understood as leaving others alone to the positive engagement with others that true dialogue demands."[59]

When one reflects on the contentious nature of the debate over affirmative action in the United States, it is clear that the centrality of money, power, and personal advantage in American life are unspoken issues that drive the discussion. Justice for the victims of racism will not come without some cost to the beneficiaries of the inherently racist structures of the current system, regardless of whether those individuals have engaged in specific acts of racist behavior themselves. Racial issues continue to blind large groups within the blue-collar, lower-middle, and middle-classes to the increasing precariousness of their economic situation.[60] Instead of questioning the direction of the U.S. economy, particularly the growth of income inequality and the decline of economic security for the middle and working classes, political attention is directed to affirmative action, which is attacked for supposedly providing "unfair" access to jobs and educational opportunities for African Americans, a group that continues to be disproportionately poor and is notably underrepresented in positions of power and influence in the United States. As the Brown University committee noted in its report, "innumerable letters sent to the steering committee made clear [that] many Americans reject, indeed resent, the suggestion that they bear some responsibility for actions in which they took no part, actions that may have occurred before they were born. The very notion collides not only with deeply ingrained beliefs about individual responsibility, but also with quintessentially American ideas about historical transcendence, the capacity and fundamental right of human beings to shake off the dead hand of the past and create their lives anew."[61]

Another important issue raised when the affirmative action debate is considered in the context of solidarity is whether anyone is really listening to African Americans when they speak about race in the United States. In the weeks following then Senate majority leader Trent Lott's racially insensitive comments in 2002, National Public Radio brought together an interracial group of employees from the National Historical Society to discuss the controversy.[62] In response to a statement by a white woman in her twenties, who said she felt "ashamed" and "attacked" in community meetings when blacks talked about the ongoing legacy of slavery, an African American man in his fifties responded with the following remarks:

> I don't want you to feel ashamed, because you didn't own any slaves. But what I want you to understand is my pain, because we, as African Americans, from the way I see it—we came out of slavery running. We have never had an opportunity to mourn.... And I have always understood slavery.... It was an economic thing. I can understand that. Everybody practiced that. But one of the things that I never understood—and I remember asking my mother—"Why do the whites hate us? They have everything. They got the best schools. They got the best books. I don't understand why they hate us. I don't understand when they hung us, why did they mutilate our bodies like they did?" You understand what I am saying? Nobody has ever answered those questions for me. I understand slavery. I am willing to let that go; let the nation go.... But I think that what we need to do is just to go somewhere and just cry without someone accusing us of being weak, without somebody criticizing our behavior. I remember, as a kid, I used to look at America as the mother of us all, and I was just this kid that she didn't want. So I straightened my hair and that wasn't right. I bleached my skin and that wasn't right ... and then I fixed my language and that wasn't right. And then there was a time when I just gave up on America. I got mad at it, and that wasn't right. You understand what I am saying?[63]

At the end of this statement, the speaker was in tears. His words impart a palpable sense of agony, and his need to mourn affirms theologian Gregory Baum's view that mourning is an appropriate way to share solidarity with victims of oppression. The dehumanizing character of American racism is part of the harsh legacy of slavery that commodified human beings to such a degree that their inherent humanity was quickly effaced in the minds of many within the mainstream culture. Listening in a spirit of solidarity reveals the enduring pain with which individuals who feel a constant sense of rejection by their society continue to struggle. African Americans are still often traumatized by the past and its ongoing implications in their daily lives. Conversation and storytelling, accompanied by real listening, allow "[t]he sometimes useless language of the law [to be] put aside.... One instead tells stories that capture and transmit common human emotions such as pain, loss, separation, desperation."[64] This kind of listening is an important underlying strength in the organization of truth and reconciliation commissions, and their work demonstrates that societies and legal systems can move beyond false neutrality in an effort to overcome difficult histories. Although beyond the scope of this chapter, the truth and reconciliation model may suggest another type of response, rooted in solidarity and respect, to the enduring legacies of racism and discrimination in the United States.

In his 1967 encyclical letter titled *Populorum progressio,* Pope Paul VI spoke of the demands on the rich that might potentially spring from solidarity with the poor and a recognized duty to promote social justice: "This demands great generosity, much sacrifice, and unceasing effort on the part of the rich man. Let each one examine his conscience, a conscience that conveys a new message for our times. Is he prepared to support out of his own pocket works and undertakings organized for the most destitute? Is he ready to pay higher taxes so that the public authorities can intensify their efforts in favor of development?"[65] Pope Paul's words suggest a parallel with the situation of African Americans in the United States. Real solidarity with the victims of an American ideology of racism may require specific acts of generosity and sacrifice in response. Political initiatives, such as the creation of affirmative action programs, can serve as signs that this recognition is not mere pretense but a true shift in understanding on the part of those in power that has ramifications for the entire community.

Constructing an Affirmative Action Policy Rooted in Solidarity

How would an affirmative action policy that proceeded from a commitment to solidarity differ from what Justice O'Connor announced in *Grutter*? At the very least, there would be two new factors that could be considered explicitly. First, the program could be race specific by attacking group-based racial discrimination through group-based remedies. Second, the key criterion for judging affirmative action's overall value to society would be its impact on those Americans least able to participate fully in the nation's common life—not its potential harm to "innocent" third parties, for "justice demands that social institutions be ordered in a way that guarantees all persons the ability to participate actively in the economic, political and cultural life of society. The level of participation may legitimately be greater for some persons than for others, but there is a basic level of access that must be made available to all. Such participation is an essential expression of the social nature of human beings and of their communitarian vocation."[66]

If it is every American's responsibility to work toward a minimal level of participation for every individual in society, those of us who are better off may have to make some sacrifices in order to promote a minimal level of engagement for those who are excluded. One obvious way of creating a program of affirmative action in higher education that also pays special attention to those who have typically been excluded on the basis of race would be to focus on the structural injustices of the U.S. system of primary and secondary public schooling. Some of the most marginalized members of our society are found in the public school systems of our cities. Not only are these systems often among the most poorly funded in the nation, but they also tend to be the most racially segregated.[67] Solidarity and justice require that special attention be given to students who must receive educations in these environments.

Public school districts are easily categorized by the students' socioeconomic profiles and the concentration of African Americans and other racial or ethnic minorities within the systems. Arguably, poor students who are educated in the most impoverished and racially segregated school districts are living on the margins of society. They suffer not only from poverty but also from an indifference to their circumstances that is due at least in part to racism. Living in intensely segregated neighborhoods and cities, these students are quickly marked as outsiders when they attempt to interact in mainstream environments. Affirmative action programs that grow out of solidarity with these students might reserve places for them in public institutions of higher learning and assess their admissibility according to separate criteria designed to identify their intellectual promise in a way that recognizes the realities of the environments in which they have been educated. Policies of this type acknowledge that educational structures prevent many poor and minority children from being competitive candidates for admission to elite universities and attempt to remedy the disadvantages these students must consequently bear.[68]

For example, as one of the most racially segregated cities in the United States, Detroit has some of the nation's worst-performing public schools. Historically, the suburban jurisdictions surrounding Detroit have been particularly hostile both to efforts to direct resources into the city that might improve the schools and to attempts to allow the city's predominately African American student population to obtain educations in the more affluent suburban public school systems. In 1974 the Supreme Court acquiesced in the segregation of poor blacks in the Detroit schools when it overruled a district court desegregation plan that would have created a metropolitan solution to segregation in the city's school district. The Supreme Court ruled that, absent a showing of constitutional violations in the suburban districts, a multidistrict remedy to the problem of school desegregation in the Detroit district was constitutionally impermissible.[69]

An affirmative action policy designed to help these students would recognize that they are uniquely disadvantaged when competing for educational opportunities at the University of Michigan. Neutrality toward these students essentially ignores an unacceptable pattern of injustice in the provision of public education in this country. Furthermore, simply giving these students a "plus" for being African American as part of a holistic admissions inquiry fails to recognize that most of them will not even make it into the University of Michigan's general applicant pool or that they will presumptively be denied admission if they do. Nevertheless, the voters of Michigan, despite *Grutter* (or perhaps because of it) remain extremely hostile to the concept of affirmative action, and in November 2006 they joined California and Washington in banning, by a wide margin, affirmative action programs based on race, gender, and ethnic status in the public arena.

A program of affirmative action that focuses on poor and segregated public school districts would also reveal other ways in which race still operates to exclude people. African Americans often find themselves in highly segregated public school districts regardless of income. The enduring nature of segregation in housing patterns disadvantages black students from a variety of socioeconomic backgrounds and might well be an additional justification for some sort of race-specific affirmative action.[70] Affirmative action directed toward students in poor and highly segregated school systems could also help identify other groups who tend to be burdened by racial or ethnic prejudice. An assessment of school districts in this way would reveal similar poverty and segregation faced by certain Latino groups and many Native Americans, particularly those who live on reservations. Indeed, affirmative action that focuses on the poverty and racial segregation within school districts need not necessarily limit itself to addressing problems associated with race. These programs could also identify disadvantaged students from a variety of backgrounds who suffer the negative results of a system of funding for public primary and secondary education that favors the wealthy and creates a pattern in the provision of public goods in which the desires of the better-off tend to come before the needs of the poor.

When engaged in a spirit of solidarity by their fellow citizens, African Americans, particularly those who have been unable to escape cycles of poverty and violence, may finally begin to feel some release from the enduring legacies of racism they have long endured and be better able to embrace the full spectrum of possibilities offered by meaningful membership in the community. Indeed, this engagement may allow for a richer understanding of

American identity, which may do a great deal more for this country than simply transform the way Americans think about race and affirmative action. Few groups in the United States are better situated than African Americans to offer critical assessments of the limitations of the American cult of economic and personal freedom.

True solidarity with African Americans may actually nurture a new solidarity among all Americans and lead us to recognize the threats to human dignity presented by blind faith in the concepts of freedom and neutrality cut off from any situation in history, culture, or community. Our discussions of social and economic issues might become both more honest and more respectful; consequently, as a society, we would be in a much better position to address constructively the growing challenges presented by our nation's ongoing rush into a culture of having rather than of being. We might then be able to turn to constructing bonds of community rooted in solidarity and social justice that recognize the profound respect for human dignity reflected in the often-quoted words of Lila Watson, an aboriginal Australian activist: "If you have come to help me, you are wasting your time, but if you have come because your liberation is bound up with mine, then let us work together."[71]

4

Enter the Poor

*American Welfare Reform, Solidarity,
and the Capability of Human Flourishing*

Martha Nussbaum has argued that in order to achieve real equality
and promote meaningful economic and social development, policymakers must determine "what people are able to do and to be."[1]
Along with Amartya Sen, Nussbaum has developed a "capabilities
approach" that recognizes a person's potential as "a combination of
various doings and beings, such as having self-respect, preserving
human dignity, taking part in the life of the community, and so on.
The capability of a person refers to various alternative combina-
tions of functionings, any one of which . . . a person can choose to
have."[2] This approach to development allows people to be seen
as ends in themselves rather than as means or tools in the hands
of others.

In this respect, Nussbaum shares key understandings of human dignity with Catholic social teaching, which also emphasizes
the importance of men and women as ends in themselves. However,
these philosophies diverge in what they consider essential criteria
for the enhancement of human dignity and the development of human capacity. Nussbaum argues that public policy should aim at
"a threshold of capacity beneath which a life would be so impoverished that it will not be human at all," and she provides a rich
array of capabilities necessary to meet this goal.[3] The focus of human well-being is driven primarily by individual needs and personal flourishing. What is less developed is an understanding of
human capacity that is rooted in our connections with others and

the well-being of the community as a whole. Catholic social thought incorporates these ideas under the concept of "solidarity." Solidarity offers a new dimension to Nussbaum's understanding of capacity, particularly in its ability to capture the importance of commitments to others, which are expressed through sharing and sacrifice as part of the essential good for everyone.

The concept of solidarity enhances Nussbaum's understandings of capacity in a manner that can be demonstrated by considering the experience of "welfare reform" in the United States. The debate over the provision of economic benefits to the poor reveals that the lack of solidarity in a society can destroy or limit the capacities of its weakest members. It also suggests that, as an important part of bringing dignity to the lives of poor people, socioeconomic development is incomplete without some attempt to nurture commitment to others throughout the society.

In this chapter I describe how a materialistic vision of society and the lack of a sense of common purpose in American life have made it extremely difficult for law and public policy to confront poverty in the United States in a way takes seriously the full humanity of poor people. After explaining how current reforms of economic assistance for those who are impoverished fail to take key cultural problems into account, I argue that the creators of welfare reform had an impoverished sense of the fundamental needs of poor people. For an alternative vision, I draw not only on Nussbaum's concept of capacity but also on the philosophical work of Paul Ricoeur and the Christian ethical perspective of theologian David Hollenbach. Ricoeur and Hollenbach demonstrate from two different perspectives that commitment to others needs to be a central part of any meaningful notion of human capacity and development. Together with Nussbaum and Sen, they lay a rich theoretical groundwork for a reassessment of American welfare reform that takes seriously the concept of capabilities, based on an enriched understanding of people's fundamental needs. This richer conceptual structure would offer poor people a more integrated role in society and check the ongoing erosion of a sense of communal responsibility in American culture.

Critiquing the Culture That Produced Welfare Reform

An intense focus on individual freedom and free-market liberalism has distorted the ways Americans view poor people and the impacts of poverty in our society. By and large, Americans take a relatively uncritical view of the current state of economic life and the costs the U.S. economic system exacts from the nation's social fabric. Many people cope with the economic and social stress inherent in American capitalism by viewing their ability to avoid poverty and dependence as a mark of strength and moral superiority. In this point of view, the poor thus become weak, morally flawed, and ultimately responsible for their own problems. In his book *The War against the Poor,* Herbert Gans has termed this the "ideology of undeservingness."[4] One important consequence of this ideology is that "[i]f poor people do not behave according to the rules set by mainstream America, they must be undeserving. They are undeserving because they believe in and therefore practice bad values, suggesting that they do not want to be part of mainstream America culturally or socially. As a result of bad values and practices, undeservingness has become a major cause of contemporary poverty. If poor people gave up these values, their poverty would decline automatically, and mainstream Americans would be ready to help them, as they help other 'deserving' people."[5]

The debates over the passage and renewal of the Personal Responsibility and Work Opportunity Reconciliation Act (PRWORA) of 1996 revealed this ideology in full flower,[6] most particularly in the view that participation in the paid labor force should be a key indication of whether a poor person deserves help from the state.[7] Even the key terms in the title of the legislation— "personal responsibility" and "work opportunity"—demonstrate the centrality of individualistic and market-oriented values in welfare policy. Upon its passage, the PRWORA was hailed by President Clinton as "the end of welfare as we know it."[8] What in fact ended was the political consensus that supported the concept of welfare as an entitlement provided by the federal government.[9]

By the mid-1990s, the conservative political reaction to the social and economic changes of the 1960s and 1970s had revealed important flaws and tensions in the system of economic provision for the poor.[10] These changes and the political reaction they helped to produce ought to have suggested to members of Congress that it was time for a broad review of the American system of entitlements. Instead, Depression-era and post–World War II entitlements that benefited those of middle and upper income, such as the home mortgage interest deduction, farm subsidies, and Social Security, became sacred cows, while the target for the reductions in federal government spending demanded by Republican politicians was aid to poor people. "[A]lthough government spending on the non-poor far exceeds expenditures directed to the poor, it is the entitlement programs aimed at the poor which have received the scrutiny of the budget-cutters and provided the ammunition to the enemies of big government."[11]

The details of the changes wrought by the PRWORA are complex, but a focus on the Temporary Assistance for Needy Families (TANF) program highlights several key aspects of the legislation. The TANF program is funded through a "block grant" or lump-sum payment to each state, and the states are given wide discretion to set their own criteria for eligibility. It also creates a block grant to support child care for low-income families. Adults who receive benefits are required to begin working within two years of receiving aid, with certain exceptions for parents of children under one year of age.[12]

Despite wide discretion given to the states in administering the program, certain limits placed on the use of the money are particularly notable in that they further the legislation's stated goals of achieving independence through work, reducing out-of-wedlock pregnancies, and encouraging the creation of two-parent families.[13] The money from these block grants cannot be used for any welfare recipient who received assistance for more than five years, although up to 20 percent of a state's welfare caseload can be exempted from this time limit. No funds may be used for a recipient who does not work after two years. Failure to comply with these and other work requirements means that a state's block grant will be reduced. States have the option to deny benefits to children born to welfare recipients, individuals convicted of drug-related felonies, and unwed parents under age 18 who do not live with an adult or attend school. In addition, newcomers from states with lower benefit amounts can be given the lower amount for up to 12 months.[14]

Much has been made of the success of the TANF programs in getting welfare recipients into jobs and off the welfare rolls. In recent legislative proposals to reauthorize TANF, Congress found that: (1) there had been dramatic increases in the employment and earnings of current and former welfare recipients; (2) welfare dependency had plummeted; and (3) the teen birth rate had dropped.[15] Given the threat the states face of lost funding, the strict time limits for benefits, the numerous reasons that can be employed to deny or terminate benefits, and a booming economy, it is not particularly surprising that the number of welfare recipients decreased in the years immediately following the creation of TANF. Yet, these touted successes also expose two fundamental weaknesses in the PRWORA. First, a prolonged economic downturn will reveal the dark side of denying poor people the economic assistance they need when unemployment is rising and few low-wage jobs are available. In fact, since 2000, as the threat of an economic recession has ebbed and flowed, caseloads have increased, work participation rates have declined, and the percentage of welfare recipients who are minorities has increased.[16]

A recent study by the Center on Budget Policy and Priorities assessing the outcome of TANF after 10 years states that the results are "more mixed than often understood" and finds that (1) child poverty increased significantly between 2000 and 2004, as did the number of children who live on incomes below half of the poverty line; (2) employment rates among single mothers were higher than they were in the mid-1990s but have fallen since 2000, and single mothers who leave TANF tend to remain poor or near-poor; (3) from 1996 to 2003 the number of single mothers who neither worked nor received welfare in an average month increased; and (4) 57 percent of the decline in caseloads during the first decade of welfare reform reflects a decline in the extent to which families who are poor enough to qualify for TANF participate in the program, rather than a reduction in the number of poor families who qualify for aid.[17]

Another disturbing aspect of the legislation is the social engineering that ties TANF benefits to "appropriate behavior" among aid recipients. The issues of decline in traditional marriage, increase in out-of-wedlock births, and changes in sexual morality are causing problems and challenges throughout American society. Yet it is the poor who are being punished for not living up to values the rest of the society seems anxious to reject. Denying benefits to poor children as a way of punishing their mothers, for example, reveals the importance of the "ideology of undeservingness" as an underlying rationale for this change in public policy.[18]

In order to understand the true import of the PWROWA, one must confront four important cultural realities about how Americans view poverty and poor people. Two of them deal with the impact racism has on Americans' attitudes toward poverty. First, since the 1960s, which was the point in U.S. history during which urban, nonwhite poor people became particularly visible to mainstream society, there has been an expanded notion of undeservingness within the dichotomy of the deserving and undeserving poor.[19] Second, all discussions of welfare policy are either implicitly or explicitly racialized. Standard tropes about the poor (e.g., "welfare queen") are racially charged and, when used in public life, are designed to decrease voter sympathy for the poor by manipulating racial fears.

The remaining two issues isolate key cultural traits that form political attitudes. First, because American society and culture are fundamentally materialist in their orientation, the assessment of poor people's membership in the broader community tends to be based on material costs and benefits. Second, any concept of the common good in our culture that might offer the poor a meaningful sense of belonging tends to be undermined by American individualism and libertarianism, which has made most Americans highly tolerant of huge disparities of wealth and generally unsympathetic to investment in public goods that might be of particular benefit to poor people.

Racism and the Poor: More Undeserving, Less "White," More Threatening

Until the 1960s, the U.S. welfare system reflected the nation's explicitly racist culture. The welfare needs of African Americans and other nonwhite groups were often completely ignored in some states, typically in the South, while in others discretionary rules were manipulated to deny or limit benefits.[20] The "deserving poor" that the system was designed to help were married, white women who had lost wage-earner husbands and needed to support legitimate children. There was no question that these "respectable" women should stay at home to raise their offspring and that this activity should be encouraged by providing financial assistance. Poor nonwhites, however, were generally expected to fend for themselves. The social and political upheaval of the 1960s forced American society to engage nonwhites and the poor as full citizens endowed with rights, regardless of entrenched racial stereotypes or the perceived immorality of their lifestyles. Over time, however, the expansion of welfare to minorities and the high concentration of the nonwhite poor in the urban ghettoes of rapidly growing cities made welfare policy the repository of the nation's unresolved and increasingly unspoken racial demons: "To understand public opposition to welfare then, we need to understand the public's perception of welfare recipients.... First, the American public thinks most people who receive welfare are black, and second, the public thinks blacks are less committed to the work ethic than other Americans. There exists now a widespread perception that welfare has become a 'code word' for race."[21]

The image of the typical welfare recipient in the United States has become the black single mother whose children have different, absent fathers.[22] For much of our society, "poor" is simply a way of saying "black" at a time when Americans' conceptions of liberal neutrality increasingly reject the idea of race-specific remedies and language when addressing social problems.[23] We are loath to acknowledge either the essential role of race-based chattel slavery and racial segregation in the formation of the nation's identity and culture or the racism inherent in our attitude toward the poor. The image of poor people has long been politically and culturally manipulated to create the impression that most are undeserving because they are unwilling to work (lazy and irresponsible—traits often culturally attributed to black men) and insist on having children out of wedlock that they cannot support (promiscuous and matriarchal—traits often culturally attributed to black women). The work requirements, punitive time limits, and emphasis on "behavior modification" through the encouragement of traditional marriage and abstinence education become somewhat more loaded when properly situated in an honestly rendered American cultural context.

Because a large percentage of white Americans believe blacks are lazy, the identification of blacks with poverty becomes a way of releasing mainstream society from any moral responsibility or communal obligation for the poor and their circumstances: "Long before the birth of the welfare state, the defenders of slavery argued that blacks were unfit for freedom because they were too lackadaisical to survive on their own. This stereotype has been traced by social psychologists through generations of white Americans. Although some evidence suggests it is not as widespread as it once was, the belief that blacks lack a commitment to the work ethic remains a popular perception among whites . . . and an important influence in their political attitudes."[24]

These political attitudes are rooted in the American individualist ideology, which, while not rejecting in principle the concept of welfare for those who "deserve" to be helped, places an inordinately high value on self-sufficiency and "making it on your own." Groups or individuals who question that ideology (either explicitly or implicitly) and those who labor under certain culturally constructed stereotypes that suggest they are insufficiently hardworking are immediately suspect and tagged as undeserving.[25]

"They Are Not My Poor": Individualism, Materialism, and a Weak Sense of Community

Along with the problem of dishonesty regarding race, many Americans also refuse to recognize that the aggressive promotion of individual autonomy in American life has undermined traditional family structures and other communal support systems that were once an essential part of the nation's social stability. The breakdown in community life has manifested itself in a number of ways, and no social group has escaped the consequences of a broad retreat from long-term marital commitment, family obligation, employment security, and civic participation.[26] However, the weakest members of society have suffered the most from these changes. Children, for example, suffer disproportionately from poverty and family breakdown.[27]

Furthermore, the rhetoric of the welfare reform debate and the plain language of the PRWORA demonstrate that materialism distorts community life and culture. Materialism has led to a certain idealization and objectification of work as the primary means of achieving social status (money) and meaning in one's life. Nonparticipation in the wage labor market is seen as parasitic and leads to social ostracism, except in certain highly circumscribed contexts (such as a married woman raising young children).[28] Thus, the position of the poor in society tends to be evaluated on the basis of a rigid cost/benefit analysis that sees poor people as either net contributors to the nation's material wealth or as drains on taxpayer resources. American culture offers the poor two primary ways of understanding their role in the broader community: as independent workers who help to create personal and societal wealth or as dependent parasites who draw on collective resources they did not help to create and therefore do not deserve.[29]

One pointed critique of welfare demonstrates the importance many Americans place on individual autonomy and a limited role for government in relieving social ills. Libertarians have argued that attempts to secure economic entitlements through rights language distorts the traditional idea of rights by moving away from an emphasis on political liberties. Self-styled "traditional" or "classical" liberals view rights as shields or weapons designed to protect individuals from the tyranny of the state, and they tend to see the creation of entitlements as an ill-conceived effort to free individuals from the consequences of life's inevitable harms, leading to the creation of "welfare rights."[30] This critique is closely related to a broader neoconservative model of civil society that also sees rights primarily as tools of defense against the state and identifies the freedom of civil society with economic liberalism and the free market.[31]

In his book *False Dawn*, John Gray makes a particularly scathing critique of the attempt by many American conservatives to recast free-market capitalism as a fundamental underpinning of liberal democracy and individual freedom:

> American capitalism [is] freedom in action. The structure of the American free market coincide[s] with the imperatives of human rights. Who dares condemn the burgeoning inequalities and social breakdown that free markets engender, when free markets are no more than the right to individual freedom in the economic realm?
>
> The philosophical foundations of these rights are flimsy and jerry-built. There is no credible theory in which the particular freedoms of deregulated capitalism have the standing of universal rights. The most plausible conceptions of rights are not founded on seventeenth-century ideas about property but on modern notions of autonomy. Even these are not universally applicable; they capture the experience only of those cultures and individuals for whom the exercise of personal choice is more important than social cohesion, the control of economic risk or any other public good.[32]

When the tenets of free-market capitalism become inseparable from the rhetoric of individual freedom, inequalities that are exacerbated by capitalism start to be seen as a necessary cost of democracy. Efforts by the state to temper economic inequalities in the interest of promoting other communal and public goods are seen as a "tyrannical" exercise of state power against the rights of free citizens.[33] This is where the American model of "freedom," the product of a general propensity toward an absolutist construction of rights, begins to reveal its tendency to breed selfishness, greed, and an indifference to the human needs of the poor. As Mary Ann Glendon has written, this "illusion of abso-luteness promotes unrealistic expectation, heightens social conflict, and in-hibits dialogue that might lead towards consensus, accommodation, or at least the discovery of common ground. . . . In its relentless individualism, it fosters a climate that is inhospitable to society's losers, and that systematically disad-vantages caretakers and dependents."[34]

American society has drifted so deeply into an absolutist construction of personal freedom that there is widespread public support for a "reform" of welfare that, in a purported effort to "help," places tremendous burdens on the poor, particularly mothers of young children, while asking almost nothing of the broader society. It also rejects a rich, humanistic understanding of community membership or citizenship for poor people, one that might value them as something beyond wage laborers or a drain on the public fisc, and it prevents the realization of many of the capacities that Nussbaum sees as fundamental to a truly meaningful human existence or "good life."

Justice and Participation for the American Poor: Paul Ricoeur's Ethics and the Catholic Vision of Solidarity

Paul Ricoeur's Ethics and Welfare Reform

Paul Ricoeur defines ethical intention as "aiming at the good life, with and for others, in just institutions."[35] He notes further that "the 'good life' is for each of us the nebulas of ideas and dreams of achievements with regard to which a life is held to be more or less fulfilled or unfulfilled."[36] Moreover, "it is in unending work of interpretation applied to action and to oneself that we pursue the search for adequation between what seems to us to be best with regard to our life as a whole and the preferential choices that govern our practices. . . . [B]etween our aim of a good life and our particular choices a sort of hermeneutical circle is traced by virtue of the back and forth motion between our idea of the 'good life' and the most important decisions of our existence."[37]

On the ethical plane, Ricoeur calls this concept of self-interpretation "self-esteem." From self-esteem, individuals move to the idea of *solicitude* for others, which is "benevolent spontaneity, intimately related to self-esteem within the framework of the aim of the 'good' life."[38] Self-esteem is thus given a dialogic dimension. For Ricoeur, solicitude is not simply an additional virtue added to self-esteem. Solicitude and self-esteem exist in critical relationship, and the two cannot be experienced or reflected upon one without the other.[39]

What makes individuals worthy of esteem is not their accomplishments but their "capacity," which is the ability to evaluate and judge oneself to be good. This judgment needs the mediating role of others to move from capacity to realization. Ricoeur's idea of capacity is intimately related to the creation of a just society. Individuals must be "capable" in order to develop the virtue of self-esteem, upon which so much of Ricoeur's ethical framework rests. Ricoeur notes that this mediating role is critical for political theory:

> [M]any philosophies presuppose a subject, complete and already fully endowed with rights before entering into society. It results that this subject's participation in community life is in principle contingent and revocable and that the individual . . . is correct in expecting from the state the protection of rights constituted outside of him or her, without bearing any intrinsic obligation to participate in the burdens related to perfecting the social bond. [This hypothesis fails] to recognize the *mediating* role of others between capacity and realization.[40]

For individuals, the quest for the good life involves working toward the virtues of self-esteem and solicitude, but this pursuit extends to institutions as well. Institutions are the points of application for the virtue of justice, which extends solicitude for the other to relationships with people that one does not know and may not see. The wish to live well in just institutions arises from the same level of morality as the desire for personal fulfillment and the reciprocity of friendship.[41] When we consider the issue of justice at an institutional level, a key concern is the problem of the just distribution of social goods.[42] Central to this problem is the heterogeneous nature of these goods and the need to determine a means of distribution of benefits and burdens among individuals in a society.[43] The ethical core of distributive justice is equality: "Equality, however it is modulated, is to life in institutions what solicitude is to interpersonal relations."[44]

The "social contract" political philosophies that Ricoeur critiques in his ethics hark back to the libertarian attacks on entitlement rights in the United States, where libertarian understandings of rights often dominate political and social policy debates and have had a profound affect on discussions of welfare reform. In Ricoeur's terms, these views demonstrate a lack of appreciation for the centrality of the mediating role of others, both in the individual quest for the good life and in the effort to create just institutions. This reality is central to understanding how social, economic, and political exclusion affect poor people in America and limit their capacities as understood by both Ricoeur and Nussbaum. Full participation in the structures of society is essential for not only the poor themselves but also their fellow citizens: "Without institutional mediation, individuals are only the initial drafts of human persons. Their belonging to a political body is necessary to their flourishing as human beings and this mediation cannot be revoked. On the contrary, the citizens who issue from this institutional mediation can only wish that every human being should, like them, enjoy such political mediation, which when added to the necessary conditions stemming from a philosophical anthropology, becomes a sufficient condition for the transition from the capable human being to a real citizen."[45]

Justice demands that the poor be fully participating members of society. In many ways, welfare reform limits their social participation by restricting their freedom to completely explore their human capacities. It is highly questionable that forcing poor mothers to work allows these women (or their children for that matter) to thoroughly exercise the capacities necessary to develop self-esteem and solicitude for others. This is not to say that under no circumstances is it appropriate for mothers who receive public assistance to work, only that a government policy that *mandates* employment in return for benefits takes a very limited view of the capacities of poor people and their role in society. When their freedom is curbed in this way, it is appropriate to question both the justice of society's institutional structures and the equitable distribution of social goods in the United States. The principle of solidarity in Catholic social thought offers additional ways to think about justice and participation for the American poor that might provide some answers to these questions.

Solidarity, the Common Good, and Christian Ethics

A Catholic understanding of rights begins with the notion of the inherent dignity of the human person, who is created in the image and likeness of God. "Rights and duties come to every human, in the first place, not based on the grounds of another social contract, but based on humans' origin."[46] Inseparable from this concept of *imago Dei* is that of human beings as intrinsically social. "Sociality is understood to be as essential a part of our humanity as rationality. That is, the person is viewed relationally—by the relationships he or she has with God, other persons, other creatures."[47]

Thus, Catholicism takes a communitarian view of people and rejects a contractarian notion of social relations, which echoes Ricoeur's understanding of the essential mediating role of others in the full development of the individual. The "communitarian perspective of Catholic social teaching has led the Church to place all rights within the context of community and to endorse a broader array of rights than the classical liberal account of rights founded on personal liberty. . . . The Catholic concern for a person's ability to participate in the life of a community rather than any individualistic notion of freedom abstracted from social relations offers an alternative formulation of entitlement rights."[48]

Theologian David Hollenbach directly addresses the exclusion of the urban poor from mainstream American life and argues that "a revival of a commitment to the common good and a deeper sense of solidarity are preconditions for significant improvement in the lives of the poor in the large cities of the United States."[49] The concept of the common good flows directly from the Catholic understanding of our sacredness and sociability: "The good of the individual never stands *against* the good of society. . . . Being thrown into each other's company is not a humiliation; letting one's self be helped belongs to magnanimity. Humans desire to stand in a relation of exchange with each other and to share their thoughts and possessions with others."[50] Translating this idea to the current circumstances of American public life Hollenbach notes that, "the common good of the public life is the realization of the human capacity for intrinsically valuable relationships, not only a fulfillment of the needs and deficiencies of individuals."[51]

Hence, the Catholic conception of the common good stresses the inherent value of human relationships: "The common good, therefore, is not simply a means for attaining the private good of individuals; it is a value to be pursued for its own sake. This suggests that a key aspect of the common good can be described as the *good of being a community at all*—the good realized in the mutual relationships in and through which human beings achieve their well-being."[52]

Human sacredness and the common good demand a recognition of and an ongoing response to the legacy of slavery and racism inherent in American culture, as well as an acknowledgment of how this legacy continues to demean individuals and detract from the common good. Furthermore, members of the community who are socially isolated or unable to participate in community life because they lack basic security, food, health care, or housing are also incapable of participating fully (if at all) in the good that is democratic self-governance.[53] "In other words, the common good of a republic fulfills needs that individuals cannot fulfill on their own and simultaneously realizes non-instrumental values that can only be attained in our life together."[54]

In his encyclical *Sollicitudo rei socialis,* Pope John Paul II described the Catholic idea of solidarity as a recognition of the moral value of the interdependence among individuals and nations. The virtue of solidarity "is a firm and persevering determination to commit oneself to the common good; that is to say to the good of all and of each individual because we are all really responsible for all."[55] Moreover, "the exercise of solidarity *within each society* is valid when its members recognize one another as persons. Those who are more influential, because they have a greater share of goods and common services, should feel responsible for the weaker and be ready to share with them all they possess. Those who are weaker, for their part, in the same spirit of solidarity, should not adopt a purely *passive* attitude or one that is *destructive* of the social fabric, but while claiming their legitimate rights, should do what they can for the good of all."[56]

Solidarity is about sharing one's life with others. The sense of responsibility and reciprocity that solidarity requires does not grow out of vague emotion or intellectual engagement but a lived experience of community.[57] Together with the common good, solidarity forms the foundation from which Catholic social teaching promotes societal obligations to the poor. These are not private notions of charity but affirmative obligations to bring the poor into full community membership in the life of a democratic republic by engaging their humanity, calling them to responsible citizenship and participation, and sharing material goods. When viewed in tandem with this aspect of Catholic social teaching, Ricoeur's ethics add a philosophical rationale for a commitment to solidarity that emphasizes the essential nature of engagement with others in the quest for an ethical life for individuals and in the creation of a society rooted in justice and equality.

The current state of American culture and civic life, both of which lack a coherent understanding of the common good, make solidarity with the poor quite difficult. Hollenbach uses the example of the isolation of poor people in urban areas as one particularly obvious example of how the structures of our society deny social justice to the impoverished, whom most metropolitan areas quarantine in certain disfavored areas. This structure is maintained and enhanced through various mechanisms, particularly archaic forms of local government and systems of funding for public services and schools that rely on property taxes; this then allows wealthy localities to hoard revenue for the exclusive benefit of their residents.[58] Recognizing this reality, Hollenbach argues that the minimal demands of justice require "lowering the structural and economic barriers that prevent the inner-city poor from sharing in the common good of their larger metropolitan areas."[59] Moreover, "this marginalization of the inner-city poor is one measure of how far short the metropolitan areas of the United States are falling from being communities whose citizens are treated with the respect they deserve. The willingness of the well-off to tolerate such conditions and even take actions that perpetuate them shows how far the larger citizenry of the United States is from an effective commitment to the common good."[60]

Welfare reform in the United States is a product of a limited view of the various possibilities for socially integrating poor people. It also reflects an impoverished notion of the shared sacrifice required to foster the solidarity that would lead to true social justice. In Ricoeur's terms, the poor are not valued because of their lack of material accomplishments, and there is little concern for the need to develop the broad range of their capacities. Welfare reform understands the role of poor people primarily in material and punitive terms.

Unable to construct an honest, shared narrative about the nation's ongoing struggle with its legacy of slavery and racism, as well as to recognize the role of racism in the persistence of poverty, American politicians use coded racialist imagery to pander to voters' prejudices, make financial assistance unpopular, and keep the poor at society's margins. Unable to confer meaning and value on virtues like self-esteem, solicitude, and social and cultural life, Americans support a welfare reform that sends poor mothers with children into the workforce so that they can justify their membership in the broader society by earning their keep. Unwilling to fund public services that they do not use, Americans consign the impoverished to isolation and degradation by expecting people without automobiles to have mobility in a car-dependent society; expecting those without decent schools to thrive in an educational meritocracy that favors the wealthy; and expecting those without money to accept without question the values of free-market liberalism.

Paul Ricoeur's ethics and Catholic social teaching offer a different vision, one in which the entire society assumes responsibility for access to decent public goods for all as one of the obligations of living in community. It is a vision that recognizes the human potential of the poor by focusing on their human capacities in ways that move beyond cost-benefit analysis and in which the objective flaws of the current economic and social structure are not regarded as acceptable prices for an atomized view of personal freedom. It is a vision that sees government as more than a referee for the aggressive pursuit of individual self-interest and in which the poor are not viewed with pity or scorn but seen as essential participants in the work of creating a truly just society.

5

Fear of the Other

Immigrants, Parvenus, and Plutocrats

Late in 2005 the Republican-controlled House of Representatives
passed the "Border Protection, Anti-terrorism, and Illegal Immigration Control Act of 2005," which turned out to be one of the most
polarizing pieces of immigration legislation the nation had seen in
decades. Among its most controversial provisions were the following:
Illegal immigrants would be charged as felons, as would those who
assisted or harbored them; all illegal immigrants who were appre-
hended would be detained at the border; pathways to legal citizenship for immigrants currently in the country illegally would be
severely restricted; no "guest worker" or amnesty programs would
be implemented; and, finally, two-layer fences would be constructed
along 700 miles of the U.S.-Mexican border.[1]

The legislation sent tremors through the country and revealed
that the American people continue to be deeply divided on the question of how one becomes a member of American society, a matter
of fundamental importance to the nation's future. In particular, the
legislation and the debate surrounding it demonstrated the inconsistency between the key political goals of the Right and orthodox
Christian understandings of human dignity. As if to emphasize the
point, shortly before the passage of the legislation, the chairman of
the Committee on Migration for the U.S. Conference of Catholic
Bishops, Bishop Gerald Barnes of San Bernardino, California,
stated that "behind these punitive provisions are people and families who will suffer needlessly. Immigrants—even those without

legal status—are not criminals."[2] Once the legislation passed, Cardinal Roger Mahoney of Los Angeles expressed the outrage of much of the Catholic hierarchy. The cardinal instructed his priests to defy provisions of the law that would require them to check for residency documents before administering certain kinds of assistance, and he stated in no uncertain terms that a Catholic could not in good conscience vote for the bill.[3] When asked whether this was a matter of prudential judgment upon which reasonable Catholics might disagree, Cardinal Mahoney responded by saying it was not: "It's an absolute because it is so punitive. It punishes people for being here in ways we have never discussed in this country. We've never had this kind of thing, ever."[4]

In the months that followed, the Senate, through a remarkable display of bipartisanship, attempted to draft compromise legislation that would soften some of the harshest aspects of the House bill. Throughout the spring, the Senate negotiated with the House in an effort to pass immigration reform legislation that politicians on both sides of the aisle agreed was long overdue. Yet, even among Senate Republicans there was deep division over these modifications.[5] "Cultural conservatives," the unassuming moniker under which the Republican Party's nativist element tends to gather, were determined to punish undocumented immigrants for their "criminal" behavior of crossing the border "without papers." They were even willing to withdraw support from President Bush in order to demonstrate their displeasure with his more moderate stance. President Bush had attempted, with little success, to take a compassionate position toward undocumented immigrants, one that sought to reconcile the costs and benefits of widespread illegal immigration. Yet, the House Republicans refused to follow his leadership, and many of them saw any attempt to legalize the status of undocumented immigrants as an unacceptable "amnesty" for "criminals."[6]

Reporting in the *Wall Street Journal*, June Kronholz offered an analysis that cast a harsh, unflattering light on the ultimate result of the House Republicans' push for immigration "reform" on their terms. After describing anti-immigrant demonstrations in New Jersey that had drawn supporters waving Confederate flags and giving Nazi salutes, she detailed a growing sense among many policy watchers in Washington that a racist and nativist Pandora's box had now been opened: "By raising illegal immigration as a political and national security issue—and then doing nothing about it—Congress has given new life to an anti-immigrant movement that had long been relegated to the political fringes."[7]

In fairness, however, the Congress was not completely unwilling to do something about immigration. As the November 2006 elections approached and it became clear that immigration was an issue that "had legs" among voters around the country, Congress pushed through legislation that authorized the construction of a 700-mile fence along the nation's border with Mexico. The "Secure Fence Act" took off in the congressional rush to adjourn for the elections.[8] It required the Department of Homeland Security to construct a double-layered fence from Calexico, California, to Douglas, Arizona, by the end of 2008 at an estimated cost of $6 billion, with initial funding of $1.2 billion separately allocated in a homeland security spending bill.[9] In late October of 2006 President Bush signed the legislation into law.[10]

Given the extraordinary cost of the fence and the Democrats' accession to the control of the Congress following the 2006 midterm elections, the project faces an uncertain future. Once again Congress failed to enact comprehensive immigration reform in 2007, and any realistic possibility for a meaningful reckoning with the nation's immigration problem will no doubt depend on the results of the 2008 presidential election. Regardless of political changes in the future, however, the Secure Fence Act remains as a reflection of the coarse state of certain aspects of democracy and political rhetoric in the United States, and its existence should give pause to anyone who believes that the humanity of immigrants is not affected by how they choose to cross a border. Through its leadership on this particular piece of legislation, the right wing of the Republican Party offered the nation a clear-eyed view of some of its core values.

Furthermore, the bipartisan support for the Secure Fence Act revealed a Congress and a president unable to exercise the leadership necessary to explain the consequences of the nation's quest for global economic leadership with reference to a free-market model. Instead, voters who were angry about the dislocations of the global economy were encouraged by their congressional representatives to blame the weakest links in the economic chain—undocumented immigrants from developing countries—for seeking employment in wealthy nations like the United States, which is exactly what the neoliberal model predicts and requires. It is easier to allow Mexicans to be cast as "barbarians at the gate" rather than reckon with our nation's role in the maintenance of economic structures that make undocumented immigration inevitable. It would be more difficult yet for Americans to consider how their individual choices contribute to the problem.

If all of this were not troubling enough, Christians have additional reasons to be outraged by the congressional response to immigration. Among the key proponents of the most punitive anti-immigration proposals during the 109th Congress were legislators closely aligned to the Religious Right. For instance, J. D. Hayworth, who lost his seat in the 2006 election, was a key leader in the passage of the "Border Protection, Anti-terrorism, and Illegal Immigration Control Act of 2005 " and had supported every issue on the Family Research

Council's legislative agenda. Founded by well-known Christian evangelical leaders like James Dobson and led in the past by right-wing Republican political activists like Gary Bauer, the Family Research Council states that its mission is to promote "family, faith, and freedom" and the "Judeo-Christian world view as the basis of a just, free, and stable society."[11]

Although much of its legislative agenda revolves around issues related to abortion, stem-cell research, same-sex marriage, and various initiatives to support a more prominent role for religion in public life, the Family Research Council also endorses repeal of the inheritance tax (or what is known in right-wing political circles as the "death tax"), reduction in funds for the National Endowment for the Arts, and a highly partisan United Nations reform plan championed by Congressman Henry Hyde, which withholds long-promised funding from the organization (a proposal that was denounced by the late Jeanne Kirkpatrick, a Republican who served as U.S. ambassador to the United Nations in the Reagan administration).[12]

Another particularly prominent House Republican supporter of punitive immigration legislation and one who has retained his congressional seat is Representative Tom Tancredo, the grandson of Italian immigrants. Tancredo has been a cosponsor of a number of key legislative initiatives promoted by the Family Research Council, and during the 109th Congress he supported the council on all of its key legislative initiatives.[13] During his political career, Tancredo has suggested eliminating public schools, bombing Mecca in retaliation for terrorism, and abolishing birthright citizenship, and he has called for the deployment of U.S. troops along the Mexican border.[14] His views dominated the House Republicans' concept of immigration legislation during the 109th Congress, and the success of the Secure Fence Act represents a triumph of his vision. According to *The Economist:*

> Mr. Tancredo's rise is a disaster for Republican politics because it threatens to expose Republican divisions while alienating Latinos, who are America's largest and fastest growing minority.... But it is a disaster that could get bigger. Mr. Tancredo reflects the fears of millions of Americans: that immigrants steal jobs, over-burden public services, and increasingly refuse to assimilate. He has a dedicated army of supporters, from Minutemen to America First activists. And he's threatening to run for the presidency. "Pitchfork" Pat Buchanan demonstrated the strength of the nativist streak in the Republican party back in 1992, when he won 37% of the vote in the New Hampshire primary against "King George" Bush.[15]

Once again, the class resentment that has been central to the transformation of the Republican Party in recent decades has reared its ugly head. This
time, however, the targets are perceived social inferiors, as well as the old-line
elites, like the Bushes, whose patrician social status limits the effects of immigration on their lives and whose economic interests are promoted by the
presence of undocumented immigrants in the labor force. A theme familiar in
American politics is being replayed in which primarily middle- and working-
class whites have set their interests against an "other" they perceive as
threatening and undesirable. Traditionally, African Americans have played the
"other" role, but as the Latino population has grown in the United States,
undocumented immigrants have taken on a similar status. White "cultural
conservatives" sense abandonment by their party's social and money elites at a
crucial point in the culture war. People they believe should be their allies
(based on a shared culture or, more appropriately in the American context,
shared "whiteness") are siding with Latino migrants, whom they perceive as a
threat to important interests of working- and middle-class Republican voters in
a way that African Americans no longer are.[16]

In order for any nation-state to maintain political integrity, it must be able
to manage its borders and determine the criteria upon which men and women
become citizens. In this respect, few would argue the legitimacy of congressional scrutiny of U.S. immigration law and policy on a regular basis. Nevertheless, the language employed by some on the Right to discuss the problem of
undocumented immigration makes it abundantly clear that this discussion is
not simply about the management of the nation's borders and the orderly
assimilation of new immigrants into the mainstream economy and culture.
The title of the original House bill explains a great deal.

The "Border Protection, Anti-terrorism, and Illegal Immigration Act" is
really as much about fear and scapegoating as it is about immigration. More
and more Americans have become agitated about the risks that the nation's
"porous" southern border poses to U.S. security. Fear of additional terrorist
acts in the wake of the atrocities of September 11 has caused many to seek
solace in an isolationist impulse that provides security behind fortress walls.
This immigration legislation uses legitimate concerns about terrorism to accomplish an objective that bears little relationship to the immigration issue
broadly understood. When a link is forged between immigration and terrorism, the immigrant as the alien "other" is absorbed into the amorphous but
extremely threatening outsider categories of "criminal" and "terrorist." What is
particularly useful about these categorizations is that, under our current
leadership, which has nurtured the heightened sense of fear that September 11

produced, criminal and terrorist others have been subjected to incessant de-humanization.

The vast majority of undocumented immigrants to the United States come from Mexico and Central America. Approximately 60 percent, or about six million people, are from Mexico, and just under 600,000 come from the Central American nations of Guatemala and El Salvador.[17] Thus, nearly 70 percent of the undocumented workforce in the United States comes from Mexico and neighboring countries to the south. Most of these immigrants are dark skinned, which makes them an easily identifiable "other" once one moves away from the major cities and border areas.[18] Some of the most extreme House Republican voices on these issues have come from congressional districts in the inland West and Southwest, places like Arizona:

> In Arizona, it becomes evident the battle over illegal immigration is, in one of its dimensions, a battle over the future of the Republican party in the state, and because of [Republican Senator] John McCain's ambitions, nationally as well. It also becomes evident that what anti-immigration zealots call an "invasion" is not in spite of federal policies but, at least in Arizona, partly because of them. For 12 years the Border Patrol has deliberately funneled the immigration flow away from settled urban areas like El Paso and San Diego...into the Arizona deserts, where intruders can be more easily spotted, tracked, and apprehended by its officers.[19]

Although it has been a state for less than a century, Arizona has long nurtured some of the United States' important right-wing political movements, and Arizona senator Barry Goldwater is often credited with reviving American conservatism in the early 1960s. In recent decades, Arizona has become a magnet for Sunbelt migrants from the East and the Midwest, as well as for economic migrants from California fleeing its high cost of living and oftentimes the extraordinary diversity of its population. Despite the suburban sprawl of greater Phoenix, which offers the homogenizing comforts of an American anyplace, Arizona is a state that borders Mexico, and it has been part of a North American Latino culture and geography that long predates its statehood. This makes it a logical landing place for Mexican migrants and a tinderbox for an increasingly angry nativist reaction against undocumented Mexican immigrants from more recent Anglo-American arrivals, many of whom seem blithely unaware of or unconcerned about the human dimension of the cheap labor that builds the houses, maintains the golf courses, and cleans the pools that make their sunny and relatively inexpensive lifestyle so appealing.

Of course, the phenomenon of undocumented immigration is a global one, and it now impacts areas of the country that have rarely seen significant immigration populations since their original European settlers. In recent years the South and rural Midwest have seen huge increases in their populations of Mexican and Central American immigrants. From 1990 to 2000 the states with the largest increases in their Hispanic populations were North Carolina (449 percent), Arkansas, Georgia, Tennessee, South Carolina, Nevada, and Alabama (229 percent).[20] The fact that Hispanic immigration is growing fastest in the heretofore relative cultural homogeneity of the Deep South is particularly noteworthy. This area of the country has traditionally had strong nativist tendencies, and the white populations of these states also tend to be Republican or Republican leaning. Moreover, apart from Nevada, these states have only very recently moved beyond a history of legalized segregation and a fairly simplistic black/white racial dichotomy that was at least unified by a common regional culture.

The cultural unity of the South, as well as parts of the Midwest, is being transformed by immigration. Much of the Hispanic immigration in the South is to rural areas, and it is not unreasonable to infer that some of the growing backlash against the newcomers is the result of their penetrating ever more deeply into parts of the country that have not traditionally been immigrant destinations. In fairness, however, large percentages of the U.S. population are uncomfortable with these new arrivals. In 2006 the CBS news team reported that 75 percent of Americans believed that the government was not doing enough to keep illegal immigrants out of the country, and a majority said they were more likely to vote for a candidate who favored tighter controls on illegal immigration.[21] Therefore, this perceived threat posed by the "other" is more basic than the threat of Islam or terrorism or immigration; the threat is simply difference, which American culture has confronted many times before.

In his book on the current immigration "crisis," Samuel Huntington has asserted that the influx of Mexicans threatens to turn the United States into a bilingual and bicultural entity similar to Canada or Belgium, although he admits that Mexican relocation as a percentage of overall immigration does not approach the rates of Irish and German resettlement in the nineteenth century.[22] In the case of the latter two groups, there was indeed much public distress about the failure of both to assimilate, and fairly harsh tactics were employed against German Americans during World War I to speed the process.[23]

What about the Mexicans? Huntington argues that the situation of these most recent immigrants is very different. Not only are they less willing to assimilate into what he terms America's "Anglo-Protestant culture," but the mainstream is also exerting less pressure on them to do so. The United States has become a much more self-consciously multiethnic or pluralist society, and many immigrants have taken on what Huntington calls "ampersand" identities through dual citizenship and immersion in ethnic enclaves. This is particularly true for the many Mexican and Central American immigrants who are still relatively close geographically to their native countries and can (again due to their large numbers) easily remain immersed within their native cultures while living and working in the United States. Huntington argues that these trends are so profound that large areas of the United States could be subject to "Hispanization" in the coming decades:

> By the mid-twentieth century, America had become a multiethnic,
> multiracial society with an Anglo-Protestant mainstream culture
> encompassing many subcultures and with a common political creed
> rooted in that mainstream culture. In the late twentieth century,
> developments occurred that, if continued, could change America into
> a culturally bifurcated Anglo-Hispanic society with two national
> languages. This trend was in part the result of the popularity of the
> doctrines of multiculturalism and diversity among intellectual and
> political elites, and the government policies on bilingual education
> and affirmative action that those doctrines promoted and sanctioned.
> The driving force behind the trend toward cultural bifurcation,
> however, has been immigration from Latin America, especially from
> Mexico.[24]

Large absolute numbers of Mexican immigrants, Mexico's geographic contiguity to the United States, the significant presence of undocumented immigrants, and the heavy concentration of many of them in certain regions of the country all contribute in Huntington's view to a need to differentiate their situation from that of previous large immigrant waves and make the prospect of their assimilation much less certain: "As their numbers increase, Mexican Americans feel increasingly comfortable with their own culture and often contemptuous of American culture. They demand recognition of their culture and the historic Mexican identity of the American southwest. They increasingly call attention to and celebrate their Hispanic identity and Mexican past."[25] Huntington believes that these trends, left unchecked, will create a Hispanic North American identity that will compete for dominance with the traditional Anglo-American one.

One might easily take issue with Huntington simply by challenging his argument as alarmist and unduly attentive to the evidence of high levels of assimilation among Mexican immigrants, as other writers have.[26] A question Huntington avoids and one that calls into question the legitimacy of the concerns he raises is whether a society committed to liberal democratic values can embark on a campaign of fence building and militarization of its borders in order to preserve its "Anglo-American identity" while at the same time remaining committed to any coherent idea of human dignity or human rights. Politicians like J. D. Hayworth and Tom Tancredo managed to push through extremist anti-immigrant legislation by playing to the fears of an electorate discomforted by social and economic change. They also capitalized on the ease with which the poor and the different can be associated with crime, poverty, and public-aid dependency in American political rhetoric. Hayworth wrote a book titled *Whatever It Takes: Illegal Immigration, Border Security, and the War on Terror*, in which he argues that "rampant illegal immigration has a huge impact on crime and prison populations. It is an enormous burden on our health care, education, and welfare systems. It is changing our culture. But the biggest threat comes from the deadly combination of porous borders and weapons of mass destruction finding their way into the hands of terrorist groups."[27]

Hayworth also details the way in which illegal immigrants are, according to him, "hastening the downfall" of Social Security, stealing jobs from American workers, and taking advantage of public health and education benefits at the expense of U.S. citizens. Tancredo has written a book as well— *In Mortal Danger: The Battle for America's Border and Security*—which takes up the same basic question as Hayworth's. Tancredo focuses on the nation's moral and cultural decline, which he likens to Rome's, and he lays out threats to the nation's sovereignty posed by illegal immigration.[28] Longtime right-wing populist Patrick Buchanan has also added his voice to the debate in his more explicitly racialized *State of Emergency: The Third World Invasion and Conquest of America*. Buchanan also raises the spectre of the "Hispanization" of the Southwest, which could result from the uncontrolled immigration of Mexicans and other Latin Americans, and argues that the United States and the rest of the Western world are poised for mongrelization and cultural destruction by the poor of the Third World.[29]

The "othering" of immigrants through racialization and criminal association is fairly widespread in the wealthy nations of the West. In her book on immigration in southern Europe, Kitty Calavita explains that Third World immigrants in Spain and Italy live in the shadows and under suspicion, despite various efforts to provide them with conditional or temporary legal status. Many remain undocumented and underground, and even those who have some sort of legal status slip in and out of legality due to the temporary or contingent nature of their status, as well as the difficulty of obtaining the consistent work necessary for permanent residency.[30] Because they are seen primarily as workers serving an economic purpose, laws designed to offer them a legally recognized status often have the perverse effect of helping to maintain their poverty and exclusion by creating "a suspect population and invit[ing] a political backlash against this useful labor force, in part because such marginal populations present fiscal and social problems, and in part because of the ideological dissonance associated with the construction of an excluded underclass in these liberal democratic societies.[31]

In addition, Calavita argues that poverty and exclusion help to lead to criminalization because it sets immigrants apart, stigmatizes them, and produces a heightened visibility that makes them more likely to attract attention. In Italy, immigrants, who make up 3 percent of the population but constitute 30 percent of the prison population, are much more likely to be stopped, questioned, and arrested by the police because of physical characteristics that make it obvious that they "do not belong," and they are five times more likely than native Italian citizens to be convicted in court.[32] This is not to say that immigrants do not commit crimes or even that they do not commit proportionately more crime than the natives, but "immigrants are usually young men (with women now beginning to close the gender gap), a category that is more disposed to crime in every population. Whatever the causal factors that produce immigrant crime—demographics, labeling, hostility over mistreatment, economic desperation, or psychological distress—one thing is clear: it draws a disproportionate response from law enforcement and in turn reaffirms collective stereotypes of the immigrant as a potential criminal."[33]

As African Americans know so well, the "other" as criminal is often inseparable from poverty and racial stigmatization. Calavita argues that immigrants are marked by both their economic marginality and their perceived racial difference and are ultimately stigmatized as "not suitable" for inclusion. In the United States, whiteness became something that could be conferred on groups once the majority culture viewed them as having shed their undesirable attributes of poverty and criminality. In cases such as the Irish, racialized otherness bore no resemblance to the reality of skin color. The same can be said of certain immigrants in southern Europe. Racial otherness, according to Calavita, is not simply a product of phenotype:

> Contemporary immigrants to Spain and Italy are racialized through several interrelated processes, the broad outlines of which are similar to those of previous times and places—including those applied to Spanish and Italian immigrants to America and northern Europe less than a century ago. Among these processes is . . . criminalization. . . . The stigma of difference marks non-EU immigrants as highly visible

Others who are not only suspicious by virtue of their difference, but conspicuous in their strangeness. . . . Subject to economic marginality and its myriad deprivations, assumed to be prone to crime, and always in the spotlight, immigrants' criminalization is overdetermined by a factor of three, with the common denominator being their racialization.[34]

Like most Mexican and Central American migrants, the men who executed the tragedies of September 11 were dark skinned, "foreign" others. The American Right has, in the language of this legislation and in the rhetoric it now uses to discuss immigration, turned the nation's undocumented aliens into "criminals" who threaten the nation's "security." The slippery slope to "terrorists" hardly seems accidental, not to assert that undocumented aliens are terrorists per se but to draw an association of alien criminality that paints with a broad stroke. The strategy of associating dark-skinned people with crime and lawlessness also has a long and sordid history in U.S. politics, as does nativism, etched in our history in the legacy of the Ku Klux Klan.

Mexican and Central American immigration has been racialized in the United States through a growing popular and academic chorus that has raised an alarm about the loss of America's Anglo-American identity. Yet, Anglo-Protestant culture cannot hold the country together. First, it is arguable that any coherent understanding of such a culture still exists. Certainly its religious components are contested, with the rapid approach of the Anglican communion toward schism but one example of a breakdown on any consensus of the meaning of "Anglo-Protestantism." James Kurth has argued that American Protestantism, understood as part of a cultural consensus among the nation's elites, has "deformed" into "expressive individualism—with its contempt for and protest against all hierarchies, communities, traditions, and customs— [and] represents the logical conclusion and ultima ratio of the secularization of the Protestant religion. The Holy Trinity of original Protestantism, the Supreme Being of Unitarianism, and, finally, the United States of the American Creed have all been dethroned and replaced by the imperial self."[35]

Second, Anglo-Protestantism no longer supports a group identity and a cogent history that can bind the diverse cultural elements that now occupy American elite culture. For example, Canada has a much stronger claim to a history of a unified, self-consciously Anglo-Protestant and Anglophilic elite, but it does not seek to ground its future unity in this past. An Anglo-Protestant vision demeans or disregards the important contributions made by French Catholics and First Nations peoples to the creation of Canadian identity and nationhood. Pretending that there was an Anglo-Canadian halcyon era when "everything worked" is to deny important truths about the nation's history and is not a compelling basis from which to construct a future for a modern Canada. Indeed, even Britain is struggling to determine what it means to be British. British elites have come realize that Englishness, which gave rise to Anglo-Protestantism, cannot be a glue for a Britain of the future, for it does not even acknowledge the diversity represented by the Union Jack, much less the influence of the former empire's cultures, which have helped to turn London into one of the world's great cosmopolitan centers.

What is true about Canada and Britain is even more so for the United States. There are many reasons for rejecting the assertion of "Anglo-Protestant" identity as a unifying force in American life. A particularly compelling argument that takes us back to the nation's origins has to do with the nation's relationship to Africa and slavery. American identity was clearly a product of a relationship with Africanness and slavery in all of its economic, social, and moral ramifications, as well as with Englishness and Protestantism. A country that is not yet 150 years away from legalized and racialized slavery and only 40 years beyond rigid, legalized, racial segregation cannot dismiss the impact of these experiences in the construction of its identity. The inability of the United States to integrate the African and European aspects of its culture was in part represented by an Anglo-Protestant obsession with whiteness and racial hierarchy. Increasingly, Americans have tired of distorting their personal lives and histories in order to prop up Anglo-Protestant culture as a unifying ideal for the United States.

The immigration issue has also demonstrated the inherent instability of a Republican coalition formed of internationally oriented money elites and their nativist, culturally conservative, domestic political allies. Nevertheless, the Republicans in the House and Senate have been pushed to the right on this issue because a wellspring of support exists among their core voter constituencies for taking a hard line toward illegal immigration. What is startling is that, until recently, many voters, particularly among the white working and middle classes of the South, Midwest, and inland West who have been carefully cultivated by the Republican Party, have resisted linking their economic and social discontent to the money elites that have a prominent place in the Republican Party. Instead of asking hard questions about economic arrangements in the United States that have consistently favored the wealthy since the 1980s, many Americans have decided instead to vent their frustrations on the weakest group within the population: undocumented Mexican and Central American immigrants.

William Pfaff has described how the American market-capitalist model came into being through explicit political and ideological choices that embraced monetarist economic theory, rejected state intervention in society as inconsistent with human freedom, and adopted an individualist egoism that justified extreme income inequality: "This change transformed labor into an anonymous commodity and put both blue-collar and white-collar staff into competition with an effectively unlimited global labor supply, resulting in employment insecurity, reduced or static wages, diminished or eliminated benefits and pensions, and the destructive social pressures of falling living standards. In the United States, the new model of corporate business has evolved toward a form of crony capitalism, in which business and government interests are often corruptly intermingled."[36]

Income inequality in the United States has been expanding consistently since the 1970s, and the richest 1 percent of Americans take a larger share of the nation's earned income than at any time since 1928.[37] The share of income earned by the top 10 percent of U.S. income earners has grown by a third in the last 30 years, and during the same period, the share earned by the top 13,000 households earning more than $10.8 million has nearly quadrupled.[38] Two recent studies have found that the United States has the lowest rate of social mobility—defined as the relationship of a child's income to that of the parents—of all of the OECD (Organization for Economic Cooperation and Development) nations, and this is particularly true for Americans at the bottom of the income scale.[39] Yet, during the height of the row over immigration, President Bush signed a bill that extended tax cuts to the nation's wealthiest citizens worth $70 billion.[40]

Expelling illegal immigrants will do little to make Americans feel more secure about their futures in a world where international borders are increasingly porous and economic security for the average wage earner is ever more precarious. Yet, rather than turn their economic insecurity back on the nation's political and economic elites in demands for a more humane economic system, Americans have accepted the global, neoliberal model as a given and have, with the assistance of key members of the political establishment, directed their anger at an easily identifiable and easily punished "other." The issues of income inequality and immigration have also contributed to the polarization of politics. A recent study by social scientists at the Massachusetts Institute of Technology (MIT) has found that, as income inequality has grown in the United States, political polarization has increased as well. Since the 1980s, the Republican Party has become more conservative, and it has moved sharply away from redistributive policies:

Noncitizens today are growing in number, and they tend to be at the bottom of the income distribution. . . . The changing economic position of noncitizens is politically relevant. It is likely to contribute to the failure of the political process in the United States to generate redistribution that would eliminate growing disparities in wage and income inequality....The income of the median voter has *not* declined relatively over the last thirty years. How has the median voter's economic position been sustained while that of the median family has declined? Part of the answer...is that lower-income people are increasingly likely to be noncitizens. The median income of noncitizens has shifted sharply downward, and the fraction of the population that is noncitizen has increased dramatically.[41]

As economic inequality intensified over the last 30 years, Republicans became increasingly successful at the polls. During the same period both legal and illegal immigration grew dramatically, and the percentage of white or First World immigrants within the noncitizen group fell by half.[42] The noncitizen group became not only poorer but also "darker," making it that much easier to consign its members to outsider status. Although immigration alone does not explain the growth in income inequality or the heightened polarization of U.S. politics, a relationship between increased immigration and income inequality would help to explain Republican voters' enhanced hostility toward immigrants and the Democrats' diminished tolerance for them. During the same period, middle-income voters have seen a rise in their real income and wealth, and when taxing the income of the top earners or redistributing income to the poorest was at issue, public policies have moved in a less redistributive way.[43]

The Dignity of the Face: Strangers into Citizens

Migration has always been a part of life in human civilizations. Indeed, Christians should see in the lives of immigrants and migrants reminders of the life of Christ, who, along with Mary and Joseph, was forced to take refuge in Egypt to escape the wrath of King Herod.[44] The Hebrew Bible in particular is filled with stories that track various migrations of the Jewish people: "Migrants and refugees are a reminder that all of us before God are 'aliens and transients.' Their presence among us is a source of mutual enrichment for humanity as well as an encouragement toward dialogue and unity. Moreover, their presence is a sign of the Risen Christ. When people of different origins are welcomed, God is revealed."[45]

The current tone of the immigration debate should therefore be a cause of deep distress for Christians and perhaps even, as theologian Gregory Baum has suggested, a time for mourning. Christians should lament the economic and political structures in the United States that have so easily turned vulnerable human beings into instruments of economic gain, cheap political rhetoric, and nativist hate. Mourning is, nevertheless, an inadequate response, for Christians are also called to promote the common good and to do so in solidarity with those whose dignity is most threatened. The flow of undocumented laborers into the United States is part of a larger global phenomenon that is being repeated in most of the wealthy nations of the developed world. As the director of the Jesuit Migration Network, Father Rick Ryscavage, has noted:

> economic factors are central to any good analysis of migration. The economic gap between rich and poor countries continues to grow and this gap surely motivates migration. A migrant can earn a dramatically higher wage in the United States than inside Mexico. But to reduce the reasons behind migration to an individual economic choice would be highly misleading. The decision to migrate is so complex that it cannot be understood fully through the lens of one discipline like economics. Sociologists have consistently found that factors such as family reunification, physical safety, educational opportunities, and transnational social networks influence the decision to migrate.[46]

Nations throughout the developed world have become the logical focus of the aspirations of millions of people in the developing world who seek to better their economic prospects, further their educations, or escape violence and repressive political regimes. Perhaps if more Americans were better students of their own history, they might see among current migrants experiences that reflect stories within their own families and certainly reminders of great social upheavals that have beset the nation in the past. In the early and mid-twentieth century, the United States witnessed one of the greatest internal migrations in modern history when African Americans uprooted themselves from the rural South and moved to the urban centers of the Northeast and the Midwest. Although these migrants were nominally citizens, they lacked many basic citizenship rights, particularly in the South. Upon their arrival in the North, most were herded into ghettoes and forced to accept employment on terms that were much less favorable than those offered to whites. In many senses, African Americans were probably at least as foreign (and certainly no more welcome) to whites in the urban North as Mexican migrants are to many Americans today.

Despite these hardships, the migrants continued to stream out of the South, primarily for reasons identified by Father Ryscavage. No matter how bad life was in Chicago, New York, or Detroit, for many African Americans, leaving the South was simply a matter of survival and an essential quest in their effort to obtain a more dignified existence. Furthermore, many moved north to join parents, siblings, or other relatives who had already made the journey. But migrating to the northern states did not necessarily mean cutting off ties to the South. The fact that the migration occurred within the boundaries of one nation certainly made it easier to journey back and forth, although for many blacks, returning to the South presented real obstacles and risks.[47]

Yet, as social and economic conditions changed in the southern states, something rather dramatic occurred. By the end of the twentieth century, the flow of African Americans out of the South had reversed, as many of the original migrants and large numbers of their descendants returned to the states they had left long ago but clearly not forgotten.[48] Changing economic and social conditions in the South, a strong connection to the South as both a place and a culture, the loss of job opportunities in many northern urban centers, and disaffection with the anomie and violence of inner-city urban culture all contributed to the reversal.[49]

As we grapple with current immigration and relocation issues, the African American migration may well be instructive because the circumstances of African Americans in the early and mid-twentieth century, as well as the political and economic conditions of the South during that time, serve as an interesting proxy for the situations of many developing world migrants and nations today. The global "south" occupies a position in the world economic order that mirrors the South's former poverty within the United States. In their pastoral letter on immigration, the Catholic Bishops of Canada cited 2005 data from the United Nations that found that the one billion people in the developed world controlled 80 percent of the globe's gross domestic product, while the five billion people in the developing world shared the remaining 20 percent.[50]

Modern technology and transportation allow people to travel from poor areas in the global south to the wealthy nations in the global "north" with an ease and swiftness akin to domestic travel within the United States 50 or more years ago. Many of the migrants that come from Mexico and Central America make a trip by bus, train, automobile, or foot that would not have been unfamiliar to many African Americans who left the Deep South around the time of World War II. The experience of African Americans also raises the prospect that many migrants may one day return to their countries of origin should circumstances in those countries improve.

That people who face extreme economic and social difficulties will leave behind all that they know and love and endure tremendous hardship on a journey into the unknown is hardly surprising. The desire for a life of safety,

comfort, and dignity is universal, and Catholic social teaching has long recognized the right to emigrate, particularly when one's ability to sustain the
basic conditions necessary for a life of dignity is threatened. As the American
and Mexican bishops pointed out in their 2003 pastoral letter on immigration,
Strangers No Longer, Pope Pius XII affirmed this basic principle in modern
church teaching in his 1952 encyclical *Exsul familia*.[51] Pope John XXIII expanded on these ideas in *Pacem in terris*, when "he embraced the right to
migrate as well as the right to not have to migrate," while also placing limits on
migration "when there are just reasons for it."[52]

By John Paul II's papacy, there had been further elaboration on family
reunification, just wages, and undocumented migrants, and the current state
of Catholic social teaching can be further summarized as follows: "Institutions
in host countries must keep careful watch to prevent the spread of temptation
to exploit foreign laborers, denying them the same rights enjoyed by nationals,
rights that are to be guaranteed by all without discrimination. Regulating
immigration according to criteria of equity and balance is one of the indis-
pensable conditions for ensuring that immigrants are integrated into society
with the guarantees required by recognition of their human dignity. Immigrants are to be received as persons and helped, together with their families,
to become part of societal life."[53]

The choice that the world migration phenomenon poses for wealthy nations like the United States, if these nations are to truly commit themselves to
the logical extensions of their democratic commitments, is the one posed by
Michael Walzer in *Spheres of Justice:* "Can states run their economies with live-
in servants, guest workers excluded from the company of citizens?"[54] For
Walzer, the answer was clearly "no," and more than 20 years ago he recognized
the destabilizing effect on liberal democracy of the presence of large numbers
of individuals within the polity who had no chance of ever becoming citizens.
He argued that as a matter of political justice, democratic societies cannot
tolerate a status of permanent alienage, which is indeed the position the undocumented or "illegal" immigrant occupies in the United States today. This is
true for both individuals and groups. We must make certain choices if our
society is to remain committed to liberal democratic values:

> The process of self-determination through which a democratic state
> shapes its internal life must be open, and equally open, to all
> those men and women who live within its territory, work in the local
> economy, and are subject to local law. Hence, second admissions
> (naturalizations) depend on first admissions (immigration) and are
> subject only to certain constraints of time and qualification never to

the ultimate constraint of closure. When second admissions are closed, the political community collapses into a world of members and strangers, with no political boundaries between the two, where strangers are subjects of the members. . . . No democratic state can tolerate the establishment of a fixed status between citizen and foreigner (though there can be stages in the transition from one of these political identities to the other). Men and women are either subject to the state's authority, or they are not; if they are subject, they must be given a say, and ultimately an equal say, in what that authority does. Democratic citizens, then, have a choice. If they want to bring in new workers, they must be prepared to enlarge their own membership; if they are unwilling to accept new members, they must find ways within the limits of the domestic labor market to get socially necessary work done. And those are their only choices.[55]

One reason to reconsider Walzer's observations is that they were prompted in part by the example of guest workers in Europe, and a similar program has been suggested by some as a solution (certainly an improvement) to the current status of undocumented workers in the United States. Walzer's analysis suggests that guest worker programs that do not offer more are chimeras, and he has argued that "every new immigrant, every refugee taken in, every resident and worker must be offered opportunities of citizenship."[56] President Bush's proposals have included "paths to citizenship" for the undocumented, but the right wing of the Republican Party has repeatedly rejected this attempt at a humane and just solution.

In an interview on National Public Radio, Rep. Tom Tancredo announced his intention to run for the presidency and made clear his opposition to any guest-worker program that would provide paths to citizenship for undocumented migrants currently in the United States. Tancredo proposed instead a policy of strict enforcement of the laws against hiring such workers, which would in his view serve two purposes. First, for many it would eliminate a key incentive for crossing the border illegally and eventually cut off the flow of undocumented laborers from Mexico. Second, undocumented workers who were currently employed would conceivably be flushed out when they were unable to find employment or when employers terminated their service for fear of being prosecuted by the federal government. When pressed by reporter Melissa Block about what would ultimately happen to these migrants when they were unable to find work and denied social services, Tancredo agreed after prompting that they would be deported, which he noted would simply be a matter of meaningful enforcement of the current law.[57]

What Tancredo did not discuss was the migrants' personal suffering and the economic dislocation the nation would experience as a result of a legal crackdown on the employers of undocumented laborers. He also did not mention the means that would be required to round up millions of human beings for deportation, men and women who may now have been in the United States for many years and perhaps even have American-born children. These people may have "broken the law" by remaining in the United States without appropriate documentation, but does the punishment Tancredo proposed fit the crime? Culpability for the situation in which the undocumented find themselves spreads far beyond the individual migrants and their families and indeed implicates the structures of the American and global economies and the elites who control them. A report from the right-leaning Heritage Foundation has stated the following in support of a guest-worker program: "An honest assessment acknowledges that illegal immigrants bring real benefits to the supply side of the American economy, which is why the business community is opposed to a simple crackdown. There are social costs as well, given America's generous social insurance institutions. . . . The argument that immigrants harm the American economy should be dismissed out of hand. The population today includes a far higher percentage (12 percent) of foreign-born Americans than in recent decades, yet the economy is strong."[58]

If immigrants, documented and undocumented, are contributing to the U.S. economy and society, what are our responsibilities to them in return? A legal status that offers no possibility of permanent full membership in the community—citizenship, in other words—is unacceptable. As currently structured, however, U.S. law is not particularly receptive to the possibility of offering citizenship status to the undocumented: "It is almost impossible to gain legal entry to the United States unless a person has an employer or family sponsor who is already a legal resident in the country. Even then, the wait for visas can stretch for years. . . . The demand for workers in less skilled jobs will continue to increase in the next 10 years. Fewer native born workers will be available to fill these jobs because they are growing older and more educated. Yet, only about 5,000 legal visas are available for such jobs annually. The U.S. immigration system does not match the demands of the U.S. labor market."[59]

It appears that a major "structure of sin" existing in the United States today is the importation of low-skilled and unskilled labor from developing countries to serve as our "live-in servants," who thereafter are forced to live in legal limbo and fear of deportation because, for most, citizenship is all but unattainable. Left dangling by the legal system and able to engage the political system only by proxy, they become targets of nativist resentment during a time of rapid social and economic change. Our political structure has shown itself incapable of addressing the current system's failures in a way that will respect the dignity of those who labor in the shadows on our behalf, so we allow the system to continue because we are unwilling to forgo the benefits that we reap from the vibrant market economy they help support. At the very least, Christians are called in solidarity with these migrants to promote meaningful dialogue about changing this system. Before anything else can happen, however, we must confront the reality that respect for human dignity, human rights, and liberal democratic principles excludes the possibility of massive deportations of undocumented immigrants.

Will Kymlicka has noted that "most Western democracies are having to rethink their approach to citizenship to respond to the challenges raised by migration."[60] One approach Christians might take to raise the level of the immigration debate in the United States is to consider Canada's experience. Kymlicka offers Canada as an example of a country that has achieved a relative consensus on citizenship policy, and he cites five reasons for this.[61] First, it is comparatively easy to become naturalized in Canada. The requirements are not particularly burdensome (a three-year residency requirement, for example). Second, being Canadian is not considered an exclusive identity, and there is no obligation to renounce the citizenship of one's country of origin to become Canadian. Canadians understand that many new migrants and immigrants will have dual loyalties and overlapping identities at least initially, and public approval of multiculturalism is fairly strong. Naturalization, in essence, is seen as one of the early steps in the process of assimilation into Canadian society.

Third, Canada commits public monies to encourage and facilitate naturalization by funding language courses and naturalization campaigns. Kymlicka sees these efforts as indicating public support for inclusion. Fourth, noncitizens have equal access to civil rights, social benefits, and the labor market (with a few exceptions) and are protected by strong antidiscrimination laws. Although they cannot vote and can be deported for certain crimes, their overall legal status is not particularly precarious. Finally, the overall trajectory of Canada's policies has been toward more openness and greater inclusion. In particular, nativist and anti-immigrant campaigns have not gained significant political traction in Canada, and Canadians overall seem to see an openness to immigrants as being in their national-self interest.[62] "We can think of immigration, citizenship, and multiculturalism as a three-legged stool, each leg of which supports (or weakens) the other two. Where one leg is weak, people begin to worry about the motives and consequences of the other two legs as well. Conversely, confidence in one leg can help generate optimism and trust in the other two."[63]

Canada's lack of a border with a large, populous, developing nation makes its circumstances somewhat different from those of the United States, but in the modern world, this does not insulate wealthy nations from global immigration and migration patterns. The relatively open border between the United States and Canada also makes the latter an easy destination for anyone who has already entered the United States. Nevertheless, the peculiarities of its circumstances do not diminish the ways in which Canada's naturalization policies address some of the concerns Walzer has raised. Indeed, an excellent opportunity for religious action in the public sphere involves programs and policies that are designed to turn migrants and immigrants into citizens. In the United Kingdom, for example, Anglican and other Protestant congregations, Catholic parishes, the Muslim community, and grass-roots community groups in Greater London have formed a coalition that has launched numerous campaigns to promote the dignity of low-wage, undocumented economic migrants. In May 2006 the cardinal archbishop of Westminster, Cormac Murphy-O'Connor, said Mass in London's Westminster Cathedral to celebrate a "May Day for Migrants." He also helped to launch a living-wage campaign sponsored by the Community Organising Foundation, which for several years had been offering instruction in community organizing for economic migrants in cooperation with Christian and Muslim religious communities all over London. At the mass, the cardinal told the migrants assembled in the packed cathedral that:

> while our nation benefits from the presence of undocumented workers, too often we turn a blind eye when they are exploited by employers. Illegal migrants should not be treated as criminals; no one leaves their country in search of work in another country unless they are desperate to do so. The presence in our city of hundreds of thousands of undocumented workers creates a social misery all of its own. . . . Is it not time to consider, as other countries have done, ways of regularizing their situation—those who are working in the country and do not have a criminal record—to the benefit of our economy and to enable them to play a fuller part in society?[64]

This coalition of believers is a sign of hope and an example of the solidarity with the dispossessed urged by Catholic social teaching. Religious believers in democratic, pluralist societies play a critical role in the struggle to create and maintain healthy, diverse communities in which the dignity of everyone is acknowledged. The most recent campaign of the London coalition has served as a theme for this chapter. Called "Strangers into Citizens," it seeks to draw London's undocumented migrants out of the shadows and into British political, economic, and cultural life. We need not fear our sisters and brothers from the developing world who seek to better their lives in partnership with us. We should see these people as potential citizens and new members of our community who will help to enrich and renew us. Our embrace of them will help us resist the calls to fear from certain segments of our political leadership who seek to maintain power through an incessant search for enemies in our midst.

6

Christian Cosmopolitans and Respect for Pluralism

Liberating Church from Nation

In October of 2006 an act of unspeakable violence devastated the calm of the tiny town of Nickel Mines, Pennsylvania. After barricading himself in a one-room Amish schoolhouse with a group of young girls, a local milkman shot ten of the girls, ultimately killing five, and then turned the gun on himself, taking his own life. The entire world was moved by the tragedy not only because of the brutality and senseless violence that took so many young lives but also because of the remarkable grace and courage of the Amish community following the events. The Amish people occupy an almost iconic status in American life. Despite living in a culture that is obsessed with technological innovation and material wealth, the Amish shun both and live simple, agrarian lives that have changed little since the nineteenth century.

Moreover, in a nation that is leading a war in Iraq justified in part by the rhetoric of a life-or-death struggle between democratic Christendom and "Islamofascism," the Amish commit themselves to vision of Christianity rooted in pacifism and nonviolence. In the wake of the murderous rampage at their school, the Amish community in and around Nickel Mines opened their homes and their funerals to the killer's family, asked God to forgive him, and modeled for the world a faith commitment so rooted in the healing grace of mercy that the American chattering classes and much of the nation along with them were struck dumb with awe and respect. "How could they *do* that?" many asked. They could do it because they take their faith seriously, struggle daily to live by its teachings, and draw strength from a life in community that offers meaning and dignity to all of its members. The Amish recognize the transcendence that comes from meaningful personal encounters with other human beings, even when that "other" is a person one desperately wants to hate.[1]

The astounding dignity of this small Amish community in the face of the heartbreaking murder of its children has much to teach all of us about the current state of religion in American public life. The witness of the Amish in Nickel Mines should remind Christians that, using Christ as our model, we are often called by the Gospels to take courageous and countercultural stands. A liaison between the Religious Right and the Republican Party that justifies the imperial ambitions of U.S. capitalism, foments ongoing conflict with the Islamic world, and scapegoats poor Mexicans and Central Americans as threats to the stability of "American" civilization distorts Christianity into a nationalistic creed in the service of a culture driven by power and wedded to privilege. Although this religious nationalism may be explained to some extent as a response to the destabilizing effects of modern value pluralism and economic globalization, at its root it is a heresy that privileges the desires of some human beings at the expense of the dignity of others: "The nation offers itself as the dominant institution for formulating cultural identities and as a vehicle for implementing both individual and group interests. It can easily become the most general form of feeling of 'us.' Outside the nations are 'the others,' the competition, the threat, perhaps the enemies. Now that traditional religions have become unsure, this profane system of reference can take on totalitarian, quasi-religious characteristics. . . . It is a likely starting point for ideologies with a claim to absoluteness."[2]

The American Right has constructed a vision of nation that assumes we are under constant threat, thereby justifying a relentless mission of identifying and expelling "others" and sealing ourselves off from dangers posed by outsiders. This is no doubt due in part to a felt need to create unity in the ever-increasing diversity of American society, and September 11 constituted an obvious threat around which the nation could unify. However, in the years that have followed, we have witnessed a Republican government that appears to have lost the commitment to human dignity forged in the aftermath of World War II, at Nuremberg, in the creation of the United Nations, at the Second Vatican Council, and in the movements of nonviolent civil disobedience led by Mahatma Gandhi, Martin Luther King Jr., and Nelson Mandela. American Christians should instinctively recoil from a political vision that seeks to take the world back to a time in which obedience to the state was seen as exerting more authority over one's actions than the dictates of a properly formed Christian conscience. Does the United States' mission in the world include a renewed legitimation of unchecked state power—be it through the theory of the "unitary executive" or through unilateral international action? Must Christians be afraid to speak truth to this power because some Christians assert that the nation acts as a force only for good in the world?

In addition, M. Cathleen Kaveny has noted that "In the United States at the turn of the twenty-first century, we . . . confront serious moral disputes among persons who see themselves as belonging to the same moral tradition and as holding themselves accountable to the same values and the same account of the virtues."[3] Kaveny argues that, in the United States, many of the intractable debates over highly contested legal and public policy questions among religious believers are the products not of factual disputes but of clashes in the style of moral discourse used to enter into dialogue. Many on the Religious Right have resorted in recent years to a "prophetic" style of engagement with fellow believers and with society at large in relation to much debated issues like abortion, homosexuality, and, most recently, America's global leadership and the fight against radical Islam, a style that does not lead to "fruitful discussions about differences, but instead signals the breakdown of conversations, and frequently, the breakdown of community."[4] While powerful when employed appropriately, Kaveny's work demonstrates that the Religious Right's repeated insistence on a prophetic rhetorical style has had devastating consequences for cohesion among Christians in the United States and has proved counterproductive to the advancement of key Christian values in the dialogue of liberal pluralism.

What exactly is a "prophetic" rhetorical style in this context? Prophesy has deep roots in the three Abrahamic faith traditions—Christianity, Judaism, and Islam—but as a Catholic theologian and a legal scholar, Kaveny uses the Christian and Jewish traditions as her primary sources. In the Hebrew scriptures, the voice of the prophet served a number of purposes, but one in particular was to give voice to God's perspective on the relationship between the Israelis and God, most notably when Israel was failing to live up to the obligations of its covenant with God. Quoting Abraham Heschel, Kaveny notes, "the prophet was an individual who said 'No' to his society, condemning its habits and assumptions, its complacency, waywardness, and syncretism. . . . His fundamental objective was to reconcile man with God."[5] Thus, in the modern context, "those who engage in prophetic discourse (or prophetically symbolic activity) are attempting to break through a community's entrenched habits of apathy and injustice in order to prevent them from smothering the fundamental values and commitments upon which the community is founded. . . . Nevertheless, it cannot be denied that those constructive intentions frequently remain unrealized, and that attempts to invoke prophetic language only exacerbate moral balkanization and even moral cynicism. The use of prophetic discourse is risky business, both for the prophet and for the community."[6]

When used at the appropriate time, the prophetic voice has an important role to play in the life of a society that has lost its moorings. However, prophesy exists in tension with our practical reason, a form of which has long been known in the Catholic tradition as *casuistry*. "We all employ casuistical discourse to the extent to which we deliberate about the rightness or wrongness of a particular action. . . . Casuistry is a way of engaging in practical reasoning—it is a form of our day-to-day moral discourse, in which we consider the rightness or wrongness of particular actions in light of applicable moral principles, particular features of the action and particular characteristics of the agent performing it."[7] Most of our reasoning is casuistical, but casuistic reasoning can be employed disingenuously when we use it to rationalize decisions we have made cut off from moral discernment or deliberation or when our process of moral reasoning is distorted in some fundamental way.[8] For example, Kaveny recounts how the Virginia courts explicitly acknowledged the full humanity of African Americans in the wake of the Civil War, but she points out that the acknowledgement had no appreciable impact on the state's antimiscegenation laws and the rationales used to uphold them for another 100 years. Prophesy serves as a remedy to these types of situations by acting as a kind of "moral chemotherapy. It is a brutal, but necessary response to aggressive forms of moral cancer, whose uncontrolled growth threatens to corrupt practical reasoning, and ultimately destroy the very possibility of it."[9]

Finally, Kaveny offers an overall assessment of the appropriate relationship between prophesy and casuistry:

> Chemotherapy can be dangerous. It kills healthy cells as well as diseased ones. In order to improve the overall health of the patient, therefore, it must be used both accurately and sparingly. So, too, must the moral chemotherapy of prophetic discourse. . . . The use of prophetic language in a particular context disrupts the normal functioning of a deliberative community. It renders the normal interactions of mutual reason-giving impossible because the audience's only avenues of response to a prophetic statement are either to acquiesce in the prophet's demands or to engage in what amounts to an *ad hominem* attack. . . . Prospective prophets need to remember that

not every moral-practical disagreement signals the breakdown of conditions for the possibility of practical reasoning. . . . For example, it is one thing to be opposed to welfare programs because the poor are not worthy of assistance; it is quite another to be opposed to them because one does not believe they actually assist the poor. The former position is inconsistent with a basic Christian world view, the latter position is not, whether or not it is ultimately correct.[10]

The American Religious Right has far too often availed itself of prophetic rhetoric in an attempt to beat fellow citizens into submission to what they claim is the will of God or obedience to the truth. Abortion, homosexuality, secularization of the public sphere, and now "Islamofascism" have all been identified as signs of the Western moral tradition on the brink of the abyss, and radical measures—constitutional amendments, suppression of the powers of the judiciary, wars—are all being called for in order to save the nation from destruction. It is not that the Religious Right is necessarily mistaken in its all of its concerns regarding the virulence of certain cancers within the body politic, but in Kaveny's terms their chemotherapy threatens to kill the patient.

There are, of course, those Christians who sincerely believe that the United States has a providential mission in world affairs. Stephen Webb has argued that "America is so determined . . . by the conviction that we have a special destiny in world history that only a careful account of the doctrine of providence can shine a clear light on the course that lies ahead. Given the indisputable dominance of America in world affairs—what we might call the Great Fact of our day—it is pernicious to deny any providential meaning to America's shaping of the globe."[11] Webb acknowledges that a providential vision of God using the United States for a special purpose is something that tends to be found on the right of the political spectrum and, more specifically, among evangelical and fundamentalist Christians, but he argues that a proper understanding of providence is a bit more difficult to pigeonhole politically. Groups on both sides of the political spectrum have used providential arguments for the country's rise as a great power: "Any theological analysis of nationalism, globalism, and the future of the church requires a strong grasp of providence. . . . Any analysis of the transnational destiny of the church must include reflection on how God is using the most powerful nation in the world. A providential reading of world history must account for America's miraculous rise to power, and it must give an interpretation of God's blessings for America as well as America's responsibilities for those blessings."[12] Webb hopes to revive the doctrine of providence more generally among Christians so that modern theology can grapple more profoundly with the ways in which God works in the world through a nation like the United States. He sets his project in opposition to a theological view that is typically identified with Stanley Hauerwas and John Howard Yoder—that Christians are *in* the world but not *of* it and that the task of the Christian is to establish a community of discipleship on Christian terms.

For Yoder, a Mennonite, Christian community meant a commitment to pacifism, and his views resonate concretely in the life and culture of the Amish. Although Hauerwas does not fully embrace the radical pacifism and potential church/world dualism that many see in Yoder, he has argued that:

> the oft-made charge that Yoder (or Hauerwas) is a sectarian simply fails to take seriously Yoder's emphasis that the church should be a community that models for the world what the world can be. That I refuse to provide an account of legitimacy for the state may seem to be irresponsible to some. . . . A refusal to develop accounts of legitimacy, moreover, does not mean that discriminating judgments cannot be made by Christians about the limits and possibilities of the societies in which they find themselves. Such judgments, however, should not ever prevent Christians from becoming missionaries in societies that they might well regard as politically oppressive."[13]

In order to understand how Christians might serve the political community in which they find themselves, Hauerwas agreed with Yoder that democracies are best understood, at least theoretically, as rule by an elite to whom authority has been entrusted in the name of democratic ideals. Democracy provides a means for challenging the reasons these elites give for their decisions and allows those who are subject to them to hold their rulers to account. Understood not so much as majority rule but as minority leverage, Hauerwas believes that Christians might reasonably see democracy as a preferable form of government.[14]

The role for Christians in the world envisioned by Catholic social teaching lies somewhere between a belief in a prophetic vision of American providence and a desire for withdrawal from the world arguably envisioned by Yoder. The Catholic view is nevertheless much closer to Hauerwas and therefore to Yoder than to evangelical understandings of a special God-inspired destiny for the United States. Although Catholic social teaching argues for a Christian engagement with the world and citizen involvement with the democratic process, the teaching broadly understood may also require a withdrawal from a national polity that seeks self-aggrandizement at the expense of the legitimate needs of nonmembers. Catholic social teaching insists on a solidarity with people worldwide that makes nationalist favoritism difficult to justify on moral terms.

Claims for basic justice raised by those outside the nation-state would certainly exert priority over loyalty to a national government that perpetuates or contributes to injustices abroad.

The demand for justice and peace is global, excluding claims to "chosenness" for any one nation in favor of a Christian humanism more philosophically consistent with cosmopolitanism. This is not a rootless, self-indulgent cosmopolitanism that knows no patriotic duties or loyalties, but a rooted cosmopolitanism that is grounded in local communities of memory and meaning, and which embraces the moral imperatives of a commitment to human dignity that transcends political borders. This rooted, Christian cosmopolitanism demands a rejection of certain notions of nation-state sovereignty currently embraced by right-wing politics in the United States, and it has profound implications for understandings of citizenship and community membership in pluralist democracies. Although located particularly in their religious traditions, political societies, and local cultures, Christian cosmopolitans owe what is best understood as a pragmatic loyalty to the nation-state. There is nothing in Christian teaching that suggests that the nation-state as a particular form of geopolitical organization is divinely ordained. History teaches us that geopolitical boundaries are ephemeral, and, apart from a general admonition to obey legitimate authority, there is nothing in serious Christian theology that suggests they have a particular moral claim on a Christian conscience. As Pope John Paul II stated, "Since it is not an ideology, the Christian faith does not presume to imprison changing socio-political realities in a rigid schema, and it recognizes that human life is realized in history in conditions that are diverse and imperfect. Furthermore, in constantly reaffirming the transcendent dignity of the person, the church's method is always that of respect for freedom."[15]

Christians are called to respect legitimate authority and to recognize the state as a natural product of our life in community, but our allegiance to state power is based first and foremost on the state's commitment to its primary purpose—the promotion of human dignity and the common good. Yet, given the increasingly plutocratic power structure of the United States today, our looking to the nation-state to serve this purpose may be misplaced. Catholic theologian William Cavanaugh has argued that the faith that many Christian ethicists place in the state as a protector and promoter of the common good does not withstand scrutiny given the way the nation-state has developed in the modern West: "The nation-state is neither community writ-large nor the protector of smaller communal spaces, but rather originates and grows over and against truly common forms of life. This is not to say that the nation-state cannot and does not promote and protect some goods, or that any nation-state is entirely devoid of civic virtue or that some forms of ad hoc cooperation cannot be useful. It is to suggest that the nation-state is simply not in the common good business."[16]

Cavanaugh also argues that the sheer size of the nation-state and the "absence of any generally agreed rational standard to adjudicate among... interests" means that "decisions on the distribution of goods are made on the basis of power, which is most often directly related to access to capital.... Deliberation is carried on by a political elite of lawyers, lobbyists and other professionals. For the same reason, the unitive community that the idea of nation offers is an illusion. The nation-state is not a genuine community, a functioning rational collectivity whose bonds make possible the virtues of ac- knowledged dependence necessary for the common good."[17] Cavanaugh sees a need for the church to demystify the nation-state and contends that it "must break its imagination out of captivity to the nation-state. The Church must constitute itself as an alternative social space...[and] needs, at every oppor- tunity to 'complexify' space, that is, to promote the creation of spaces in which alternative economies and authorities flourish."[18]

How the common good and human dignity are understood within socie- ties in which widespread pluralism exists will often be a source of some debate. Thus, Christians "should show in practice how authority can be reconciled with freedom, personal initiative with solidarity and the needs of the social framework as a whole, and the advantages of unity with the benefits of di- versity. They should recognize differing points of view on the organization of worldly affairs and should show respect for individual citizens and groups who defend their opinions by legitimate means."[19] One source of hope for the future of the global political order from the Christian perspective and a de- velopment that the Catholic Church has supported explicitly through its social teaching is the emerging international consensus around human dignity through a commitment to international human rights. The protection of hu- man rights is certainly a Christian moral imperative, for it recognizes that human beings are the ultimate ends of social, political, and economic life. Indeed, Catholic social teaching has embraced a broader conception of human rights than has typically been the case in the American liberal tradition.

The main point of divergence is that the social teaching views rights as rooted in our social nature and within a framework of solidarity that stresses a communal, as opposed to an individualist, perspective on rights language. For example, David Hollenbach has described the Second Vatican Council's ap- proach to human rights as "affirm[ing] the rights that have been classically defended by the liberal democratic tradition of the West and that are enshrined in the Bill of Rights of the Constitution of the United States. That these rights are not understood in an individualistic way is evident since *Gaudium et Spes* follows the work of John XXIII in *Pacem in terris* by affirming social and economic rights, which are more difficult to justify on liberal and individualistic grounds. These include the rights to 'access all that is necessary for living a genuinely human life, for example food, clothing, housing."[20] Recall, however, that this embrace of a broad framework of social, political, and economic rights by the Catholic social tradition has been particularly troubling to American neoconservatives. Nonetheless, the Christian agenda and the U.S. agenda are not one and the same.

A commitment to human rights and fundamental human dignity is severely threatened, if not violated, when the United States seeks to legitimate the expansion of the use of military aggression as a means of promoting democracy and when it encourages an international economic agenda that consistently preferences the desires of the rich nations at the expense of basic necessities for the poor.[21] Although a respect for the common good may demand basic obedience to government authority from citizens, is this a government to which American Christians owe unquestioned loyalty simply because we live within the borders of the United States? We may be witnessing a government that is losing a connection to fundamental moral principles and increasingly finding ourselves in the position of African Americans in the pre–Civil Rights South. Through acts of civil disobedience and nonviolence, African Americans and other Americans of goodwill showed their respect for human life and a dedication to the common good while at the same time rejecting the legitimacy of state-sanctioned violations of what have come to be seen as basic human rights. At the very least, the thoughtful Christian is obliged to question and perhaps even challenge through the democratic process the governing authority when that authority begins to undermine the common good. The government owes its citizens reasons for its actions, reasons that situate those actions within the bounds of a meaningful commitment to global solidarity and human dignity. To reprise Stanley Hauerwas, the church cannot survive if it believes that its fundamental task is to "make America work," based on a vision of God that is vague and attenuated and dims "the reality of God found in cross and resurrection":

> The attenuated god of American Christianity is necessary for a people who believe they are the future of humankind. I believe, therefore, Christians can do nothing more significant in America than to be a people capable of worshipping a God who is to be found in the cross and resurrection of Jesus of Nazareth. The worship of such a God will not be good for any society that desires a god made in the

image of the bureaucrat. A people formed by the worship of a cru-
cified God, however, might just be complex enough to engage in
the hard work of working out agreements and disagreements with
others one small step at a time.[22]

A Cosmopolitan Rejection of the American "Tribal Fantasy"

Consistent with the increasingly distorted claims of the nation-state identified
by Cavanaugh, Samuel Huntington has argued that the cultural core of
American identity is an "Anglo-Protestant" culture that was brought to North
America by the nation's founding English settlers. Despite the presence of
Native Americans, the almost simultaneous arrival of African slaves, various
large waves of immigration from Catholic Europe, and, later, Asian immigrants from China and Japan, Huntington sees the Anglo-Protestant culture as
the unifying cultural feature of American life: "Throughout American history,
people who were not white Anglo-Saxon Protestants have become Americans
by adopting America's Anglo-Protestant culture and political values. This
benefited them and the country. [The Anglo-Protestant] elite's religious and
political principles, its customs and social relations, its standards of taste and
morality, were for 300 years America's, and in basic ways they still are—
despite our celebration of 'diversity.' ... Millions of immigrants and their
children achieved wealth, power, and status in American society precisely
because they assimilated themselves to the prevailing American culture."[23]

Huntington is concerned that this cultural consensus is in danger of being
lost and that the ensuing consequences may be severe. However, as I argue
in the previous chapter, his fear of a loss of America's Anglo-Protestant culture is unduly alarmist, and it overemphasizes the unifying aspect of Anglo-
Protestantism in American life. Anthony Appiah maintains that a common
culture is something that derives from "values and practices (almost) universally shared and known to be so" and that such practices have to be at the core
of what most Americans would call their individual cultural lives.[24] Appiah
finds it hard to imagine that countries with the kind of diverse ethnic, racial,
and religious makeup that has long characterized the United States could ever
share this type of commonality, which he associates with small-scale, traditional societies that involve regular face-to-face contact, shared language, and at
least a core of common cultural practices: "I am inclined to say that there is not
now and there has never been a centering common culture in the United
States.... The reason is simple: the United States has always been multilingual and has always had minorities who did not speak or understand

English. . . . Americans have always differed significantly even among those who do speak English. . . . The notion that what has held the United States together historically over its great geographical range is a citizenry centered on a common culture is—to put it politely—not sociologically plausible."[25] In Appiah's view, what the United States did have (and may still have in some ways) is a dominant, as opposed to a common, culture: "It was always true that there was a dominant culture in these United States. It was Protestant, it spoke English, and it identified with the high cultural traditions of Europe and, more particularly, of England. This dominant culture included much of the common culture that centered most members of the dominant classes—the government and business and cultural elites—but it was familiar to many others who were subordinate to them. And it was not merely an effect but also an instrument of their domination."[26]

Huntington confuses the pragmatic adoption of Anglo-Protestant values by those outside the circle with an absorption into a common culture, and he is probably caught up in what Appiah might call a "tribal fantasy" of an Anglo-Protestant United States: "Here is one model of the role of the national culture: we might call it the tribal fantasy. There is an ideal—which is to say imaginary—type of a small scale, technologically uncomplicated, face-to-face society where most interactions are with people whom you know, that we usually call traditional. In such a society almost every adult speaks the same language. . . . To share a language is to participate in a complex set of mutual expectations and understandings. . . . There is a second crucial feature of the common culture in the tribal fantasy: it is that the common culture is, in a certain sense, at the heart of every individual and every family."[27]

No doubt some European immigrants to the United States were able to become part of the dominant culture—perhaps through intermarriage or religious conversion. This would have involved, however, a more or less complete abandonment of the cultures, languages, and religions of their birth and perhaps even a rejection of family members. Most Americans did not follow this path either because they chose not to or because it was forbidden to them. They were nevertheless encouraged or forced to take up key attributes of the dominant society if they were to have any hope of economic or social progress in a nation dominated by Anglo-Protestants. Appiah argues that, for most Americans, it is not Anglo-Protestant culture that centers their lives or their view of what it means to be American. Rather, it is their attachment to the democratic freedoms and institutions that make possible a commitment to the values and traditions that actually *do* center their lives: "The French and American revolutions invented a form of patriotism that allows us to love our country as the embodiment of principles, as a means to the attainment of moral ends. . . . If among the ideals we honor in America is the enabling of a certain kind of human freedom, then we cannot, in consistency, enforce attachment either to the state or to the principles. In valuing the autonomous choices of free people, we value what they have chosen because they have chosen it: a forced attachment to a fine principle does not diminish the principle, but the force makes the attachment unworthy."[28]

It is not necessary, Appiah argues, for citizens to be centered on a common culture in a nation like the United States. What is needed is a shared commitment to common institutions and the conditions necessary for a common life. This dedication allows us to sustain the pluralism to which our democratic values commit us. Life in a modern, diverse democracy cannot attempt to replicate the world of the tribal fantasy because it must encompass a wide range of beliefs and meanings for its citizens. It must, in other words, live out its allegiance to equality in a meaningful way, and it is difficult to imagine how this might be done if all citizens are required to center their lives on a core culture that encompasses areas like religion and language. Indeed, this is the very dilemma that has forcefully confronted the nations of Western Europe in recent years. What does it mean to be English or French or German in a modern nation-state that embraces the values of liberal pluralism? Can Muslims be European and still be Muslims? Under Appiah's view they can, as long as they respect the institutions and values of democracy in a way that offers the same freedoms to others.

Inevitably, of course, some of these freedoms will conflict. At some point one's right to fully practice a Muslim faith may be inconsistent (at least for some) with freedoms others claim for themselves. Given this challenge, might even a pluralist democratic nation need a centering culture to support a commitment to a common political culture? This critique is a variation of Michael Sandel's argument against minimalist liberalism and the "proceduralist state." Sandel has argued for a liberalism that recognizes the claims of solidarity and memory that come from our membership in communities with particular histories, beliefs, or religious ways of knowing. In contrast, the type of liberalism now dominant in the United States proceeds from the idea that, "since people disagree about the best way to live, government should not affirm in law any particular vision of the good life. Instead, it should provide a framework of rights that respects persons as free and independent selves capable of choosing their own values and ends. Since this liberalism asserts the priority of fair procedures over particular ends, the public life it informs might be called the proceduralist republic."[29] Sandel explains why this form of liberalism as the basis of the modern welfare state is subject to attack, particularly from libertarian arguments so resonant in political discourse:

It is vulnerable . . . to the libertarian objection that redistributive policies use some people as means to others' ends, and so offend the
"plurality and distinctness" of individuals that liberalism seeks above
all to secure. In the contractual vision of community alone, it is
unclear how the libertarian objection can be met. If those whose fate
I am required to share are, morally speaking, *others,* rather than
fellow participants in a way of life with which my identity is bound,
then liberalism as an ethic of sharing seems to be open to the same
objections as utilitarianism. Its claim on me is not the claim of a
community with which I identify, but rather the claim of an arbi-
trarily defined collectivity whose aims I may or may not share.[30]

Appiah recognizes this problem—let us call it the communitarian
objection—to some extent and acknowledges that there may be central debates
that cannot be resolved purely on the basis of assent to a common political
culture. He responds by offering a pragmatic approach that accepts some
limits to the ability of pluralist society to please all comers but at the same time
suggests an abiding faith in the ability of people with divergent views to accept
a political community that does not reinforce every belief at the center of their
cultural life. The liberal political culture must offer possibilities of change
when extremely important values essential to maintaining the integrity of the
political culture are at stake. In this regard, he offers the experience of African
Americans under Jim Crow as an example of both a failure of the political culture to uphold its core values and of the culture's redemption through a
process that focused on those values. In some instances, however, as some
would argue the case of abortion demonstrates in the United States, there
might not be a satisfactory resolution for some citizens: "If as a result of the
processes of democracy, laws are passed that are deeply repugnant to you—as
is perfectly possible in a society not centered on a common culture—you may
well reach the point where you consider that you have been . . . repudiated by
the state. The price of having no common culture to center our society is that
possibility; but the cosmopolitan patriot believes that the creation of a common
culture rich enough to exclude this possibility would exact a higher price."[31]

Christians might reflect on Hauerwas's comment that the church cannot
survive if its fundamental task is "to make America work." By the same token,
the liberal, pluralist state cannot survive if its fundamental task is to center the
culture on a particular vision of Christianity that makes the Christian community's values coterminous with the state's. Appiah offers instead the vision
of "cosmopolitan patriots" who are committed to the nation's animating liberal
principles but who also recognize that in some extreme cases (limited, we

hope) certain key values of their core centering culture may not be vindicated by the state apparatus. Ideally, the core liberal values should be those that overlap significantly with principles common to many people. Appiah calls these "thin" moral concepts: "Thin concepts seem to be universal; we aren't the only people who have the concepts of right and wrong, good and bad; every society, it seems, has terms that correspond to these thin concepts, too. Even thick concepts like rudeness or courage are ones you find everywhere. But there are thicker concepts still that really are peculiar to particular societies. The most fundamental level of disagreement occurs when one party to a discussion invokes a concept that the other simply doesn't have. This is the kind of disagreement where the struggle is not to agree, but just to understand."[32]

As an example of agreement on a thin concept that is evident despite a fairly explicit external cultural difference, Appiah considers the matrilineal family in his native Ghana. In his youth, a typical family structure was one in which men were the primary financial support of their *sisters'* children; thus, the relationship between a man and his biological children appeared, to European sensibilities, more akin to that of an uncle, whereas the father/child relationship in the Western sense was oriented toward nieces and nephews. These explicit differences notwithstanding, the matrilineal system nevertheless ensured that all children born into a family group were properly nurtured, socialized, and financially supported, which is also central to the Western model of nuclear family organization: "There are, in short, different ways of organizing family life. Which one makes sense to you will depend, in good measure, on the concepts with which you grew up. As long as a society has a way of assigning responsibilities for the nurture of children that works and makes sense, it seems to me, it would be odd to say that one way is the right way of doing it and all the others wrong. . . . There are thin, universal values here—those of good parenting—but their expression is highly particular, thickly enmeshed with local customs and expectations and the facts of local social arrangements."[33]

The communitarian objection to cosmopolitanism is an important one, particularly for Christians who take seriously our essentially social nature and the importance of the common good and solidarity to any understanding of human dignity in the social order. As I have argued earlier in this book, the lack of a coherent American narrative identity that encompasses the lives and experiences of African Americans and poor people has been the source of a great deal of incoherence in U.S. law as it has struggled to confront honestly the legacy of slavery and the reality of persistent poverty in a land of "freedom" and "opportunity." Appiah's cosmopolitanism is not inconsistent with those observations, for it offers a realistic assessment of how the United States functions as a pluralist democracy. Whatever might be the community-binding benefits of an honest narrative about the nature of the American society, it has become abundantly clear that a core, centering culture cannot be imposed on the United States as a whole. It is simply impossible to imagine the circumstances under which the necessary agreement might be obtained without a level of coercion that would contradict modern Christian and secular understandings of human rights.

African Americans, for instance, are most unlikely to obtain any further recognition for their unique experience as Americans (despite its centrality to the "truth" of the nation's founding) because many Americans remain resolute in their refusal to accept the contradictions that slavery and its aftermath raise for any construction of American identity. But more pragmatically, the world is moving on, and African Americans may be better served by a cosmopolitan ethos that links them more profoundly to the struggles for human dignity currently being waged in Africa, Asia, and Latin America. As the devastating nature of the marriage of the Religious Right and a right-wing political agenda has demonstrated in the United States, the cost of forcing a common culture on an unwilling nation is extremely high and could well push the political community to a breaking point. What Appiah's cosmopolitan vision offers is a more realistic understanding of the nature of democratic agreement on the level of national politics, an agreement that will by necessity be rooted in thin principles. At the same time, real communities of meaning centered on culture—like the Amish, for instance—will be able to exist and thrive through a cosmopolitan ethos that values and endeavors to preserve a world in which difference is a good worth nurturing:

> There are two strands that intertwine in the notion of cosmopolitanism. One is the idea that we have obligations to others, obligations that stretch beyond those to whom we are related by the ties of kith and kin, or even the more formal ties of a shared citizenship. The other is that we take seriously the value not just of human life, but of particular human lives, which means taking an interest in the practices and beliefs that lend them significance. People are different, the cosmopolitan knows, and there is much to learn from our differences. Because there are so many human possibilities worth exploring, we neither expect nor desire that every person or every society converge on a single mode of life.[34]

I turn now to these ideas and their implications for a different kind of engagement with American democracy and the international community for creedal Christians.

The Cosmopolitan Imperative in Liberal Pluralist Democracies

One common caricature of the cosmopolitan position is that it requires a rejection of the particular, the local, and the national. The result is the absorption of individuals into an amorphous world community with little real meaning. This view, however, neglects much of what recent pro-cosmopolitanism arguments have offered. Martha Nussbaum has arguably provided one of the most widely discussed arguments for the moral soundness of cosmopolitanism. She has noted that a heavy emphasis on patriotic pride in the circumstances of the modern world is "both morally dangerous and, ultimately, subversive of some of the worthy goals patriotism sets out to serve—for example, the goal of national unity in devotion to worthy moral ideas of justice and equality.[35]

Nussbaum traces the evolution of the cosmopolitan view back to the Greek Stoic philosophers, who believed that "to be a citizen of the world one does not need to give up local identifications, which can be a source of great richness in life. They suggest that we think of ourselves, not devoid of local affiliations, but as surrounded by a series of concentric circles. The first one encircles the self, the next takes in the immediate family, then follows the extended family, and then, in order, neighbors or local groups, and fellow countrymen.... Outside all these circles is the largest one, humanity as a whole."[36] The fundamental dignity of human beings must be recognized wherever they are, and, given the increasing ease with which the world's people interact, this moral imperative takes on increased relevance, for, "if we really do believe that all human beings are created equal with certain inalienable rights, we are morally required to think about what that conception requires us to do with and for the rest of the world."[37]

In *Frontiers of Justice*, Nussbaum continues the development of her capabilities approach to solve key problems of justice that exist within liberal social contract theory. One problem that is particularly relevant to a cosmopolitan understanding of human dignity is the quest for justice for all of the world's citizens.[38] Although she remains sympathetic to the contractarian view of liberalism elucidated by John Rawls, Nussbaum recognizes that the Catholic natural law tradition offers a particularly compelling framework for understanding the human person in ways that Rawlsian liberalism cannot. Drawing on the natural law theory of international relations as expounded by seventeenth-century philosopher Hugo Grotius, Nussbaum embraces the natural law conception of the human person in which Grotius's theory is grounded, which sees people as characterized by an inherent dignity, or moral worth, and by sociability: "Thus [Grotius's] political theory begins from an abstract idea of basic entitlements, grounded in the twin ideas of dignity (the human being as an end) and sociability. It is then argued that certain specific entitlements flow from those ideas, as necessary conditions of a life with human dignity."[39] She notes further that "What I want to bring out about Grotius' theory is that it begins with the content of an outcome, in the sense of an account of basic entitlements of human beings whose fulfillment is required by justice; if these requirements are fulfilled, then a society (in this case 'international society') is minimally just. The justification of the entitlement set is not procedural, but involves an intuitive idea of human dignity as an argument to the effect that a certain entitlement is implicit in the idea of human dignity.... Grotius evidently believes that a society based upon sociability and respect rather than upon mutual advantage can remain stable over time."[40]

Nussbaum employs this natural law conception of human dignity to support the capabilities approach, which maintains that entitlements are a necessary part of a just social order that respects human dignity (similar to the approach taken in Catholic social teaching). It is a response to utilitarian excesses of contemporary economic analysis, the insistence on mutual advantage as the rationale for formulating political principles in contractarian versions of liberal theory, and the inability of social contract theory to globalize the theory of justice beyond the nation-state. Following Grotius once again, she notes that human beings have a common good and seek a common life:

> This intelligence is a moral intelligence. The three central facts about human beings that this moral intelligence apprehends are the dignity of the human being as an ethical being, a dignity that is fully equal no matter where human beings are placed; human sociability, which means that part of a life with human dignity is a common life with others organized so as to respect this dignity; and the multiple facts of human need, which suggests that this common life must do something for us all, fulfilling needs up to a point at which human dignity is not undermined by hunger, or violent assault, or unequal treatment in the political realm. Combining the fact of sociability with the other two facts, we arrive at the idea that a central part of our own good, each and every one of us—insofar as we agree that we want to live on decent and respectful terms with others—is to produce, and live in, a world that is morally decent, a world in which all human beings have what they need to live a life worthy of human dignity.[41]

Capabilities are what human beings must have in a minimally just and decent world, and securing them for people worldwide requires international cooperation at an institutional level. This does not mean that Nussbaum supports the idea of a "world state" (she rejects this explicitly), nor does it require the elimination of sovereign nations. Nussbaum believes that national sovereignty has moral importance "as a way people have of asserting their autonomy, their right to give themselves laws of their own making," but this importance does not supersede the states' moral obligations to secure basic capabilities for their citizens.[42] Nussbaum thus adopts a "rooted cosmopolitanism" similar to Appiah's, in which locality and particularity remain important as part of the diversity and pluralism that cosmopolitanism seeks to protect. At the same time, the basic moral requirements of human dignity embraced by the cosmopolitan require some weakening of the state's political claims on the individual inasmuch as they are inconsistent with the fundamental truths about people. Furthermore, Nussbaum's doubts about the ability of social contract theory to reflect human sociability and our richly layered moral life echo similar concerns about social contract theory as expressed in the philosophical work of Lévinas and Ricoeur. Thus, Nussbaum's capabilities approach and the cosmopolitan philosophical outlook underlying it draw ever closer once again to important insights of Catholic social teaching.

The cosmopolitan critique of nationalism does not necessarily reject the loyalties and attachments that would traditionally be associated with patriotism. The nation-state is a relatively new phenomenon in world history, particularly for people in the developing world. Even in the "old" democratic nations of the developed world, the nation-state concept is groaning under the weight of its twentieth-century excesses and unrealistic aspirations. What the more rooted cosmopolitanism of Appiah and Nussbaum makes clear is that nationalism is becoming a bankrupt ideology. Even Alasdair MacIntyre, a strong supporter of the coherent narrative identities that tend to thrive in cohesive local cultures, has voiced a sharp critique of behavior normally associated with nationalism and considers patriotism as both a virtue and a vice. In his view, one must be extremely careful to extract patriotism from "mindless loyalty to a particular nation which has no regard at all for the characteristics of that particular nation."[43] He states that "moral behavior requires abstracting oneself from social particularity and partiality, whereas patriotism requires me to exhibit peculiar devotion to my nation and you to yours. It requires me to regard such contingent social facts as where I was born and what government ruled over that place at that time, who my parents were and who my great-great-grandparents were and so on, as deciding for me the question of what virtuous action is—at least insofar as it is the virtue of patriotism which is in question. Hence, the moral standpoint and the patriotic standpoint are systematically incompatible."[44]

Charles Taylor has argued that democratic societies need a common identity and that this often tempts them to exclude because democracy has a strong need for mutual understanding and cooperation in order to work.[45] This is true not only in societies that have a long tradition of ethnic cohesion but also in diverse societies like the United States. In all of these cultures either intense pressure was exerted on newcomers to conform to the dominant social model or measures were introduced to prevent the integration and assimilation of groups that were seen as incapable of assimilating into the mainstream community. Since the 1960s, however, various groups outside of the mainstream have been less willing to subsume key aspects of their identity in order to conform to the dominant cultural ideal.

In addition, previously excluded groups have been allowed into the social mainstream, and global migration has made it more difficult to control who enters the society in the first place: "Migrants . . . no longer feel the imperative to assimilate. One must not misidentify the switch. Most migrants want to assimilate substantively to the societies they have entered; and they certainly want to be accepted as full members. But they frequently want, now, to do this at their own pace and in their own way, and, in the process, they reserve the right to alter the society even as they assimilate to it."[46] In other words, migrants and other outsider groups recognize the multicultural and increasingly pluralist nature of most wealthy modern democracies, and they reject a vision of their place in those societies that suggests they have no role in the shaping of the culture. Few modern nations remain coterminous with culturally cohesive peoples, and the phenomenon of global migration is making the few that might arguably still exist the exceptions that prove the rule.

One reason for this is the success (most notably since the 1960s) of the pluralist democratic model provided by what Will Kymlicka and Wayne Norman call the "countries of immigration"—the United States, Canada, and Australia.[47] Once a "national" community of a democratic state encompasses a culturally diverse population in a highly interdependent global economy, the cosmopolitan arguments for global obligations become particularly salient. The values of liberal democracy as they have evolved since the Second World War require a respect for difference that has fundamentally changed the global cultural environment and more accurately reflects the kinds of cultural diversity and accommodation that have long been a reality in the United States, as well as that which exists in the multicultural, postcolonial democracies of the developing world.[48]

Multicultural societies mean that groups within a nation-state may well maintain attachments to an international diaspora community. It is no longer possible for countries seriously committed to liberal democratic values to insist that citizens shed diaspora identities because they are perceived threats to national unity. However, as Appiah and other cosmopolitans point out, the obligations we have to those outside of our nation are due not only to shared ethnic, linguistic, or cultural identities but also to certain obligations that derive from our shared humanity. The capabilities approach of Martha Nussbaum is another way (within the tradition of cosmopolitanism) of considering these needs in a way that embraces a broad conception of human dignity.[49]

Understood in the rooted sense of Appiah and Nussbaum, cosmopolitanism offers an important link between secular language about the global common good and the dignity of the human person, which aligns naturally with both the system of international human rights and Catholic social teaching. Indeed, Nussbaum's important insight into how the Stoics understood the human community has a direct parallel in Christian theology: "A favored exercise in this process of world thinking is to conceive of the entire world of human beings as a single body, its many people as so many limbs."[50] Christians will recognize this image as the same as that in Paul's first letter to the Corinthians: "As a body is one though it has many parts, and all the parts of the body, though many, are one body, so also Christ. For in one spirit we were all baptized into one body, whether Jews or Greeks, slaves or free persons, and we were all give to drink of one Spirit.[51] The Christian image of the "mystical body of Christ" provides another important way to articulate universal principles of respect for human beings despite our differences. Paul noted in particular that it was the body's weakest or least visible parts that often take on the greatest importance: "Indeed, the parts of the body that seem to be weaker are all the more necessary, and those parts of the body that we consider less honorable we surround with greater honor, and our less presentable parts treated with greater propriety, whereas our more presentable parts do not need this."[52]

Achieving Common Cause by Promoting Human Dignity and Human Rights in Global Civil Society

The modern world demands a new, global orientation to the challenges posed by humanity's shared existence on the planet. There are few issues that arise today in any particular nation that remain completely contained within the geopolitical boundaries of the nation-state. Armed conflict, terrorism, disease, environmental degradation, economic policy, and social change all cause repercussions to the lives of human beings around the world. Of course, the interrelatedness of humanity has always been with us, if only because people have migrated from place to place for various reasons since the beginning of their presence on earth. The explosion of technological knowledge, however, has made these movements easier and quicker, and it has also enabled human beings to impact one another dramatically without ever actually having a personal encounter. All of this suggests that the global social order is real and that the global common good and solidarity demand serious attention. It is simply irresponsible (and certainly for Christians, immoral) for Americans to behave as if their needs and desires have special priority over those of other members of the human family simply because the United States happens to be the world's richest and most powerful nation.

Does America's fear for its domestic security because of 3,000 deaths in a terrorist attack on a single day justify the war that is now estimated to have taken the lives of from 52,000 to 600,000 Iraqi civilians since 2003?[53] Is an American life worth more than an Iraqi life? Are rich people more deserving of protection than poor people? Are the citizens of Western-style democracies more human—more civilized—than those in Islamic states? One might be forgiven for thinking that these questions were answered in the human rights revolution that occurred in the wake of the Second World War, but the early years of the twenty-first century seem to be signaling a retreat from that promise. In his book *Can Human Rights Survive?* Conor Gearty states that "internment, torture, coercive interrogation, covert surveillance, and other manifestations of lawless state power are no longer simple wrongs to be avoided and severely punished when they occur; rather they have become a set of supposed solutions to supposed ethical dilemmas that need now to be considered and debated. . . . The unspeakable is no longer unspoken. Even the greatest of our human rights taboos—the prohibition on torture and inhuman and degrading treatment—has become just another point of view—and to some people an eccentrically absolutist one at that."[54]

What should be particularly troubling for American Christians is that an administration and a political party that have maintained power with widespread Christian support have been key contributors to making the unspeakable acceptable, and this has led a retreat from a vision of human rights that the United States was at the forefront of creating. This turn of events should demonstrate to Christians that a vision of human dignity tied primarily to the political vagaries of internal nation-state politics is simply not capable of nurturing the kind of global solidarity envisioned by Catholic social teaching over the long haul, nor can it be expected to be particularly concerned about the global common good. As for a commitment to human dignity, Christians must recognize that meaningful partnerships can be formed across secular and interreligious divides to encourage what Pope Paul VI called "authentic human development." In the face of recent assaults, Gearty's call to protect the achievements of the human rights revolution offers an important opportunity for creedal Christians to consider whether our faith's cosmopolitan commitment to human dignity, particularly the precarious dignity of the poor, the weak, and the outcast, must take precedence over unquestioned devotion to American exceptionalism, dominance, and power. Although the thought may be comforting, it is naive to assume that the United States acts not primarily to promote the interests of its elites but for some amorphous "good" in the world, as if the American empire could remained untainted by corruptions of power that have hobbled every powerful imperial nation throughout history.

The economic and political agendas of certain right-wing elites in the United States have played a significant role in eroding decades of real progress toward meaningful commitments to human dignity across cultural and ideological boundaries. Bound up with that, Gearty argues that the promise represented by the human rights revolution is threatened by three crises that particularly threaten advances in human rights. The first crisis is one of authority, which springs from the value pluralism and the challenge to knowable truth that defines our current era. Whereas religious believers might take some solace in the truth claims of their faiths, "the human rights believers are lonely and vulnerable. . . . They cannot thrive outside of pluralism: to the extent that human rights instincts are to be found in the world of certainty where religious believers are still at home then it is as a benign branch of whatever the prevailing religion happens to be. But pluralism as a shelter for human rights leaks with doubt; in a place where everything is true, nothing can be *really* true."[55]

A second crisis is that of legalism. The legal codification of human rights norms has presented both opportunities and hazards. The entry of such standards into the mainstream of the domestic legal systems of (primarily) democratic nation-states has had real emancipatory effects for many people who have long been repressed or existed on the margins of their societies. Enmeshing these norms into the legal system gives them extraordinary reach and power.[56] On the other hand, the reception of human rights in democratic societies has tended to occur at the highest levels of legal abstraction—in bills of rights and constitutional provisions, and although this may give human rights a certain moral authority:

> What is the nature of this new-found authority? What are the underlying truths about human rights that have been dormant in the political process, but which have now been liberated by this transfer of the trusteeship of the idea from the political to the judicial sphere? . . . In recovering its certainty in what is right and what is wrong, human rights law seems invariably to find itself reverting to

a particular philosophical tradition that has certainly had its uses in past generations but which is not particularly helpful or persuasive today.... On this view, our core or essential human rights are made up of a number of rights that people have which *precede* politics or which are *above* politics. They are not rights which are achieved (and sustained) *through* politics.[57]

Christians would of course disagree with Gearty's view that core human rights do not precede the state or politics. Nevertheless, Christians need to reckon with this idea if we are to be a relevant part of the conversation about human rights in modern pluralist democracies. In his most recent book, Michael Perry argues that the morality of human rights—the idea that each and every human being has inherent dignity and is inviolable—is best justified metaphysically on religious grounds, and he finds secular arguments for the *morality* of human rights, as opposed to secular arguments about particular human rights claims, less compelling.[58] In other words, Perry embraces the foundationalist position for human rights that Gearty rejects.

To some extent, Gearty's position is similar to Richard Rorty's views, which Perry examines in some detail. Rorty argued that, rather than attempting to discern common transcultural elements that undergird the idea of human rights as a basis for global agreement, the goal of Western human rights supporters should be to strengthen the human rights culture created by the West. Rorty believed that we in the West should seek to convert others to our human rights culture.[59] To this Perry responds that "for many (most?) of us who embrace the cause of human rights, the fundamental wrong done, when the inherent dignity of any human being is not respected—when any human being is violated—is not that our local ("Eurocentric") sentiments are offended. The fundamental wrong done is that, somehow, the very order of the world—the normative order of the world—is transgressed."[60]

Despite Gearty's rejection of the foundationalist or natural law–grounded view of the case for human rights, Gearty's overall position offers a great deal of common ground for Christian and secular supporters of human rights. Indeed, what is generally apparent in the arguments made to support human rights is a deep and abiding respect for people. Like Nussbaum, Gearty demonstrates a fierce commitment to the participation of all citizens as the key source of legitimate political authority in a democracy. It is essential for citizens to have an opportunity to live a life of dignity if their participation in the polity is to be meaningful. A life of dignity that leads to participation in community links us again to important principles in Catholic social teaching like solidarity and the preferential option for the poor. These are values

Christians can support, regardless of the theoretical justifications underlying them, as part of a commitment to living out their faith as engaged members of the pluralist communities of the modern world. A dedication to the participation of all in a democracy means accepting the reality of the secularization of public discourse. As Jeffrey Stout has explained:

> Ethical discourse in religiously plural modern democracies is
> secularized . . . only in the sense that it does not take for granted a set
> of agreed-upon assumptions about the nature and existence of
> God. . . . It means that no one can take for granted, when addressing a
> religiously plural audience, that religious commitments have de-
> fault authority in this context. It does not entail any limitation on
> what an individual can presuppose in the first sense. On the contrary,
> the discursive practice is secularized . . . precisely because many of
> the individuals participating in it do have religious commitments that
> function as presuppositions in some of their own deliberations
> and pronouncements.[61]

Notwithstanding his skepticism about rights that precede the state, Gearty sees real value in future alliances between progressive secular and religious citizens who are committed to human rights, and he recognizes the potential danger of a secularist worldview that turns human genius into a false god.[62] "Humanitarian instincts are too precarious in global civil society to make it sensible to reject support from certain sources merely on account of quarrels in the distant past. This remains the case even if the content of human rights remains a source of radical dispute on certain core issues."[63]

The third human rights crisis that Gearty identifies is national security:

> In the ethical grammar that underlies our way of describing the
> world, danger and fear are fast replacing dignity and hope as
> the terms that come first to mind when we describe the shape of the
> world in which we live. . . . I identified the core idea behind human
> rights as being the equality of esteem in which we are all held in
> virtue of our humanity. This unfolds into a respect for dignity which
> demands both an end to cruelty and humiliation on the one hand
> and a commitment to human flourishing on the other. . . . Terrorism
> laws challenge . . . the core proposition underpinning human
> rights. . . . In place of equality of esteem they offer, very particularly,
> inequality of esteem, judging people not by the fact that they simply
> are but by where they are and where they are from and by which
> culture of faith it is to which they belong.[64]

Whereas the domestic legal systems of democratic states have over the last 60 years integrated expanded modern understandings of fundamental human rights and put protections and procedures in place that allow individuals accused of criminal acts to be treated by the state and its agents in a fashion that respects their inherent dignity, the "national security" system of justice that has of late been employed in the United States works diligently to remove "terrorists" from these protections on the basis of their status as unredeemable, inherently evil others who by their acts have forfeited rights to protections granted to "civilized" persons. The argument used to justify these actions is implicitly that we in the West, who created and implemented a comprehensive system of human rights, must stand ready to protect it from those outsiders who do not respect it and seek to destroy it. That those outsiders are themselves human becomes secondary. This is a position that should be deeply troubling for Christians. In his discussion of capital punishment, Michael Perry has asked whether one can forfeit one's inherent dignity and determines that the answer from modern Catholic theology is clearly "no."[65] "The morality of human rights holds that each and every (born) human being has inherent dignity. There is no exception for depraved criminals. . . . The Catholic Church now teaches that every human being, innocent or not, has inherent dignity—a dignity that cannot be forfeited and is therefore inalienable."[66]

An encyclical document sometimes included in compendia of the primary documents of Catholic social teaching (but one that receives fairly modest attention) is *Evangelii nuntiandi*, or "Evangelization in the Modern World." In these modern, rather skeptical times, evangelization tends to smack of a certain intolerance and lack of respect for others, certainly inasmuch as the quest to evangelize is perceived as emanating from a desire to "save" others from their freedom to choose. In *Evangelii nuntiandi*, however, Pope Paul VI describes a method of evangelization well suited to current times and arguably much more likely to produce success: "The task of evangelizing all people constitutes the essential mission of the Church."[67] Yet, in specifying what evangelization actually is, Paul VI made it very clear that the primary method of evangelization should be through the witness of life:

> Above all the Gospel must be proclaimed by witness. Take a Christian, or a handful of Christians who, in the midst of their own community, show their capacity for understanding and acceptance, their sharing of life and destiny with other people, their solidarity with the efforts of all for whatever is noble and good. Let us suppose that, in addition, they radiate in an altogether simple and unaffected way their faith in values that go beyond current values and

their hope in something that is not seen and that one would not dare
to imagine. . . . Through this wordless witness these Christians stir up
irresistible questions in the hearts of those who see how they live:
Why are they like this? Why do they live this way? What or who is it
that inspires them? Why are they in our midst? Such a witness is
already a silent proclamation of the Good News and a very powerful and effective one. . . . Other questions will arise, deeper and more
demanding ones, questions evoked by this witness which involves
presence, sharing, solidarity, and which is an essential element, and
generally the first one, in evangelization.[68]

Modern pluralist democracy in an era of global capitalism appears hungry
for the witness of a cosmopolitan, lived Christianity that is fiercely committed
to the dignity of all human beings and rooted in "presence, solidarity, and
sharing." This witness brings Gospel values to light in a world of shifting or
easily penetrable geopolitical boundaries and should be coupled with a respect
for the principle of subsidiarity, which can not only offer a structural principle
for human rights, as Paolo Carozza has argued, but also support a vision of
Christian engagement with the world that proceeds from a respect for pluralism. "Human rights and subsidiarity can both be summarized as ideas that
advance the understanding of the common good as based in the totality of
conditions necessary for a full and flourishing human life."[69] What this means
for the Christian cosmopolitan witnessing through example and engagement
is reflected in Carozza's description of the interaction between respect for the
individual and pluralism in subsidiarity and the same values in international
human rights as they relate to religious freedom:

The freedoms contemplated by human rights instruments deliberately create an ordered space for the liberty to pursue a range of
goods. In other words, the idea of human rights, just as much as the
principle of subsidiarity, necessarily entails an affirmation of a degree of pluralism and diversity in society. Consider, for instance, the
freedom of religious belief and worship: a person's authentic search
for and adherence to the meaning of life and the cosmos is fundamental to human dignity, yet one's human right "to manifest his
religion or belief in teaching, worship, and observance" is independent of the object of belief and worship or the doctrines and practices
of the believer.[70]

The Christian cosmopolitan recognizes that creating a global culture of
respect for the essential link between human dignity and freedom to choose

one's beliefs protects her freedom to believe as well as protecting the beliefs of others. She recognizes that benefits of pluralism rooted in respect for diversity redound to every member of the community, no matter who happens to be in charge at a given moment in time. Despite the aggressive American rhetoric of democracy and freedom as the key to global peace and prosperity, Christians would be wise to remember that forcing others to do as we do and to believe as we believe is not a path to peace. It is the source of unending conflict.

As I have demonstrated in earlier chapters, we have in recent years witnessed a renewed contempt for international cooperation and universalism from certain right-wing political elites. We have also seen an increasing sacralization of the American nation-state and a casting of the nation's role in the world in pseudo-Christian terms. Finally, an enemy has been offered up whose acts have relieved us from the necessity to conceive a genuine respect for their humanity, much like the rendering of the "Hun" in World War I. Additionally, what is deeply troubling for Christians is that the civil religion presented by the Right has counseled us to reject or ignore the entreaties for peace and international cooperation made by religious figures from outside the homeland. An attempt to reclaim power for the nation-state by stoking the flames of fear of "outsiders" and rejecting our international obligations does little to prepare the American people to meet the demands of a future characterized by increased global engagement. Indeed, for Christians, this xenophobic stance draws us away from our faith's universalist tradition and toward the false, discredited idol of Christian nationalism.

Catholic social teaching recognizes the need for attention to global solidarity and the common good in a world where national borders increasingly do not define self-contained ethnic, linguistic, religious, and economic communities. We all must heed the call to wide-reaching responsibility that is completely lacking in the rhetoric of neoliberalism, religious nationalism, and libertarianism. Christian cosmopolitanism offers a more hopeful response, rooted in the transcendent dignity of the human person and convinced that human freedom and diversity are worth preserving and celebrating. It is committed to democratic pluralism and the dialogue with others that it requires. It is not driven by fear of either difference or change. Finally, it welcomes new members to particular communities in which Christians reside on the basis of shared commitments to the core ideas that shape our life in common and to the dialogue necessary to define them further in the quest for global peace and justice.

Conclusion

In this book I have endeavored to awaken the consciences of American Christians who do not see their faith reflected in either the "values" agenda of the Religious Right or the economic and foreign policies of the Republican Party. I also hope to appeal to other Americans of goodwill from different religious traditions who work for the common good from a perspective that reflects a sense of values shared with other religious believers. I aim, moreover, to arouse a sympathetic response in nonreligious people who are committed to a vision of dialogue in a pluralist society that supports the right of both religious and nonreligious voices to shape our common life. My use of Catholic social teaching is a way of demonstrating that religious believers can offer thoughtful arguments in public debate that are rooted in logic and a commitment to democratic pluralism, arguments that are accessible to—and capable of being engaged by—all of the members of a democratic society.

The United States is no less susceptible to the temptations of wealth and power than any other great nation in history. However, it is inappropriate, perhaps even idolatrous, for Christians to justify the nation and its actions through political maneuvers in which the church is given the power to impose a moral and cultural vision on the American people in return for bestowing its blessing on an economic and foreign policy agenda that is far removed from core values of orthodox Christian theology and social teaching. Furthermore, the strong libertarian, individualist, and materialist impulses in

American culture tend to blind many Americans to the ways in which the United States may be particularly ill suited to claim any moral mission rooted in Christianity for itself and its people.

Any suggestion that the United States is a "Christian" nation ignores significant evidence to the contrary and relies on a rendering of Christianity that is only very loosely connected to orthodox interpretations of the Gospels. The Christianity of the American empire is a caricature that is designed to justify the lives and worldviews of key groups in the nation's population, a use of Christianity that would not have been unfamiliar to the French and British elites and middle classes at the turn of the twentieth century. Power seeks to justify itself in any way it can. A top-down version of Christianity that blesses the current economic arrangements and social structures becomes an apologia for the distorted values of a nation's middle and upper classes, and this role for religion has already demonstrated its weaknesses throughout history. We need not repeat those mistakes.

I argue for a more bottom-up vision of Christianity, one that is much better suited to a respect for democratic pluralism and properly engaged with modern Christian social thought. This Christianity is cosmopolitan in its outlook but is rooted in the particular traditions of peoples, their histories, and the places that are dear to them. It leads by example and seeks to propose, rather than impose, the truth of its beliefs. Most important, it does not direct its primary energies to supporting the powerful and justifying the rich. Instead, it looks to relationships with the weak, the poor, and the marginalized as the foundation for meaningful community and solidarity, thereby enabling what Martha Nussbaum has termed a "purified patriotism" within the context of an increasing recognition of responsibilities to those outside the nation-state.

Nussbaum has further argued that the internal goal of national community within a pluralist democracy should be to create a model for the way in which we all ought to live. By domestically fostering just institutions that promote the capabilities that nurture human dignity, democratic citizens, particularly those in wealthy nations, are better able to appreciate their call to global responsibility. A nation of this type is one of which its citizens can be proud and in which they can have meaningful dialogue and relationships with "others"—those with whom, in Lévinas's terms, they have no natural affinity but who still demand their attention as a moral matter. A purified patriotism allows for an embrace of a more cosmopolitan sense of duties to humanity around the world, rooted in the practices of sharing and solidarity practiced at home. In the modern world, this vision is remarkably consistent with Christians' responsibilities as envisaged by the concepts of human dignity, solidarity, and the common good in Catholic social teaching.

For those of us who are no longer interested in a passive acceptance of legal, political, and social arrangements that enrich and embolden those in power at the expense of the weak, a commitment to solidarity and promotion of the common good has political consequences. I have demonstrated that, in the United States, legal approaches to provide for the poor offer little opportunity for impoverished Americans to enter into a relationship with the broader community that would encourage a dialogue about how entrenched and intractable poverty limits their meaningful participation in the nation's common life. Furthermore, this legal regime prevents poor people—both explicitly and through their witness—from raising questions about the roles material acquisition and low-wage labor play in propping up middle-class identity in our culture.

A similar unwillingness to engage the "other" prevents many African Americans from being full, dignified participants in American society. Because U.S. law seeks to solve the problem of African American marginalization through an expansion of autonomy, the lessons that the African American experience can provide to the broader American culture about group identity and its relationship to sharing and suffering are lost. Americans are also denied an opportunity to rethink and reshape their society in ways that honor the nation's African forebears and provide balance to libertarian freedom rhetoric, which is centered on the experience of the white, Anglo-American, male "founders." Embracing America's African heritage would suggest that being an American is not exclusively the product of freedom and choice but has also been the result of bondage and suffering.

This more honest rendering of who we are might also help us to recast our current debate on immigration. We might see those seeking to cross our borders not as "law breakers" and "illegals" but as sojourners who, in their search for dignity, seek a relationship with us. This relationship may or may not end in an expansion of our community to include them as full members. Nevertheless, in either case, we recognize (as Ricoeur has demonstrated) that the mediating role of others is necessary if our quest to create a just society is to have any hope of success. The lack of an equitable distribution of social goods on a global scale is a primary cause of migration around the world. It will remain an impediment to international justice—and therefore an ongoing source of migration—unless those of us in the wealthy nations take seriously our encounter with the face of the migrant and recognize the economic, social, and political transformation that the encounter is destined to unleash.

Serious Christians must be fierce in the defense of human dignity at home and abroad, and we must recognize that we cannot consider our personal needs and desires without reference to others. Is the ongoing expansion of the U.S. economy so sacred that it cannot be slowed or modified in an effort to stop the degradation of the planet or improve the opportunities for a decent life for the world's poorest people? We must recognize and be able to articulate that individuals alone do not have absolute control over their lives and prospects. Structures do matter, and global structures matter more than ever before. Structures of sin also exist, rooted in our personal failures and those of our communities, to acknowledge and confront human need and suffering in a pursuit of justice.

Finally, we must take on the challenge of global solidarity with a commitment to a truly cosmopolitan Christianity that will help to forge international responsibility. Elites around the world are benefiting from the freedoms unleashed by wide-reaching markets, technological innovation, and the decline of the salience of nation-states. They must also be made aware of their obligations. Christian cosmopolitans, ever attentive to the universal implications of their faith commitments, should be ready to call them to account in a worldwide economy that heretofore has enriched only a limited few while the abundant poor remain trapped in lives filled with poverty, violence, disease, and fear.

Notes

NOTES TO INTRODUCTION

1. From one of the great documents of the Second Vatican Council, *Gaudium et Spes*: "Believers and unbelievers agree almost unanimously that all things on earth should be ordained to humanity as to their center and summit. . . . For sacred scripture teaches that women and men were created "in the image of God," able to know and love their creator and set by him over all earthly creatures that they might rule them and make use of them while glorifying God. 'What are women and men that you are mindful of them, their sons and daughters that you care for them? You have made them little less than angels, and crown them with glory and honor. You have given them dominion over the works of your hands; you have put all things under their feet' (Psalms 8:5–8)." Vatican Council II, *Gaudium et Spes*, in *Vatican Council II: Constitutions, Decrees, Declarations*, ed. Austin Flannery (Northport, N.Y.: Costello, 1996), 12.

2. In the Catholic tradition, this is probably best exemplified by the acceptance of the church's ideas of religious freedom and freedom of conscience, which led to a rejection of centuries of magisterial teaching and the promulgation of *Dignitatis humanae personae* by the Second Vatican Council in 1965. For a discussion of the transformation of Catholic thinking in this area see John T. Noonan Jr., *A Church That Can and Cannot Change: The Development of Catholic Moral Teaching* (Notre Dame, Ind.: University of Notre Dame Press, 2005), 154–158.

3. Catholic social teaching parts with Anglo-American contract-based theories of rights, often traced to the writings of Hobbes and Locke. In contrast, phenomenological philosophy on the European continent, drawing on the work of Kant and Hegel, has had profound influences on Catholic

social thought. Paul Ricoeur and Emmanuel Lévinas are examples of modern continental European philosophers in the phenomenological tradition who have rejected
contractarian understandings of human relationships in favor of concepts that stress
human interdependence as essential to individual development.

4. The key stumbling blocks in the path to unity for Roman Catholicism and
most of the orthodox traditions involve matters of ecclesiology, particularly the primacy of the pope. Cardinal Walter Kasper, president of the Pontifical Council for
Promoting Christian Unity, has noted "broad agreement" between the Roman
Catholic and Orthodox churches on doctrinal matters. See E. Curtis and M. Hirst,
"Amid the Cold, Signs of a Thaw," *Tablet*, Jan. 21, 2006, 12–14. Relations with the
Anglican communion have foundered in recent years primarily because of differences
over the ordination of women to the priesthood. The Roman Catholic and Lutheran
churches have been engaged in an ongoing dialogue on restoring full communion
since 1965. A significant sign of progress in the process was the Joint Declaration on
the Doctrine of Justification, signed in Augsburg, Germany, in 1999.

5. For an excellent discussion of the unwillingness of key Catholic Republicans
to take responsibility for their enthusiastic support of President Bush's failed policy in
Iraq, see "Bishops and Their Critics," *Commonweal*, Apr. 20, 2007, 5.

6. For example, as the instigator of the current devastation in Iraq, does the
United States have an obligation to accept a significant number of Iraqi war refugees?
Thus far, only a very few have been granted entry to the United States. Given the
fear of terrorism since the attacks of September 11, the strong hostility directed toward
the large numbers of Mexican migrants in the United States, and the failure of
immigration reform legislation in 2007, it appears highly unlikely that Congress will
be able to summon the political consensus necessary to provide sanctuary to a
large number of Iraqi war refugees. For more discussion of this issue see ABC News,
"Forced from Iraq: Now America's Moral Obligation?" at http://abcnews.go.com/WN/
TheAgenda/Story?id=3426088&page=2 (accessed Feb. 15, 2008).

7. "No to war! War is not always inevitable. It is always a defeat for humanity.
International law, honest dialogue, solidarity between States, the noble exercise of
diplomacy: these are methods worthy of individuals and nations in resolving their
differences." Pope John Paul II, "Address of His Holiness, Pope John Paul II, to the
Diplomatic Corps," Vatican City, Jan. 13, 2003.

8. In this book I rely on an understanding of the role of elites that was developed
by sociologist Edward Shils. Sociologists have defined "society" as "the outermost
social structure for certain groups of individuals who, whatever might be their attitude
toward it, view themselves as members and experience their identities as being determined by it." Liah Greenfield and Michel Martin, "The Idea of the Center: An
Introduction," in *The Center: Ideas and Institutions*, ed. Liah Greenfield and Michel
Martin (Chicago: University of Chicago Press, 1988), viii. Shils uses the concept of the
center to locate both the central system of values in a society and the institutions
and persons who embody the value system (ix–x). Generally, various types of elites
occupy the center. "The center exercises authority and power; it also espouses and
embodies beliefs about things thought to be of transcendent importance, that is

'serious.'" Edward Shils, "Center and Periphery: An Idea and Its Career" (251). With the waning of a prescriptive culture based on the habits and values of white, Anglo-Saxon Protestants, wealth has become the primary determinant of elite social status in the United States. Education is also an important indicator of social status. Increasingly, a social and political divide has emerged between what I call the *educational elite* and the *money elite*. The former tend to occupy key positions in the traditional professions, government and civil service, the arts, and the academy. These individuals may or may not be wealthy, but few would be found outside of the middle- and upper-middle class. The money elite dominate the corporate and business sectors of the U.S. economy, and many have entered the elite through earned or, in some cases, inherited wealth.

9. Jeffrey Stout, *Democracy and Tradition* (Princeton, N.J.: Princeton University Press, 2004), 13. On the one hand, Stout rejects the views of liberal secularists like Richard Rorty, who see religious views as inadmissible in democratic conversation. At the same time, he is unwilling to accept the views of traditionalists such as Alasdair MacIntyre and Stanley Hauerwas, who view modern democracy as "the antithesis of tradition . . . an atomizing, inherently destructive social force" (11).

10. "A liberal cosmopolitan of the sort I am defending might put its point like this: We value the variety of human forms of social and cultural life, we do not want everybody to become part of a homogenous global culture, and we know this will mean that there will be local differences (both within and between states) in moral climate. So long as those differences meet certain general ethical constraints—so long, in particular that certain institutions respect basic human rights—we are happy to let them be." Anthony K. Appiah, "Cosmopolitan Patriots," in *For Love of Country: Debating the Limits of Patriotism*, ed. Martha C. Nussbaum (Boston: Beacon, 2002), 25–26.

11. Seymour Martin Lipset has made this same point in much of his writing. Canadians, he has noted, "have a great advantage over Americans since, while very few of the latter study their northern neighbor, it is impossible to be a literate Canadian without knowing almost as much, if not more as [sic] most Americans about the United States." Seymour Martin Lipset, *American Exceptionalism: A Double-edged Sword* (New York: Norton, 1996), 34. Moreover, American thinkers from a wide variety of disciplines still rely heavily on the observations of American life by eighteenth-century French aristocrat Alexis de Tocqueville in *Democracy in America*.

12. George Grant, *Lament for a Nation* (Montreal: Carleton University Press, 1982), 8n1.

13. Andrew Bacevich, *American Empire* (Cambridge, Mass.: Harvard University Press, 2002), 86.

14. Ibid., 88.

15. Michael Hardt and Antonio Negri, *Empire* (Cambridge, Mass.: Harvard University Press, 2000), xii.

16. Ibid., xiii.

17. Ibid., 15.

18. David Harvey, *The New Imperialism* (New York: Oxford University Press, 2003), 17.

19. Ibid., 16.

20. Ibid., 17.

21. Andrew J. Bacevich, *The New American Militarism: How Americans Are Seduced by War* (New York: Oxford University Press, 2005).

22. Andrew J. Bacevich, "The Cult of National Security: What Happened to Checks and Balances?" *Commonweal*, Jan. 27, 2006, 7.

23. Ibid.

24. Adam Liptak, "In Limelight at Wiretap Hearing: Two Laws, but Which Should Rule?" *New York Times*, Feb. 7, 2006, A1. The chairman of the committee, Sen. Arlen Specter, a Republican, said to Gonzales that his interpretation "defied logic and plain English," and a group of fourteen constitutional law scholars and former government officials wrote to the committee, insisting that this assertion of executive power was unwarranted (ibid.).

25. Simon Tisdall, "Washington Digs In for a 'Long War' as Rumsfeld Issues a Global Call to Arms," *Guardian*, Feb. 7, 2006.

26. "US Military Stretched to Breaking Point," *Guardian*, Jan. 26, 2006.

27. Second inaugural address of President George Bush, reprinted by the *Washington Post*, Jan. 21, 2005, A24. As Lipset has observed, "America, as a principled nation, must go to war for moral reasons. We set moral goals, such as 'to make the world safe for democracy,' as reasons to go to war.... If we fight the evil empire, if we fight Satan, then he must not be allowed to survive." Lipset, *American Exceptionalism*, 65n6.

28. Robert Harvey, *A Few Bloody Noses: The American War of Independence* (London: John Murray, 2001), 4–5.

29. Ibid., 428.

30. Ibid., 427.

31. Grant, *Lament*, 69.

32. W. McDougall, "The Colonial Origins of American Identity," *Orbis*, Winter 2005, 7, 15–16.

33. Ibid., 16.

34. Ibid., 16–17.

35. For a discussion of the profoundly important influence of German intellectuals on the early twentieth-century social encyclicals, see Philip Chmielewski, SJ, *Bettering Our Condition: Work, Workers, and Ethics in British and German Economic Thought* (New York: Peter Lang, 1992).

36. M. Cathleen Kaveny, "How Views of Law Influence the Pro-life Movement," *Origins* 34, no. 35 (Feb. 14, 2005), 560–565.

37. Ibid.

38. Joanna Walters, "All American Trouble: Furious Row as U.S. School Board Drops International Baccalaureate for Being 'Too Foreign,'" *Guardian*, Mar. 14, 2006.

NOTES TO CHAPTER I

1. Emmanuel Todd, *L'illusion économique* (Paris: Gallimard, 1998), 75 (author's translation).

2. Martin Feldstein, "The Return of Saving," *Foreign Affairs*, May/June 2006, 87–93.

3. Ibid.

4. Vikas Bijaj, "US Trade Deficit Sets Record, with China and Oil the Causes," *New York Times*, Feb. 11, 2006; BBC News, "Oil Sets Fresh Record above $109," March 11, 2008.

5. U.S. Federal News Service, "Republican Economic Policies Are Securing America's Economic Prosperity," July 10, 2006.

6. Lizabeth Cohen, *A Consumers' Republic: The Politics of Mass Consumption in Postwar America* (New York: Vintage, 2003), 8.

7. Ibid., 8–9.

8. Ibid., 397.

9. See, for example, Jonathan Watts, "A Miracle and a Menace," *Guardian*, Nov. 9, 2005, in which Watts discusses the rapid growth of capitalism in China, the benefits this growth has conferred on an expanding middle class, and the challenges China presents to the global order as it becomes a "superconsumer."

10. In 2005 Russia and the United States displayed similar levels of income inequality, with the richest 10 percent of the population earning almost 15 times the amount of the poorest 10 percent. Kommersant, "The Usual Passivity," http://www.kommersant.com/p684342/r_500/The_Usual_Passivity/. The number of millionaires grew by 17.4 percent in 2005, accounting for 0.1 percent of the population, while those below the poverty level made up 17.8 percent. On the ongoing problem of xenophobia and racism in Russia see Nassor Ali, "Russia: Attacks on Foreigners on the Rise," *New African*, April 2004, 60–63; Sophia Kishkovsky, "Attackers Pillage Moscow Art Gallery and Beat Activist Owner," *New York Times*, Oct. 22, 2006 (describing an attack on an ethnic Georgian artist and political activist by Russian skinheads); Steven Lee Myers, "In Anti-immigrant Mood, Russia Heeds Gadfly's Cry," *New York Times*, Oct. 22, 2006 (describing the move into the political mainstream of an explicitly racist and anti-immigrant political movement in Russia).

11. The birthrate for women under 20 in the United Kingdom was the second highest of 28 Organization for Economic Cooperation and Development (OECD) countries, surpassed only by women in the United States, and there is "a host of evidence that teenage births are associated with poor outcomes for the teenage mother and child, both in the short and long term." Jonathan Bradshaw, "Teenage Births," Joseph Rowntree Foundation, http://www.jrf.org.uk/child-poverty/publications.asp.

12. Fraser Nelson, "Our Hidden Shame," *Scotsman*, Jan. 8, 2006.

13. "Must Britain take the American low road to job creation through low pay and insecurity, or can it follow the European high road to better-quality jobs, underpinned by decent training, while avoiding the worst economic effects of over-regulation? If

the first of these, it is hard to imagine child poverty ever disappearing." Mary Braid, "Trying Hard to Make Good," *New Statesman*, July 10, 2006, 17. See Paul Krugman, "Helping the Poor, the British Way," *New York Times*, Dec. 25, 2006, on improvements to the lot of the poor under the Labour government since 1996.

14. On the 2006 employment law protests in France see "In Rare Praise of Dominique de Villepin," *Economist*, Mar. 18, 2006, 13–14; "Le Climbdown," *Economist*, Apr. 15, 2006, 52–53. On the economic and political challenges facing Germany's first woman chancellor, Angela Merkel, see William Drozdiak, "Creating a Merkel Miracle," *Foreign Policy*, January/February 2006, 68–72; "Letting Go: Germany Needs to Loosen Up—or Face Decline," *Economist*, Feb. 11, 2006, 16.

15. Pope John Paul II, *Sollicitudo rei socialis*, 1987, 28.

16. "Evangelicals and Catholics Together: The Christian Mission in the Third Millennium," *First Things*, May 1994, 15–22. See also Mark A. Noll and Carolyn Nystrom, *Is the Reformation Over? An Evangelical Assessment of Contemporary Roman Catholicism* (Grand Rapids, Mich.: Baker Academic, 2005).

17. "Evangelical-Catholic Pact Questioned," *Christian Century*, Mar. 15, 1995, 287.

18. Richard John Neuhaus, "The Public Square," *First Things*, August/September 1995, 67–68.

19. Daniel Golden, "A Test of Faith: A Professor's Firing after His Conversion Highlights a New Orthodoxy at Religious Colleges," *Wall Street Journal*, Jan. 7, 2006.

20. David P. Gushee and Dennis P. Hollinger, "Toward an Evangelical Ethical Methodology," in *Toward an Evangelical Public Policy: Political Strategies for the Health of the Nation*, ed. Ronald J. Sider and Diane Knippers (Grand Rapids, Mich.: Baker, 2005), 117, 119; Hannah Elliott, "Accurate Definition of 'Evangelical' Up for Debate in Theology, Politics," Associated Baptist Press, http://www.abpnews.com/1687.article.

21. See, for example, Michael Gerson, "A New Social Gospel," *Newsweek*, Nov. 13, 2006, 40–43.

22. See, for example, Jim Wallis, *God's Politics: Why the Right Gets It Wrong and the Left Doesn't Get It* (San Francisco: Harper, 2005); Anthony Campolo, *Letters to a Young Evangelical* (New York: Basic, 2006). Campolo's book is described on his website as one that "enjoins Evangelicals young and old to resist the intimidating rhetoric of the Religious Right and think for themselves." See http://www.tonycampolo.org/store.php#LTYE. Campolo also seeks to connect evangelicals to forms of Catholic spirituality and prayer life, noting that perhaps Protestants "left too much behind" after the Reformation. Campolo, *Letters*, 31.

23. Laurie Goodstein, "Evangelical's Focus on Climate Draws Fire from Christian Right," *New York Times*, Mar. 3, 2007.

24. Gushee and Hollinger, "Toward an Evangelical Ethical Methodology," 119–120.

25. Randall Balmer, *Blessed Assurance: A History of Evangelicalism in America* (Boston: Beacon, 1999).

26. John McGreevy, *Catholicism and American Freedom: A History* (New York: Norton, 2003), 12–13.

27. Jeremy Leaming, "James Dobson: The Religious Right's 800-Pound Gorilla," *Church and State*, February 2005, 14.

28. Dan Gilgoff and Bret Schulte, "The Dobson Way," *U.S. News and World Report*, Jan. 17, 2005, 62–71.

29. Ibid. For more discussion of the political agenda of the Religious Right following George Bush's reelection, see Debra Rosenberg and Rebecca Sinderbrand, "Of Prayer and Payback," *Newsweek*, Nov. 22, 2004, 46; Doug Ireland, "Republicans Relaunch Antigay Culture Wars," *Nation*, Oct. 20, 2003, 18–23; "Falwell Pleads for Funds to Recruit Christian Voters for 2006 and Beyond," *Church and State*, February 2005, 20.

30. John C. Danforth, "In the Name of Politics," *New York Times*, Mar. 30, 2005. See also Peter Slevin, "St. Jack and the Bullies in the Pulpit," *Washington Post*, Feb. 2, 2006. Danforth has released a book that elaborates on these ideas; see John Danforth, *Faith and Politics: How the "Moral Values" Debate Divides America and How to Move Forward Together* (New York: Viking, 2006).

31. Patrick Hynes, "Christian Republicans," American Spectator, http://www.spectator.org/dsp_article.asp?art_id=8948.

32. Paul M. Weyrich, "Republicans Who Think as Does Jack Danforth," Free Congress Foundation, http://www.freecongress.org/.

33. Charles Babington, "Conservatives' Tactics against Miers May Backfire Next Time; Liberals Say the Rules Keep Changing," *Washington Post*, Oct. 30, 2005; Ralph Z. Hallow, "Conservatives Ill-at-Ease in Dissent; Factions Are Split on Whether a New High Court Pick Alone Can Heal Rifts on the Right," *Washington Times*, Oct. 30, 2005.

34. This summary of the events leading to Terri Schiavo's death is adapted from various news reports and from Steven G. Calabresi, "The Terri Schiavo Case: In Defense of the Special Law Enacted by Congress and President Bush," *Northwestern Law Review* 100 (2006): 151–152.

35. Ibid., 153–154.

36. Rachel Graves, "The Terri Schiavo Case: Schiavo Dies but Debate Lives," *Houston Chronicle*, Apr. 1, 2005.

37. Daniel Eisenberg, "Lessons of the Schiavo Battle," *Time*, Apr. 4, 2005, 22–30.

38. Calabresi, "Terri Schiavo Case,"158.

39. Wes Allison and Anita Kumar, "What Terri's Law Cost the Republicans: Faith and Consequences," *St. Petersburg Times*, Dec. 18, 2005.

40. Nina J. Easton, "Rift Emerges in GOP after Schiavo Case," *Boston Globe*, Apr. 9, 2005.

41. See, for example, Paul Lauritzen, "Caring at the End: How the Schiavo Case Undermined Catholic Teaching," *Commonweal*, Mar. 10, 2006, 14–16; Gilbert Orr and Robert Meilaender, "Ethics and Life's End: An Exchange," *First Things*, August/September 2004, 31–37.

42. Alasdair MacIntyre, "Politics, Philosophy, and the Common Good," in *The Alasdair MacIntyre Reader*, ed. Kevin Knight (Notre Dame, Ind.: University of Notre Dame Press, 1998), 235, 238.

43. Blaine Harden, "O'Connor Bemoans Hill Rancor at Judges," *Washington Post*, July 22, 2005.

44. Jimmy Carter, *Our Endangered Values* (New York: Simon and Schuster, 2005), 8.

45. Ibid., 53.

46. Ibid., 42.

47. Robert Nozick, "The Entitlement Theory of Justice," in *The Libertarian Reader*, ed. David Boaz (New York: Free Press, 1997), 81.

48. Ibid., 195.

49. Friedrich A. Hayek, *Law, Legislation, and Liberty.* Vol. 2: *The Mirage of Social Justice* (Chicago: University of Chicago Press, 1978), 3.

50. Ibid., 110.

51. Ibid., 113.

52. Ibid., 7.

53. Ibid., 69.

54. Ibid., 68.

55. Ibid., 66.

56. "The minimalist state is the most extensive state that can be justified. Any state more extensive violates people's rights." Nozick, "Entitlement Theory of Justice," 81. Nozick goes on to describe the inherent flaws in the concept of distributive justice, a principle central to Catholic social teaching.

57. "We can debate a lot of economic data but not income inequality. Every serious study shows that the US income gap has become a chasm. Over the past 30 years, the share of income going to the highest earning Americans has risen steadily to levels not seen since shortly before the Great Depression." Steven Rattner, "The Rich Get (Much) Richer," *Business Week*, Aug. 8, 2005, 90. For a perspective on the issue that attributes the phenomenon to skill-based technological change, see A. Steelman and J. A. Weinburg, "What's Driving Wage Inequality?" *Federal Reserve Bank of Richmond Economic Quarterly*, Summer 2005, 1–17.

58. See David Rodgers, "Republicans Mount New Push to Cut Estate Tax," *Wall Street Journal*, July 27, 2006; David Rodgers, "House Republicans Move to Tie Wage Increases to Estate Tax Cut," *Wall Street Journal*, July 29, 2006; David Nather, "Frist Loses Estate Tax Showdown," *CQ Weekly*, Aug. 7, 2006.

59. For a full account of Left libertarianism and a response to key critiques, see Peter Vallentyne, Hillel Steiner, and Michael Otsuka, "Why Left-Libertarianism Is Not Incoherent, Indeterminate, or Irrelevant: A Reply to Fried," *Philosophy and Public Affairs* 33, no. 2 (2005): 201.

60. Jacques Maritain, *The Person and the Common Good* (Notre Dame, Ind.: University of Notre Dame Press, 1985), 47–48.

61. Alasdair MacIntyre, *After Virtue: A Study in Moral Theory* (Notre Dame, Ind.: University of Notre Dame Press, 1981), 12–22.

62. James Q. Wilson, "Divided We Stand: Can a Polarized Nation Win a Protracted War?" *Wall Street Journal*, Feb. 15, 2006.

63. Joseph Bottum, "The New Fusionism," *First Things*, June/July, 2005, 32–36.

64. Eric Schmitt, "Uproar in House as Parties Clash on Iraq Pullout," *New York Times*, Nov. 19, 2005.

65. Richard John Neuhaus, "Communion and Communio," *First Things*, August/September 2004, 86–104; Frans Josef van Beek, "Denying Communion to Politicians," *Commonweal*, June 4, 2004, 19–21; Joe Feuerherd, "The Battle for the Catholic Vote," Salon, http://dir.salon.com/story/news/feature/2004/10/31/catholics/index.html. For an excellent overview of the controversy, see M. Cathleen Kaveny, "Prophesy and Casuistry: Abortion, Torture, and Moral Discourse," *Villanova Law Review* 51 (2006): 524n82.

66. See Frank Bruni, "Threats and Responses: Vatican, Threat of Iraq War Draws World Leaders, with Different Views, to the Pope's Door," *New York Times*, Feb. 22, 2003; Mark and Louise Zwick, "Pope John Paul II Calls War a Defeat for Humanity: Neoconservative Iraq Just War Theories Rejected," *Houston Catholic Worker*, July/August 2003.

67. The Vatican's *Compendium of the Social Doctrine of the Catholic Church* is explicit: "The Magisterium condemns the savagery of war and asks that war be considered in a new way. In fact, it is hardly possible to imagine that in an atomic era, war could be used as an instrument of justice. War is a scourge and is never an appropriate way to resolve problems that arise between nations, it has never been and it will never be because it creates new and still more complicated conflicts." Pontifical Council for Justice and Peace, *Compendium of the Social Doctrine of the Catholic Church* (Washington, D.C.: U.S. Conference of Catholic Bishops, 2005), 216. See also Rowan Williams, "War and Statecraft: An Exchange," *First Things*, March 2004, 14–22.

68. George Weigel, "Moral Clarity in a Time of War," *First Things*, January 2003, 23.

69. Ibid., 24.

70. Williams, "War and Statecraft," 15.

71. William T. Cavanaugh, "Killing for the Telephone Company: Why the Nation-State Is Not the Keeper of the Common Good," *Modern Theology* 20, no. 2 (2004): 268.

72. Michael Northcott, *An Angel Directs the Storm: Apocalyptic Religion and American Empire* (London: Tauris, 2004), 100.

73. James Kurth, "The Protestant Deformation and American Foreign Policy," *Orbis*, Spring 1998, 221.

74. Ibid., 226.

75. Ibid., 227.

76. Ibid., 229.

77. John L. Allen Jr., *All the Pope's Men: The Inside Story of How the Vatican Really Thinks* (New York: Doubleday, 2004), 315–316.

78. See Susan Page, "Church Going Closely Tied to Voting Patterns," *USA Today*, June 6, 2004, http://www.usatoday.com/news/nation/2004-06-02-religion-gap_x.htm.

79. "Vatican Condemns Cartoons of Mohammed," Zenit, http://www.zenit.org/article-15193?l =english.

80. Joseph Bottum, comment on "The Easy Charge Is Hypocrisy," First Things on the Square Blog, comment posted Feb. 7, 2006, http://www.firstthings.com/onthesquare/?p=173 (accessed Feb. 18, 2008).

81. See "U.S. Government Calls Anti-Islamic Cartoons 'Offensive,'" International Information Programs, http://usinfo.state.gov/xarchives/display.html?p=washfile-english&y=2006&m=February&x=20060203165442cpataruko.3103907; "Straw Comments on Cartoons Depicting the Prophet Mohammed," Foreign and Commonwealth Office, http://www.fco.gov.uk/servlet/Front?pagename=Open Market/Xcelerate/ShowPage&c=Page&cid=1007029391629&a=KArticle&aid=1138869062592&year=2006&month=2006-02-01.

82. Bottum, "Easy Charge."

83. Heinrich Schneider, "Patriotism, Nationalism, and the Duties of Citizens," in *Religion and Nationalism,* ed. John Coleman and Miklos Tomka (London: SCM, 1995), 33, 38.

84. Ibid., 33.

85. Ibid., 40.

86. Ibid., 41.

87. See Nolan McCarty, Keith T. Poole, and Howard Rosenthal, *Polarized America: The Dance of Ideology and Unequal Riches* (Cambridge, Mass.: MIT Press, 2006).

88. Robert George, "The Tyrant State," *First Things,* November 1996, 39–42. For an overview of the entire debate, in which key voices in the American neoconservative movement argued that the U.S. government was dangerously close to no longer being the legitimate representative of a large segment of the citizenry, see Richard John Neuhaus, *The Anatomy of a Controversy* (Dallas: Spence, 1997).

NOTES TO CHAPTER 2

1. Johan Verstraeten, "Re-thinking Catholic Social Thought as Tradition," in *Catholic Social Thought: Twilight or Renaissance?* ed. Jonathan Boswell, Francis P. McHugh, and Johan Verstraeten (Leuven, Belgium: Leuven University Press, 2000), 64.

2. See ibid., 59–60.

3. Ibid., 61.

4. Robert Ellsberg, Introduction, *The Logic of Solidarity: Commentaries on Pope John Paul II's Encyclical 'On Social Concern,'* ed. Gregory Baum and Robert Ellsberg (Maryknoll, N.Y.: Orbis, 1989), ix.

5. John XXIII was the first pope to address a social encyclical in this way, with *Pacem in terris* in 1963.

6. See Mary Ann Glendon, "What Happened at Beijing," *First Things,* January 1996, 30–36.

7. See Virgil Nemoianu, "The Church and the Secular Establishment: A Philosophical Dialog between Joseph Ratzinger and Jürgen Habermas," *Logos* 9, no. 2 (2006): 16–42.

8. See Chantal Delsol, "Actualité de la pensée sociale catholique dans les sociétés individualistes contemporaines," in Boswell et al., ed., *Catholic Social Thought*, 117, 118–119.

9. See Michael Schuck, "Early Modern Roman Catholic Social Thought, 1740–1890," in *Modern Catholic Social Teaching: Commentaries and Interpretations*, ed. Kenneth R. Himes et al. (Washington, D.C.: Georgetown University Press, 2005), 99–124; Philip Chmielewski, SJ, *Bettering Our Condition: Work, Workers, and Ethics in British and German Economic Thought* (New York: Peter Lang, 1992), 143.

10. David O'Brien and Thomas Shannon, eds., *Catholic Social Thought: The Documentary Heritage* (Maryknoll, N.Y.: Orbis, 1997), 9.

11. Ibid., 13.

12. See Stephen Pope, "Natural Law in Catholic Social Teachings," in Himes, ed., *Modern Catholic Social Teaching*, 50.

13. See Pope Pius XI, *Quadragesimo anno* (1931), 101–110.

14. S. Heileman, "Is There a Future for Catholic Social Teaching?" in Jonathan Boswell, Francis McHugh, and Johan Verstraeten, eds., *Catholic Social Teaching: Twilight or Renaissance?* (Dudley, Mass.: Peeters, 2000), 13–14.

15. Ibid., 22–23.

16. Vatican Council II, "*Lumen gentium*," in *Vatican Council II: Constitutions, Decrees, Declarations*, ed. Austin Flannery (Northport, N.Y.: Costello, 1996), para. 36.

17. Vatican Council II, "*Gaudium et spes*," in *Vatican Council II*, para. 29.

18. David Hollenbach, "Commentary on *Gaudium et spes*," in Himes, ed., *Modern Catholic Social Teaching*, 266, 284–285.

19. Pope Paul VI, *Populorum progressio* (1967), para. 47.

20. Ibid., para. 22–23.

21. Gustavo Gutiérrez, *A Theology of Liberation: History, Politics, and Salvation*, 2d ed., trans. and ed. Sr. Caridad Inda and John Eagleson (Maryknoll, N.Y.: Orbis, 1988), xv–xvi.

22. Pope John Paul II, *Sollicitudo rei socialis* (1987), para. 42.

23. Pontifical Council for Justice and Peace, *Compendium of the Social Doctrine of the Catholic Church* (Washington, D.C.: United States Conference of Catholic Bishops, 2005), para. 162.

24. Ibid., para. 163.

25. Ibid., para. 105.

26. Ibid., para. 107.

27. U.S. Conference of Catholic Bishops, *For I Was Hungry and You Gave Me Food: Catholic Reflections on Food, Farmers, and Farmworkers* (2003), http://www.usccb .org/bishops/agricultural.shtml.

28. Ibid.

29. See L. Roos, "The Human Person and Human Dignity as Basis for the Social Doctrine of the Church," in *Principles of Catholic Social Teaching*, ed. David A. Boileau (Milwaukee: Marquette University Press, 1998), 53, 57.

30. Ibid.

31. Ruth Abbey, *Charles Taylor* (Princeton, N.J.: Princeton University Press, 2000), 6.

32. Richard Kearney, "Ricoeur," in *A Companion to Continental Philosophy*, ed. Simon Critchley and William R. Schroeder (Malden, Mass.: Blackwell, 1998), 443–444.

33. Agnès Poirier, "The High Road to Decadence: To Understand the World Better, Britons Need to Be Freed from Their Monolingual Misery," *Guardian*, Dec. 20, 2006.

34. Jon Marcus, *America Slow to Take International Outlook, New York Times Education Supplement*, Oct. 31, 2003, 12.

35. Jon Marcus, "American Lack of Foreign Knowledge 'Dangerous,'" *New York Times Higher Education Supplement*, Dec. 2, 2005, 13; Edward B. Fiske, "States Prepare for the Global Age" (2005), available at Asia Society, http://www.internationaled.org/statesprepare for the globalage.pdf (accessed Apr. 10, 2008).

36. Emmanuel Lévinas, *Alterity and Transcendence*, trans. Michael B. Smith (New York: Columbia University Press, 1999), 101.

37. Ibid., 88.

38. Ibid., 10–104.

39. Ibid., 106.

40. Delsol, "Actualité de la pensée," 118.

41. "*Gaudium et spes*," in *Vatican Council II*, para. 26.

42. Southern African Catholic Bishops' Conference, *God's Agents of Hope: Sustaining Democracy in South Africa* (2004), http://www.sacbc.org.za/pdfs/justice_and_peace/Election%20brief.pdf.

43. See Pope John Paul II, *Centesimus annus* (1991), para. 31.

44. Ibid.

45. "*Gaudium et spes*," in *Vatican Council II*, para. 71.

46. For further elaboration on the three forms of justice, see U.S. Conference of Catholic Bishops, *Economic Justice for All: Pastoral Letter on Catholic Social Teaching and the U.S. Economy* (Washington, D.C.: United States Conference of Catholic Bishops, 1986), para. 69–76.

47. Bishops of England and Wales, *The Common Good and the Catholic Church's Social Teaching*, para. 70–71, http://www.catholicchurch.org.uk/resource/cg/cg003.htm.

48. See "2004 Republican Party Platform," 39, http://www.gop.com/media/2004platform.pdf.

49. Pontifical Council for Justice and Peace, *Compendium of the Social Doctrine*, para. 168.

50. "*Gaudium et spes*," in *Vatican Council II*, para. 26

51. Pontifical Council for Justice and Peace, *Compendium of the Social Doctrine*, para. 355.

52. U.S. Conference of Catholic Bishops, *Economic Justice for All*, para. 82–83.

53. Donal Dorr, *Option for the Poor: A Hundred Years of Catholic Social Teaching*, rev. ed. (Dublin: Gill and Macmillan, 1992), 181–182.

54. See Pope Paul VI, *Populorum progressio*, para. 18–21.

55. Dorr, *Option for the Poor*, 182–183.

56. See Martha C. Nussbaum, *Women and Human Development: The Capabilities Approach* (New York: Cambridge University Press, 2000).

57. Pope John Paul II, *Sollicitudo rei socialis*, para. 38.

58. See Charles Curran, Michael Himes, OFM, and Thomas Shannon, "Commentary on *Sollicitudo rei socialis* (On Social Concern)," in Himes, ed., *Modern Catholic Social Teaching*, 429.

59. Ibid., 428.

60. Gregory Baum, "Structures of Sin," in *The Logic of Solidarity: Commentaries on Pope John Paul II's Encyclical: "On Social Concern,"* ed. Gregory Baum and Robert Ellsberg (Maryknoll, N.Y.: Orbis, 1989), 112–113.

61. Ibid., 119.

62. Ibid.

63. Ibid.

64. Max Weber, *The Protestant Ethic and the Spirit of Capitalism*, trans. Talcott Parsons (Los Angeles: Roxbury, 1998).

65. John E. Tropman, *The Catholic Ethic and the Spirit of Community* (Washington, D.C.: Georgetown University Press, 2002). Much of Tropman's earlier sociological work has been on poor people in the United States. See John E. Tropman, *Does America Hate the Poor? The Other American Dilemma: Lessons for the 21st Century from the 1960s and the 1970s* (Westport, Conn.: Praeger, 1998).

66. Tropman, *Catholic Ethic*, 2.

67. Ibid., 21.

68. Ibid., 22.

69. See Michael J. Schuck, "Early Modern Roman Catholic Social Thought, 1740–1890," in Himes, ed., *Modern Catholic Social Teaching*, 101.

70. Ibid., 108.

71. Chmielewski, *Bettering Our Condition*, 143; See also Christine Firer Hinze, "Commentary on *Quadragesimo anno* ("After Forty Years")," in Himes, ed., *Modern Catholic Social Teaching*, 154.

72. Chmielewski, *Bettering Our Condition*, 189.

73. See Hinze, "Commentary on *Quadragesimo anno*, 154–155.

74. Pope Pius XI, *Quadragesimo anno*, para. 79.

75. Paolo Carozza, "Subsidiarity as a Structural Principle of International Human Rights Law," *American Journal of International Law* 97, no. 38 (2003): 50.

76. Ibid., 42.

77. Ibid., 44.

78. Ibid., 45.

79. Pope John Paul II, *Centesimus annus*, para. 25.

80. Milton Friedman, "The Relation between Economic Freedom and Political Freedom," in *The Libertarian Reader*, ed. David Boaz (New York: Free Press, 1997), 297–298.

81. Michael Novak, *Freedom with Justice: Catholic Social Thought and Liberal Institutions* (San Francisco: Harper and Row, 1984), xiii.

82. Ibid., 34–35.

83. Ibid., 38.

84. Charles Curran, "The Reception of Catholic Social and Economic Teaching in the United States," in Himes, ed., *Modern Catholic Social Teaching*, 482.

85. See Novak, *Freedom with Justice*, 108–124.

86. Ibid., 119.

87. Ibid., 147.

88. See James Brooke, "Vatican Undercuts Leftist Theology in Brazil," *New York Times*, April 23, 1989; Leonardo Boff, "I Sat in [Galileo's] Seat: The Father of Liberation Theology Remembers the Day the Inquisition Took Over," *Index on Censorship*, 33, no. 4 (October 2004): 31–36; Dennis Doyle, "Communion Ecclesiology and the Silencing of Boff," *America*, Sept. 12, 1992, 139.

89. George Weigel, *Catholicism and the Renewal of American Democracy* (New York: Paulist Press, 1989), 16–27.

90. Ibid., 18–19.

91. Ibid., 26.

92. Ibid., 181.

93. The seminal work for the argument that Americans have become remarkably more atomized in recent decades is Robert Putnam, *Bowling Alone: The Collapse and Revival of American Community* (New York: Simon and Schuster, 2000). The book has generated a great deal of discussion and various articles challenging or supporting its thesis. Nevertheless, there is no real debate about the obvious decline in the relevance of traditional social groups, religious institutions, and communities of memory in the lives of most Americans.

94. Richard John Neuhaus, "An Argument about Human Nature," in *A New Worldly Order*, ed. George Weigel (Washington, D.C.: Ethics and Public Policy Center, 1992), 124.

95. See George Weigel, "Prologue," in Weigel, *New Worldly Order*, 5.

96. Michael Novak, "Tested by Our Own Ideals," in Weigel, *New Worldly Order*, 139.

97. Daniel Finn, "Commentary on *Centesimus annus*," in Himes, ed., *Modern Catholic Social Teaching*, 462.

98. Gregory Kalscheur, SJ, "John Paul II, John Courtney Murray, and the Relationship between Civil Law and Moral Law: A Constructive Proposal for Contemporary American Pluralism," *Journal of Catholic Social Thought* 1, no. 2 (2004): 264.

99. Ibid., 267–269.

100. Ibid., 268.

101. Ibid., 270.

NOTES TO CHAPTER 3

1. James Boyd White, "What's Wrong with Our Talk about Race? On History, Particularity, and Affirmative Action," *Michigan Law Review* 100 (2000): 1929.

2. Ibid., 1938–1939.

3. I recognize both that the concept of race is infinitely more complex than the black/white binary construction of race allows and that this construction excludes the important voices of other groups that have suffered racial discrimination in American society. See Juan F. Perea, "The Black/White Binary Paradigm of Race," *California Law Review* 85 (1997): 1213. I employ it here as emblematic of the destructive nature of racism. By making race a "black/white" issue, millions of individuals who fit in neither category were robbed of a meaningful identity in American society. Furthermore, blacks were forbidden from acknowledging multiethnic backgrounds. Fundamentally, however, racism in the United States was about the determination of who was black and who was white.

4. I use the descriptive term "Anglo-American" before "liberalism" to describe the unique modern understanding of liberalism as it has developed in the Anglo-American world, particularly through the philosophical works of Dworkin and Rawls. An accompanying strain of liberalism that is particularly prominent in the United States is the libertarian variety that is rooted in the works of Hobbes, Locke, and Mill and finds its modern philosophical voice in the works of Robert Nozick.

5. Clint Bolick, *The Affirmative Action Fraud: Can We Restore the American Civil Rights Vision?* (Washington, D.C.: Cato Institute, 1996), 24–25.

6. As Thomas Guglielmo points out, "America, during the past century tended to draw a 'color line' which separated 'whites' from the 'colored races'—groups such as 'Negroes,' 'Orientals,' and sometimes 'Mexicans.'" *White on Arrival: Italians, Race, Color, and Power in Chicago, 1890–1945* (New York: Oxford University Press, 2004), 3. The existence of this color boundary influenced many aspects of Americans' daily social, political, and economic lives by creating opportunities even for those who, like the Italian immigrants, were considered to be of questionable ethnic descent but were nevertheless able to place themselves in the "white" group, and isolating those of the "colored races" (6, 26–27).

7. Charles Taylor, *Philosophical Arguments* (Cambridge, Mass.: Harvard University Press, 1995), 186.

8. Michael Sandel, *Democracy's Discontent: America in Search of a Public Philosophy* (Cambridge, Mass.: Belknap Press of Harvard University Press, 1996), 24.

9. Ibid., 14.

10. Ibid.

11. Taylor, *Philosophical Arguments*, 247.

12. Will Kymlicka and Ruth Rubio Marín, "Liberalism and Minority Rights: An Interview," *Ratio Juris*, June 1999, 135–136.

13. "We citizens of the United States, and of other liberal democracies, do not now live in a time that is 'after liberalism.' We Americans are all liberals now. . . . That is, we are not merely democrats (small 'd') but *liberal* democrats. We are all committed both to the true and full humanity of every person and, therefore, to certain basic human freedoms (liberties)." Michael J. Perry, *Under God? Religious Faith and Liberal Democracy* (New York: Cambridge University Press, 2003), 36.

14. Ibid.

15. Sandel, *Democracy's Discontent*, 15.

16. Will Kymlicka and Wayne Norman, "Citizenship in Culturally Diverse Societies: Issues, Contexts, Concepts," in *Citizenship in Diverse Societies,* ed. Will Kymlicka and Wayne Norman (New York: Oxford University Press, 2000), 24.

17. See Kymlicka and Marín, "Liberalism and Minority Rights," 136.

18. The controversy over the veiled racist comments of former Senate majority leader Trent Lott in 2002 shows how powerfully race continues to resonate in American life. To this one might add the "shocking" revelations of the fathering of mixed-race children by Thomas Jefferson and Strom Thurmond. Although African Americans have longed accepted these stories as true, it has taken DNA tests and, in Thurmond's case, dramatic personal revelations by an African American daughter to give "mainstream" credibility to these stories. Historical truths about race in American life as lived by African Americans have typically had little or no validity in our culture until they have been authenticated by science or by someone white.

19. For a general discussion of how race, ethnicity, and color have played an important role in burdening certain racial groups with the inability to transcend oppression, see Guglielmo, *White on Arrival,* 3.

20. Michael Novak, *Free Persons and the Common Good* (Boulder, Colo.: Madison Books, 1989), 56.

21. Ibid., 59.

22. *Adarand Contractors, Inc. v. Peña,* 515 U.S. 200, 239 (1995).

23. See M. Cathleen Kaveny, "Discrimination and Affirmative Action," *Theological Studies* 57 (1996): 286, 301.

24. James Boyd White, *Justice as Translation: An Essay in Cultural and Legal Criticism* (Chicago: University of Chicago Press, 1994), 20.

25. Ibid., 102.

26. *Grutter v. Bollinger,* 539 U.S. 306, 329 (2003), quoting *Regents of Univ. of California v. Bakke,* 438 U.S. 265, 310 (opinion of Powell, J.).

27. Ibid.

28. Ibid., 330, quoting *Adarand Constructors, Inc.,* 515 U.S., at 227.

29. Ibid., 331, citing *Richmond v. J.A. Croson Co.,* 488 U.S. 469, 493 (1989) (plurality opinion).

30. Ibid.

31. Ibid.

32. Ibid., 332 (quoting brief for Respondents Bollinger et al., I).

33. Ibid., 331–334.

34. Ibid., 336.

35. Ibid.

36. Ibid., 2343.

37. Ibid.

38. Ibid., 2343, 2345–2346.

39. White, "What's Wrong with Our Talk about Race?" 1942.

40. Brown University Steering Committee on Slavery and Justice, "Slavery and Justice," 7–8, http://www.brown.edu/Research/Slavery_Justice/.

41. Cheryl I. Harris, "Whiteness as Property," in *Critical Race Theory: The Key Writings That Formed the Movement*, ed. Kimberlé Chrenshaw et al. (New York: New Press, 1995), 276, 278.

42. Ibid., 279, quoting *Johnson v. Butler*, 4 Ky. (I Bibb) 97 (1815).

43. See Kimberlé Crenshaw, "Race Reform and Retrenchment: Transformation and Legitimation in Antidiscrimination Law," in *Critical Race Theory*, 103, 113. Moreover, she states that "Race-consciousness also reinforces whites' sense that American society truly is meritocratic, and thus it helps to prevent them from questioning the basic legitimacy of the free market. Believing both that blacks are inferior and that the economy impartially rewards the superior over the inferior, whites see that most blacks are indeed worse off than whites are, which reinforces their sense that the market is operating 'fairly and impartially'; those who logically should be on the bottom are on the bottom" (116).

44. Ibid.

45. Derrick Bell, "Racial Realism," in Chrenshaw et al., eds., *Critical Race Theory*, 304.

46. See Sandel, *Democracy's Discontent*, 15.

47. U.S. Conference of Catholic Bishops, *"Brothers and Sisters to Us": A Pastoral Letter on Racism* (Washington, D.C.: Author, 1979).

48. Perry, *Under God?* 36.

49. Michael J. Perry, *The Idea of Human Rights* (New York: Oxford University Press, 1998), 11–12. Perry notes, however, that the fact that religious views are the only "intelligible" ones does not mean that they are necessarily persuasive or plausible.

50. Charles E. Curran, *Catholic Social Teaching: A Historical and Ethical Analysis 1891–Present* (Washington, D.C.: Georgetown University Press, 2002), 132.

51. Hervé Carrier, SJ, *The Social Doctrine of the Church Revisited: A Guide for Study* (Vatican City: Pontifical Council for Justice and Peace, 1990), 11.

52. Curran, *Catholic Social Teaching*, 133.

53. Pope John Paul II, *Sollicitudo rei socialis* (1987), para. 39.

54. Ibid., para. 40.

55. See White, *Justice as Translation*, 3–4.

56. Pope John Paul II, *Sollicitudo rei socialis*, para. 38.

57. See David Hollenbach, SJ, *The Common Good and Christian Ethics* (New York: Cambridge University Press, 2002). Hollenbach uses the Catholic understanding of solidarity and the common good to argue for new relationship between suburbanites and residents of the inner cities, who are disproportionately black and poor (173–211).

58. Ibid., 40.

59. Ibid., 154.

60. On the growth of income inequality in the United States, see Paul Krugman, "A Touch of Class," *New York Times*, Jan. 21, 2003; on the precariousness of the economic situation of the middle class, see Elizabeth Warren, *The Two-income Trap: Why Middle-Class Mothers and Fathers Are Going Broke* (New York: Basic Books, 2003).

61. Brown University Steering Committee, *Slavery and Justice*, 43. This anger at certain people benefiting more than others in a competitive economic system and the perception that the advantage is unfair relates to the issues identified by Kimberlé Crenshaw: Americans place an unreasonable degree of confidence in the social and economic sorting done by the free market and are extremely skeptical of any adjustments in the system that might assist those whom the marketplace has, in their mind, identified as "losers." See Crenshaw, "Race Reform and Retrenchment," 1380–1381.

62. See "Analysis: Racism in America in Light of Trent Lott's Comments at Strom Thurmond's Birthday and Retirement Party, Part One," NPR, Dec. 20, 2002, http://nl.newsbank.com/nl-search/we/Archives.

63. Ibid., comments of Wilbert Glover.

64. Teresa Phelps, *Shattered Voices: Language, Violence, and the Work of Truth Commissions* (Philadelphia: University of Pennsylvania Press, 2004), 70. Phelps's work emphasizes the role that the acknowledgment of these stories by the state and those traditionally in power plays in "capturing the reality of a piece of a shared past." It is not essential that all of the details of the stories be factually accurate, but a real recognition of the storyteller's humanity and the subjectivity are necessary.

65. Pope Paul VI, *Populorum progressio* (1967), para. 46.

66. U.S. Conference of Catholic Bishops, *Economic Justice for All: Pastoral Letter on Catholic Social Teaching and the U.S. Economy* (Washington, D.C.: Author, 1986), para. 78.

67. Norman Chemerinsky has noted that "schools are more segregated today than they have been for decades, and segregation is rapidly increasing. Most notably, wide disparities exist in funding for schools." Erwin Chemerinsky, "Separate and Unequal: American Public Education Today," *American University Law Review* 52 (2003): 1461. He sites research by Harvard professor Gary Orfield to demonstrate that, from 1986 to 1999, the percentage of African American students attending majority black schools increased from 62.9 percent to 70.2 percent and that a similar pattern holds for Latino students (1463).

68. This proposal is similar to that of a program that was instituted by one of the most elite higher education programs in France, the Institute of Political Studies, known there as "Sciences Po." Sciences Po offers special courses for students from France's poorest neighborhoods (which tend to be heavily populated by Muslim immigrants from north Africa) and from its most economically depressed region, Lorraine. These students receive counseling and special courses, and the high schools ultimately select certain students to take a special 45-minute oral examination conducted by a panel from Sciences Po (instead of the two-day examination the other applicants take). Although these students are reported to be performing at the same level as their classmates, right-wing groups in France have protested the policy as a violation of the French republican tradition of "equality of opportunity." See Burton Bollag, "A French Court Supports an Elite University's Affirmative Action Program," *Chronicle of Higher Education*, Nov. 21, 2003, 34.

69. See *Milliken v. Bradley*, 418 U.S. 717 (1974). "*Milliken* has had a devastating effect on the ability to achieve desegregation in many areas. In a number of major

cities, inner city school systems are substantially black and are surrounded by almost all-white suburbs. Desegregation obviously requires the ability to transfer students between the city and suburban schools. There simply are not enough white students in the city, or enough black students in the suburbs, to achieve desegregation." Chemerinsky, "Separate and Unequal," 1469.

70. Using the example of Prince George's County, Maryland, Sheryll Cashin has demonstrated how African Americans, regardless of income, are disadvantaged in the provision of public services and economic investment when they live in suburban communities with substantial black populations. See Sheryll Cashin, "Middle-class Black Suburbs and the State of Integration: A Post-integrationist Vision for Metropolitan America," *Cornell Law Review* 86 (2001): 729–776. "African Americans fare better—at least in terms of government services, local taxes, and access to educational opportunity—in integrated settings. While middle-class black enclaves may be premised on a confident separatism, the rightfully proud residents of these communities must face a painful reality. . . . Externalities beyond their control are inevitable—a chief external factor being the race-laden private decisions of people and institutions not to invest in, locate in, or cooperate with all-black communities" (733).

71. Lila Watson's quote can be found on the blog "If You Have Come to Help Me . . ." at http://northlandposter.com/blog/2006/12/18/lila-watson-if-you-have-come-to-help-me-you-are-wasting-your-time-but-if-you-have-come-because-your-liberation-is-bound-up-with-mine-then-let-us-work-together/ (accessed Apr. 10, 2008).

NOTES TO CHAPTER 4

1. Martha C. Nussbaum, *Women and Human Development: The Capabilities Approach* (New York: Cambridge University Press, 2000), 5.

2. Martha C. Nussbaum and Amartya Sen, "Introduction," in *The Quality of Life,* ed. Martha C. Nussbaum and Amartya Sen (New York: Oxford University Press, 1993), 3.

3. Nussbaum, *Women and Human Development,* 81–83.

4. Herbert J. Gans, *The War against the Poor: The Underclass and Antipoverty Policy* (New York: Basic Books, 1995), 6.

5. Ibid.

6. See Public Law 104-193, 110 Stat. 2105 (codified as amended in scattered sections of 42 U.S.C.).

7. The historical dichotomy of the deserving and undeserving poor is central to any coherent understanding of American economic support for poor people. In his study of 500 years of English poor laws, William Quigley traces the statutory origins of the deserving/nondeserving poor distinction to the Statute of Laborers of 1349. For those willing to work, the statute regulated wages during a period of acute worker shortages. For those who preferred to beg, which before this time had been a socially acceptable way for unemployed poor people to sustain themselves, the statute allowed able-bodied individuals to be seized and put to work. See William P. Quigley, "Five Hundred Years of English Poor Laws, 1349–1834: Regulating the Working and

Non-working Poor," *Akron Law Review* 30 (1996): 84–92. "The regulation of the non-working poor depended completely on whether the poor person was able to work. If they were able to work, the choice was work at the wages offered or prison. If they were unable to work, then they were not prohibited from begging" (90).

8. "Predictably labeled a 'crisis,' welfare became an issue in the 1992 presidential campaign, when candidate Bill Clinton promised to 'end welfare as we know it.' Welfare dependency, he said, had become 'a way of life.'" Joel F. Handler and Yeheskel Hasenfeld, *We the Poor People: Work, Poverty, and Welfare* (New Haven, Conn.: Yale University Press, 1997), 5.

9. From the 1930s through the 1970s, U.S. welfare policy provided a system of social insurance (to protect workers against income loss from retirement, disability, unemployment, death of a breadwinner) and means-tested public assistance (welfare), which transferred income to certain deserving categories of destitute nonworkers. This meant a de facto separation of the welfare income transfer program from the world of work and labor market policies. Hugh Heclo, "The Politics of Welfare Reform," in *The New World of Welfare,* ed. Rebecca M. Blank and Ron Haskins (Washington, D.C.: Brookings Institute Press, 2002), 169, 172.

10. "[A] program that stays the same while the society around it is changing can actually amount to a transformed policy. Such policy morphing is essentially what happened to Washington's welfare program as the American society and economy evolved around it. . . . Other developed countries have also had to substantially modify, if not abandon, the older male-breadwinner vision of income security, but in the United States the path to doing so has been uniquely contentious and socially divisive" (ibid., 173).

11. Kenneth R. Himes, "Rights of Entitlement: A Roman Catholic Perspective," *Notre Dame Journal of Law, Ethics, and Public Policy* 11 (1997): 509. Himes argues that, from the perspective of the Catholic tradition, the entrenched tendency for American democracy to preference unnecessary benefits for the rich over the fundamental needs of the poor and the disadvantaged raises fundamental questions about the ability of the nation's economic and political system to offer basic justice to all of its citizens: "The Church's teaching appeals to our national and individual conscience to remember that in whatever strategies we adopt it is the rights of the most needy which have priority over the entitlement claims of the rest of us" (529).

12. See Vee Burke, "Welfare Reform: An Issue Overview," CRS Reports, http://digital.library.unt.edu/govdocs/crs/permalink/meta-crs-2066.

13. The White House, "Working toward Independence," the White House, http://www.whitehouse.gov/news/releases/2002/02/welfare-reform-announcement-book.html; Sharon Hays, *Flat Broke with Children: Women in the Age of Welfare Reform* (New York: Oxford University Press, 2003), 17.

14. See Jeffrey L. Katz, "Provisions of Welfare Bill," *Congressional Quarterly Weekly Report,* Aug. 3, 1996, 219293; White House, "Working toward Independence."

15. See *Personal Responsibility, Work, and Family Promotion Act of 2002,* H.R. 4737, 107th Cong. 4.1 (a–c), 2(a) (2002).

16. See Burke, "Welfare Reform." For instance, recent unemployment statistics indicate that African American unemployment increased a full percentage point from May to June in 2003, rising to 11.8 percent. John M. Berry, "Jobless Rate Climbs to 6.4%; 9 million Couldn't Find Work in June," *Washington Post*, July 4, 2003. The rate of black unemployment is rising twice as fast as that for whites. Louis Uchitelle, "Blacks Lose Better Jobs Faster as Middle-class Work Drops," *New York Times*, July 12, 2003.

17. See Sharon Parrott and Arloc Sherman, "TANF at 10: Program Results Are More Mixed than Often Understood," Center on Budget and Policy Priorities, http://www.cbpp.org/8-17-06tanf.htm (2006); Lauren Etter, "Hot Topic: Welfare Reform: Ten Years Later," *Wall Street Journal*, Aug. 26, 2006 (Etter argues that welfare reform has been a success in many ways, although not for everyone); Ron Haskins, "Welfare Check," *Wall Street Journal*, July 27, 2006. Haskins argues that the dire predictions about the suffering that poor people would endure under welfare reform have proved unfounded and that its accomplishments should please both Republicans and Democrats.

18. The PRWORA legislation also represents the triumph of an intellectual vision of welfare reform championed by Charles Murray and Lawrence Mead. Charles A. Murray, *Losing Ground: American Social Policy, 1950–1980* (New York: Basic Books, 1984) (Murray has argued that social programs since 1964 had failed by creating disincentives among poor people that discouraged workforce participation, education, and traditional marriage/childbearing. Murray has suggested ending AFDC and other federal Great Society poverty programs in favor of locally created and controlled assistance programs designed to move the poor toward self-sufficiency); Lawrence M. Mead, *Beyond Entitlement: The Social Obligations of Citizenship* (New York: Simon and Schuster, 1986) (Mead argues that social welfare recipients would benefit more from being expected to fulfill certain obligations in return for support. In particular, Mead's idea of a "new paternalism" toward poor people exposes key aspects of the underlying theoretical framework that animates TANF). See also Lawrence M. Mead, *The New Paternalism: Supervisory Approaches to Poverty* (Washington, D.C.: Brookings Institution Press, 1997), in which Mead explains the trend toward government programs that supervise poor people's lives in return for offering support, with "paternalism" signifying close supervision of dependents and "welfare reform" primarily meaning that aid recipients are required to work.

19. The massive internal migration of rural African Americans from the South to the industrial cities of the Northeast and the Midwest, which peaked during the mid-twentieth century, added new complexity to racial relations in the United States. The relegation of African Americans to socially and economically marginalized ghettoes at a time when most Americans were becoming urban dwellers helped to racialize the nation's understanding of poverty. On the African American migration and its social implications for American life see Nicholas Lemann, *The Promised Land: The Great Black Migration and How It Changed America* (New York: Knopf, 1991).

20. See James T. Patterson, *America's Struggle against Poverty, 1900–1985* (Cambridge, Mass.: Harvard University Press, 1986), 68–70 (Patterson states that the

emphasis on localism allowed states to apply prejudicial criteria to families seeking assistance); Heclo, "Politics of Welfare Reform," 173–174.

21. Martin Gilens, *Why Americans Hate Welfare: Race, Media, and the Politics of Anti-poverty Policy* (Chicago: University of Chicago Press, 1999), 3.

22. This perception holds despite readily available statistics that demonstrate otherwise. In 2000 the U.S. Census Bureau classified 31.1 million Americans as poor. Of this group, 21.29 million were white, and 7.9 million were black. Joseph Dalaker, "Poverty in the United States: 2000," U.S. Department of Commerce, http:// www.census.gov/prod/2001pubs/p60-214.pdf. The *rate* of African American poverty was 22 percent, as opposed to 9.4 percent for whites. Although the black poverty rate is twice as high, nearly three times as many whites are poor. Much of the perception that poverty is a "black" problem can be explained by certain racist social constructions that are inherent in American society:

> The racial image of the black welfare dependent woman and her poverty-causing, extramarital childbearing jibes with the social construction of black womanhood. Like the matriarch, who does not submit to her man's authority, the welfare dependent single mother is a "bad" woman whose dominance wrecks the natural order of things.... Like Jezebel, who is overtly sexual and lascivious, the welfare dependent single mother's hypersexuality is responsible for her anti-patriarchal childbearing. Like the breeder, whose owner imposed on her a duty to procreate, the welfare dependent single mother's extramarital childbearing is a learned response to the financial incentive provided by [welfare benefits]. (Lisa A. Crooms, "Don't Believe the Hype: Black Women, Patriarchy, and the New Welfarism," *Howard Law Journal* 38 [1995]: 626)

For more on the racialist construction of poor people in the United States and how it has contributed to a more punitive and less generous welfare program, see Gilens, *Why Americans Hate Welfare.*

23. In the 400-year history of Anglo-American settlement in what is now the United States, African Americans have either been enslaved or subject to legally and socially sanctioned racial discrimination for all but the last 40 years:

> [T]he [socially constructed] truth about black women and "welfarism"... renders "black poverty" redundant. Blackness has become the conceptual norm for poverty. No one can talk about the poor without violating the new rules of public discourse which state that race-specific measures are automatically suspect, and feigned colorblindness, no matter how illusory, is the politically popular way to remedy race and sex discrimination. This approach, however, fails to appreciate the fact that the damage has already been done. The rhetoric remains racist as long as its socially constructed meaning infuses it with a racial subtext. (Crooms, "Don't Believe the Hype," 627–628)

24. Ibid., 78.

25. Gilens, *Why Americans Hate Welfare,* 62–72.

26. For an in-depth sociological study of the breakdown in "social capital" in the United States, see Robert Putnam, *Bowling Alone: The Collapse and Revival of American Community* (New York: Simon and Schuster, 2000).

27. Sixteen percent of American children lived in poverty in 2000, but this group constituted close to a third of all of the nation's poor (of the 31.1 million poor people, 11.6 million were youngsters) (Dalaker, "Poverty in the United States"). On the devastating psychological and social effects of an entrenched "divorce culture" on the lives of middle-class children, as well as the persistence of these effects well into adulthood, see Judith S. Wallerstein, Julia Lewis, and Sandra Blakeslee, *The Unexpected Legacy of Divorce: A 25-Year Landmark Study* (New York: Hyperion, 2000); Eileen Mavis Hetherington, *For Better or for Worse: Divorce Reconsidered* (New York: Norton, 2002).

28. "In the United States . . . there is almost a manic desire to work, both for its own sake and more often in order to make money—an uncertain means to perhaps a forgotten end of greater human dignity. Work is one important element in, but not identical with, the whole of an integrated life. Social ostracism almost universally attaches to unemployment, especially in the case of those unable to support themselves financially" (David L. Gregory, "Catholic Labor Theory and the Transformation of Work," *Washington and Lee Law Review* 45 (1988): 133).

29. Amy Wax offers a particularly compelling theory of "strong reciprocity" to explain the "typical" American's hostility to providing public assistance to poor single mothers who do not work. See Amy L. Wax, "Rethinking Welfare Rights: Reciprocity Norms, Reactive Attitudes, and the Political Economy of Welfare Reform," *Law and Contemporary Problems* 63 (2000): 257–296. According to Wax, "the analysis suggests that a belief that unconditional public assistance for single mothers violates norms of reciprocity begins with a perception that welfare mothers and their families give back less to society than they receive. . . . [A]n imbalance between individual contribution and public support does not pose a problem for strong reciprocity if the individual who calls upon group support is unable to improve upon the situation or reduce her need for public funds. . . . But whether the neediness of many poor single mothers is in some sense 'involuntary' is a hotly contested question that, for many voters, yields a negative answer" (279).

30. J. L. A. García, "Liberal Theory, Human Freedom, and the Politics of Sexual Morality," in *Religion and Contemporary Liberalism*, ed. Paul J. Weithman (Notre Dame, Ind.: University of Notre Dame Press, 1997), 218–219.

31. See Peter L. Berger and Richard John Neuhaus, *To Empower People: The Role of Mediating Structures in Public Policy* (Washington, D.C.: American Enterprise Institute, 1977); Michael Novak, *The Spirit of Democratic Capitalism*, 2d ed. (Boulder, Colo.: Madison Books, 1991), 56–57.

32. John Gray, *False Dawn: The Delusions of Global Capitalism* (New York: New Press), 108.

33. See William O'Neill, "Poverty in the United States," in *Reading the Signs of the Times: Resources for Social and Cultural Analysis*, ed. T. Howland Sanks and George Coleman (New York: Paulist Press, 1993), 68, 74:

Our liberal philosophical heritage has been loath to recognize a right to the fulfillment of even basic welfare needs... Our cherished rights are principally liberties or immunities from interference by others; our duties, obligations of forbearance rather than "positive" duties of assistance to those less favored.... Justice, once the fruition of the common good, is rendered as fair or impartial rules safeguarding individuals' liberties and property rights. Vast inequalities of wealth are thereby justified, for if, as is generally assumed, our social institutions rest on fair and impartial rules, themselves derived from individual consent, poverty can no longer be regarded as a failure of moral entitlement or right. To restrict my liberty (e.g., through tax or transfer policies) rather than through voluntary charity is to "conspire against" my freedom.

34. Mary Ann Glendon, *Rights Talk: The Impoverishment of Political Discourse* (New York: Free Press, 1991), 14.

35. Paul Ricoeur, *Oneself as Another*, trans. Katherine Blamey (Chicago: University of Chicago Press, 1992), 172.

36. Ibid., 179.

37. Ibid.

38. Ibid., 190.

39. Ibid., 180.

40. Ibid., 181.

41. See Paul Ricoeur, *The Just*, trans. David Pellauer (Chicago: University of Chicago Press, 2000), xiii.

42. Ibid., 80.

43. See Ricoeur, *Oneself as Another*, 201.

44. Ibid., 202.

45. Ricoeur, *The Just*, 9–10.

46. L. Roos, "The Human Person and Human Dignity as Basis of the Social Doctrine of the Church," in *Principles of Catholic Social Teaching*, ed. David A. Boileau (Milwaukee: Marquette University Press, 1998), 53, 57.

47. Himes, "Rights of Entitlement," 516.

48. Ibid., 519–520.

49. David Hollenbach, SJ, *The Common Good and Christian Ethics* (New York: Cambridge University Press, 2002), 173.

50. L. J. Elders, "Common Good as Goal and Governing Principle of Social Life: Interpretations and Meaning," in *Principles of Catholic Social Thought*, 103, 107–108.

51. Hollenbach, *Common Good*, 81.

52. Ibid., 81–82.

53. Ibid., 82.

54. Ibid., 83.

55. Pope John Paul II, *Sollicitudo rei socialis*, reprinted in *Catholic Social Thought: The Documentary Heritage*, ed. David J. O'Brien and Thomas J. Shannon (Maryknoll, N.Y.: Orbis, 1997), 325, 421.

56. Ibid., 422.

57. Donal Dorr, *Option for the Poor: One Hundred Years of Vatican Social Teaching,* rev. ed. (Maryknoll, N.Y.: Orbis, 1992), 332–333.

58. Many commentators have pointed out the tendency for suburban municipalities to become enclaves of privilege under the legal cover of local autonomy. Huge disparities exist among jurisdictions in the level of public services they offer, and they tend to concentrate the least desirable land uses in jurisdictions with high concentrations of poor or minority residents. For example, Richard Briffault argues that "[m]ore affluent localities can ... use their regulatory authority to maintain their preferred fiscal position. To the extent that more affluent localities are able to deploy exclusionary zoning techniques as an informal wealth test that keeps out newcomers who bring less to the locality in tax base than they cost in local services, these localities can continue to offer better services and/or hold down their taxes." Richard Briffault, "The Local Government Boundary Problem in Metropolitan Areas," *Stanford Law Review* 48 (1996): 1136. Building on Briffault, Sheryll Cashin notes that this phenomenon creates a "tyranny of the favored quarter," whereby certain high-growth, high-income suburbs, representing about 25 percent of the population of many metropolitan regions, capture the lion's share of the regions' infrastructure expenditure and job growth: "Theoretical justifications for local governance should be tested against the empirical reality of the favored quarter. The collective action problem wrought by fragmented local governance creates a system in which the 'free riders' are the most privileged people in our society." Sheryll D. Cashin, "Localism, Self-interest, and the Tyranny of the Favored Quarter: Addressing the Barriers to New Regionalism," *Georgetown Law Journal* 88 (2000): 1990.

59. Hollenbach, *Common Good,* 200.

60. Ibid., 202.

NOTES TO CHAPTER 5

1. See *Border Protection, Anti-terrorism, and Illegal Immigration Control Act of 2005,* HR 4437, 109th Cong., 1st sess., *Congressional Record* 151 (Dec. 16, 2005).

2. Peter Wallsten, "Immigration Rift in GOP up for Vote," *Los Angeles Times,* Jan. 20, 2006.

3. John Allen Jr., "Mahoney on Immigration," *National Catholic Reporter,* Apr. 14, 2006.

4. Ibid.

5. See G. R. Chaddock, "A GOP Face-off over Illegal Immigration," *Christian Science Monitor,* Mar. 29, 2006.

6. See Carl Hulse and Jim Rutenerg, "Senate Passes Two Immigration Measures," *New York Times,* May 18, 2006.

7. June Kronholz, "Politics and Economics: Immigration Stalemate—Congress's Failure to Resolve Issue Feeds the Ire of Activists on Both Sides," *Wall Street Journal,* Sept. 6, 2006; Brad Knickerbocker, "Anti-immigrant Sentiments Fuel Klan Resurgence," *Christian Science Monitor,* Feb. 9, 2007.

8. See *Secure Fence Act of 2006*, HR 6061, 109th Cong., 2nd sess., *Congressional Record* 152 (Sept. 14, 2006).

9. See Jonathan Weisman, "Border Fence Is Approved; Congress Sets Aside Immigration Overhaul in Favor of 700-Mile Barrier," *Washington Post*, Oct. 1, 2006.

10. See "Border Fence Becomes Law: Bush Surrenders to GOP House on Key Immigration Issue," *Human Events*, Oct. 30, 2006.

11. See Family Research Council, http://www.frc.org/get.cfm?c=ABOUT_FRC.

12. In June 2005 Kirkpatrick, along with seven other former UN ambassadors, signed a letter urging Congress to defeat a Hyde bill that would have cut U.S. contributions to the United Nations by half. See James Morrison, "Opposing Hyde," *Washington Times*, June 15, 2005.

13. Ibid.

14. "The Tancredo Tendency," *Economist*, Apr. 8, 2006, 36.

15. Ibid.

16. See John O'Sullivan, "The GOP's Immigration Problem: Will the Elites Get a Clue?" *National Review*, Sept. 12, 2005, 34–37.

17. See Douglas S. Massey, "Testimony of Douglas S. Massey," Senate Judiciary Committee, http://judiciary.senate.gov/hearing.cfm?id=1634 (accessed Feb. 24, 2008).

18. Sarah Pulliam, "Evangelical Ambivalence Mirrors National Immigration Deadlock," *Christianity Today*, June 2007, 20–21 (Pulliam notes that key Hispanic evangelicals believe that white evangelicals do not support comprehensive immigration reform).

19. Joseph Lelyveld, "The Border Dividing Arizona," *New York Times*, Oct. 15, 2006.

20. See Samuel P. Huntington, "The Hispanic Challenge," *Foreign Policy*, Mar./ Apr. 2004, 30–45.

21. See CBS *Evening News*, Mar. 27, 2006, story 3.

22. See Huntington, *Hispanic Challenge*.

23. See Samuel Huntington, *Who Are We?: The Challenges to America's National Identity* (New York: Simon and Schuster, 2004), 187.

24. Ibid., 221.

25. Ibid., 254–255.

26. See Thomas G. Dolan, "Do Hispanics Fail to Assimilate?" *Education Digest*, November 2004, 44–48.

27. J. D. Hayworth, *Whatever It Takes: Illegal Immigration, Border Security, and the War on Terror* (Washington, D.C.: Regnery, 2006); quotes at http://www .azconservative.org/Hayworth_book.htm.

28. See Thomas G. Tancredo, *In Mortal Danger: The Battle for America's Border and Security* (Nashville: WND, 2006).

29. See Patrick Buchanan, *State of Emergency: The Third World Invasion and Conquest of America* (New York: Thomas Dunne, 2006).

30. See Kitty Calavita, *Immigrants at the Margins: Law, Race, and Exclusion in Southern Europe* (New York: Cambridge University Press, 2005), 43.

31. Ibid., 46.

32. Ibid., 141.

33. Ibid., 143–144.

34. Ibid., 145.

35. James Kurth, "The Protestant Deformation and American Foreign Policy," *Orbis,* Spring 1998, 221–239.

36. William Pfaff, "The Globalized Economy: Who Wins & Who Loses," *Commonweal,* May 19, 2006, 7.

37. See Steven Rattner, "The Rich Get (Much) Richer," *Business Week,* Aug. 8, 2005, 90.

38. Ibid.

39. See "Snakes and Ladders; Charlemagne," *Economist,* May 27, 2006, 52.

40. See "Bush Signs $70 Billion Tax-cut Extensions," *New York Times,* May 17, 2006.

41. Nolan McCarthy, Keith T. Poole, and Howard Rosenthal, *Polarized America: The Dance of Ideology and Unequal Riches* (Cambridge, Mass.: MIT Press, 2006), 116.

42. Ibid., 133.

43. Ibid., 175.

44. See Matthew 2:13–15.

45. Episcopal Commission for Social Affairs, "We Are Aliens and Transients before the Lord Our God," Canadian Conference of Catholic Bishops, http://www.cccb.ca/site/Files/PastoralLetter_Immigration.html, para. 5.

46. See Rick Ryscavage, SJ, "The Catholic Church's Rich Understanding of U.S. Immigration," *In All Things,* Winter 2006–2007, 1–2.

47. The tragic murder of Emmet Till in 1955 is but one example.

48. For a full discussion of modern African American migration patterns within the United States with accompanying data see William W. Falk, Larry L. Hunt, and Matthew O. Hunt, "Return Migrations of African Americans to the South: Reclaiming a Land of Promise, Going Home, or Both," *Rural Sociology* 69 (2004): 490–509.

49. Ibid., 492.

50. Episcopal Commission for Social Affairs, "We Are Aliens and Transients," para. 1.

51. Catholic Church, Conferencia del Episcopado Mexicana, *Strangers No Longer: Together on the Journey of Hope: A Pastoral Letter concerning Migration from the Catholic Bishops of Mexico and the United States* (Washington, D.C.: U.S. Conference of Catholic Bishops, 2003), para. 29.

52. Ibid., para. 30.

53. Pontifical Council for Justice and Peace, *Compendium of the Social Doctrine of the Catholic Church* (Washington, D.C.: U.S. Conference of Catholic Bishops, 2005), para. 298.

54. Michael Walzer, *Spheres of Justice: A Defense of Pluralism and Equality* (New York: Basic Books, 1983), 55.

55. Ibid., 60–61.

56. Ibid., 62.

57. Tom Tancredo, interview by Melissa Block, *NPR News,* Jan. 26, 2007.

58. Tim Kane and Kirk A. Johnson, "The Real Problem with Immigration . . . and the Real Solution," Heritage Foundation, http://www.heritage.org/Research/Immigration/bg1913.cfm (accessed Feb. 24, 2008).

59. Ryscavage, "The Catholic Church's Rich Understanding of U.S. Immigration," 3; see Massey, "Testimony."

60. Will Kymlicka, "Immigration, Citizenship, Multiculturalism: Exploring the Links," *Political Quarterly* 74 (2003): 195.

61. Ibid., 197.

62. Ibid., 197–199.

63. Ibid., 202. Other observers of the Canadian cultural scene have shared Kymlicka's observations. Joshua Hergesheimer has noted that Canadian identity is one in which "you can be yourself and be Canadian simultaneously. What makes you part of Canadian society is what you contribute to Canada. . . . This for us is the definition of multiculturalism: the belief that tolerance is not enough. Only by publicly recognising and institutionally protecting certain aspects of people's cultural identity will newcomers feel bound to uphold the values of a society that accepts them for who they are, instead of trying to make them homogenous replicas of some 'Canadian' identity that probably never existed." Joshua Hergesheimer, "My Country Right, Not Wrong," *Catalyst,* January/February 2007, 24.

64. Text of homily by Cardinal Cormac Murphy-O'Connor at a Mass concelebrated on May 1, 2006, at Westminster Cathedral by the three bishops of the London Catholic diocese, at http://www.rcdow.org.uk.

NOTES TO CHAPTER 6

1. For a full account of the Nickel Mines tragedy and the role of forgiveness in the Amish response, see Donald B. Kraybill, Stephen M. Nolt, and David L. Weaver-Zercher, *Amish Grace: How Forgiveness Transcended Tragedy* (San Francisco: Jossey-Bass, 2007).

2. Miklós Tomka, "Secularization and Nationalism," in *Religion and Nationalism,* ed. John Coleman and Miklós Tomka (London: SCM Press, 1995), 29.

3. M. Cathleen Kaveny, "Prophesy and Casuistry: Abortion, Torture, and Moral Discourse," *Villanova Law Review* 51 (2006): 500.

4. Ibid., 501.

5. Ibid., 506, quoting Abraham Heschel, *The Prophets,* vol. 1 (New York: Harper and Row, 1969).

6. Ibid., 508.

7. Ibid., 511.

8. Ibid., 570.

9. Ibid., 574.

10. Ibid., 576.

11. Stephen Webb, *American Providence: A Nation with a Mission* (New York: Continuum, 2004), 2.

12. Ibid., 9.

13. Stanley Hauerwas, "Democratic Time: Lessons Learned from Yoder and Wolin," *Crosscurrents*, Winter 2006, 539–540.

14. Ibid., 540–541.

15. John Paul II, *Centesimus annus* (1991), para. 46.

16. William Cavanaugh, "Killing for the Telephone Company: Why the Nation-State Is Not the Keeper of the Common Good," *Modern Theology* 20 (Apr. 2, 2004): 266.

17. Ibid., 263.

18. Ibid., 267.

19. Vatican Council II, "*Gaudium et spes*," in *Vatican Council II: Constitutions, Decrees, Declarations*, ed. Austin Flannery (Northport, N.Y.: Costello, 1996), para. 75.

20. David J. Hollenbach, SJ, "Commentary on *Gaudium et spes*," in *Modern Catholic Social Teaching: Commentaries and Interpretations*, ed. Kenneth R. Himes, OFM (Washington, D.C.: Georgetown University Press, 2005), 281.

21. See Nicholas D. Kristoff, "Iraq and Your Wallet," *New York Times*, Oct. 24, 2004.

22. Stanley Hauerwas, "On Being a Christian and an American," in *Meaning and Modernity: Religion, Polity, and Self*, ed. Richard Madsen et al. (Berkeley: University of California Press, 2001), 234–235.

23. Samuel P. Huntington, *Who Are We?: The Challenges to America's National Identity* (New York: Simon and Schuster, 2004), 61–62.

24. Kwame Anthony Appiah, "Cosmopolitan Patriots," *Critical Inquiry* 23 (1997): 628.

25. Ibid., 627.

26. Ibid.

27. Ibid., 626.

28. Ibid., 629.

29. Michael J. Sandel, *Democracy's Discontent: America in Search of a Public Philosophy* (Cambridge, Mass.: Harvard University Press, 1996), 4.

30. Ibid., 16–17.

31. Appiah, "Cosmopolitan Patriots," 631.

32. Kwame Anthony Appiah, *Cosmopolitanism: Ethics in a World of Strangers* (New York: Norton, 2006), 47.

33. Ibid., 49.

34. Ibid., xv.

35. See Martha Nussbaum, "Patriotism and Cosmopolitanism," in *For Love of Country: Debating the Limits of Patriotism*, ed. Joshua Cohen (Boston: Beacon, 1996), 4.

36. Ibid., 9.

37. Ibid., 13.

38. Martha Nussbaum, *Frontiers of Justice: Disability, Nationality, Species Membership* (Cambridge, Mass.: Belknap, 2006), 5.

39. Ibid., 36.

40. Ibid., 37.

41. Ibid., 274.

42. Ibid., 313–314.

43. Alasdair MacIntyre, "Is Patriotism a Virtue?," in *Theorizing Citizenship*, ed. Ronald Beiner (Albany: State University of New York Press, 1995), 210.

44. Ibid., 212.

45. See Charles Taylor, "Democracy, Inclusive and Exclusive," in *Meaning and Modernity*, 181.

46. Ibid., 187.

47. Will Kymlicka and Wayne Norman, "Citizenship in Culturally Diverse Societies: Issues, Contexts, Concepts," in *Citizenship in Diverse Societies*, ed. Will Kymlicka and Wayne Norman (New York: Oxford University Press, 2000), 21.

48. Burgeoning powers such as India, Nigeria, Brazil, and China all encompass a wide range of ethnic, religious, racial, and cultural groups within their populations.

49. See discussion in chapter 4.

50. Martha Nussbaum, "Patriotism and Cosmopolitanism," 10.

51. 1 Cor. 12:12–13 (New American Version).

52. Ibid., 22–24.

53. See Lizette Alvarez and Andrew Lehren, "The Conflict in Iraq, 3,000 Deaths in Iraq, Countless Tears at Home," *New York Times*, Jan. 1, 2007.

54. Conor Gearty, *Can Human Rights Survive?* (New York: Cambridge University Press, 2005), 131–132.

55. Ibid., 18.

56. Ibid., 67.

57. Ibid., 72.

58. See Michael J. Perry, *Toward a Theory of Human Rights: Religion, Law, Courts* (New York: Cambridge University Press, 2007).

59. Ibid., 26–27.

60. Ibid., 27.

61. Jeffery Stout, *Democracy and Tradition* (Princeton, N.J.: Princeton University Press, 2004), 99.

62. See Gearty, *Can Human Rights Survive?* 155.

63. Ibid., 156.

64. Ibid., 102–103.

65. Perry, *Toward a Theory of Human Rights*, 40.

66. Ibid., 40–41.

67. Pope Paul VI, *Evangelii nuntiandi* (1975), para. 14.

68. Ibid., para. 21.

69. Paolo Carozza, "Subsidiarity as a Structural Principle of International Human Rights Law," *American Journal of International Law* 97 (2003): 49.

70. Ibid., 47, quoting the Universal Declaration of Human Rights, Art. 18 (1948).

Index

Protestantism, 51–53
providential mission of, 159–60
racism in, 107, 112, 201n3
segregation in, 87, 116–17, 144,
    204n67, 205n70
siege mentality of, 12
slavery in, 15, 100–101, 106–7, 144
social mobility, 145
"States Prepare for the Global Age,"
    69–70
teenage pregnancy rate, 191n11
tribal fantasy of, 164–66
welfare reform, 124–25, 132
universalism, and the Religious Right,
    181
University of Michigan Law School, 104–5
U.S. Conference of Catholic Bishops, 109,
    133–34
utilitarianism, 167, 171

Vatican, 49, 52–54, 59, 195n67. *See also*
    Second Vatican Council
Vatican II. *See* Second Vatican Council
Verstraeten, Johann, 58
Vietnam War, 45, 46
Virginia, 158

Waco conflagration, 12
Wall Street Journal, 134
Wallerstein, Judith S., 209n27
Wallis, Jim, 28
Walzer, Michael, 149–50, 153
The War against the Poor, 121
war on terror, 12–14, 35, 141
Watson, Lila, 118
Watts, Jonathan, 191n9
Wax, Amy L., 209n29
Webb, Stephen, 159–60
Weber, Max, 79
Weigel, George, 6–7, 48–50, 88–91
Weinburg, J. A., 194n57

welfare reform
and African Americans, 124–25,
    207n16, 208n22, 208n23
in America, 124–25, 132
block grants, 122
capabilities approach, 120, 128
Clinton administration, 121, 206n8
and community, 125–27, 209–10n33
entitlements, 121, 206n11, 207n18
free-market liberalism and, 120–23, 132
hostility toward, 55
human rights, 126
justice, 127–29, 209–10n33
materialism, 123, 125–27
new paternalism, 207n18
and politics, 206n10
PRWORA, 121–23, 125, 207n18
"Rethinking Welfare Rights," 209n29
self-esteem, 127–29
and slavery, 124–25
social contract theory, 128–29
social insurance, 206n9
solidarity, 127–29
strong reciprocity, 209n29
TANF, 121–22, 207n17
undeservingness, 121, 123, 205–6n7
unemployment statistics, 209n28
Why Americans Hate Welfare, 208n22
welfare state, 63, 81–82, 166–67
Weyrich, Paul, 32
*Whatever It Takes: Illegal Immigration,
    Border Security, and the War on Terror*,
    141
Wheaton College, 27
White, James Boyd, 95–96, 103, 112
whiteness, 107, 144
Why Americans Hate Welfare, 208n22
Williams, Rowan, 50
Wilson, James Q., 44–45, 54
wiretapping, 190n24
women's movement, 29–31